Approaches to Teaching the Works of Benito Pérez Galdós

Approaches to Teaching the Works of Benito Pérez Galdós

Edited by

Liana Ewald,

David R. George, Jr.,

and

Wan Sonya Tang

The Modern Language Association of America

New York 2026

85 Broad Street, New York, New York 10004
www.mla.org

To order MLA publications, visit www.mla.org/books. For wholesale and international orders, see www.mla.org/bookstore-orders. The EU-based Responsible Person for MLA products is the Mare Nostrum Group, which can be reached at gpsr@mare-nostrum.co.uk or the Mare Nostrum Group BV, Mauritskade 21D, 1091 GC Amsterdam, Netherlands. For a copy of the MLA's risk assessment document, write to scholcomm@mla.org.

Approaches to Teaching World Literature 184
ISSN 1059-1133

Library of Congress Cataloging-in-Publication Data

Names: Ewald, Liana editor | George, David R., Jr. editor | Tang, Wan Sonya, 1983– editor
Title: Approaches to teaching the works of Benito Pérez Galdós / edited by Liana Ewald, David R. George, Jr., and Wan Sonya Tang.
Description: New York : The Modern Language Association of America, 2026. | Series: Approaches to teaching world literature, 1059-1133 ; 184 | Includes bibliographical references.
Identifiers: LCCN 2025041910 (print) | LCCN 2025041911 (ebook) | ISBN 9781603297240 hardcover | ISBN 9781603297257 paperback | ISBN 9781603297264 EPUB
Subjects: LCSH: Pérez Galdós, Benito, 1843–1920—Study and teaching (Higher) | Pérez Galdós, Benito, 1843–1920—Criticism and interpretation | BISAC: LITERARY CRITICISM / European / Spanish & Portuguese | LANGUAGE ARTS & DISCIPLINES / Study & Teaching | LCGFT: Literary criticism | Essays
Classification: LCC PQ6555.Z5 A725 2026 (print) | LCC PQ6555.Z5 (ebook)
LC record available at https://lccn.loc.gov/2025041910
LC ebook record available at https://lccn.loc.gov/2025041911

CONTENTS

Introduction

Liana Ewald, David R. George, Jr., and Wan Sonya Tang

In the field of Hispanic studies, Benito Pérez Galdós is considered the most influential writer after Cervantes and is key to understanding Spanish culture and society from the nineteenth to the twenty-first century. While much less extensive, the attention he has garnered outside of Hispanism is just as admiring. Fredric Jameson writes in *The Antinomies of Realism*, "If Zola is the Wagner of nineteenth-century realism (and George Eliot perhaps its Brahms), then Benito Pérez Galdós is its Shakespeare . . ." (95). Galdós is notable not only for his enormous literary production, which includes more than seventy novels, twenty plays, and countless short stories and articles, but also for his engagement with the aesthetic and political questions of the day and with his intellectual contemporaries elsewhere in Europe and the Americas. For more than a century, Galdós's works have been continuously translated and adapted, resulting in new versions that are similarly varied and rich. These include film, television, and stage adaptations as well as illustrated treatments such as graphic novels, comics, and children's books.

Since his death in 1920, the writer has been studied by literary scholars and cultural historians around the world, many of whom belong to the Asociación Internacional de Galdosistas. Their work has been published in numerous monographs and peer-reviewed academic journals and reflects every major paradigm of classic literary criticism as well as the latest developments in critical cultural theory. Yet despite the wealth of secondary literature available, Galdós proves to be a challenging author to teach, particularly at the undergraduate level, and he is often overlooked in English-language classrooms. This volume seeks to provide any instructor interested in teaching Galdós, regardless of their specialization, with online and print resources, diverse theoretical frameworks, and sample activities and assignments to facilitate the incorporation of the author's works into their syllabi. For instructors who specialize in Galdós and his time, this collection offers fresh critical approaches with which to engage the author's works as well as suggestions for examining those less frequently taught. For instructors with scant knowledge of the author and his sociohistorical context, the volume provides numerous ways in which Galdós might be included in broader survey courses on such far-reaching topics as gender, social class, or imperialism. In all cases, the approaches and strategies of our essayists have been tested in the classroom, where they have proved successful with students. All contributors have been especially mindful of how Galdós might be taught in translation, taking note of when sources and resources are available in English so as to encourage instructors of world literature or general humanities courses to consider adding Galdós to their curricula.

Contextualizing Galdós

Despite the diversity of critical and pedagogical approaches represented in this volume, no essay examines Galdós's work as produced in a vacuum. Contributors agree that understanding the sociohistorical context that informs the author's writing helps students comprehend and connect with the assigned works. This introduction provides a brief overview of the period in which Galdós was active to orient students and instructors unfamiliar with the history of late-nineteenth- and early-twentieth-century Spain. Bibliographic information for more detailed social histories can be found in the Materials section of the present volume.

During his lifetime, Galdós witnessed dizzying changes in the Spanish social landscape resulting from internal political, economic, and cultural shifts as well as Spain's changing place on the world stage. Soon after the Canarian author moved to Madrid in 1862, Spain passed through the turbulent political period known as the *sexenio revolucionario* ("revolutionary sexennium"), which began with the deposition of the Bourbon queen Isabel II in the Revolution of 1868; proceeded through a dynastic change in the short-lived reign of Amadeo of Savoy (1870–73), followed by the even briefer democratic experiment of the First Spanish Republic (1873–74); and ended with the 1874 restoration of the Bourbon monarchy in the person of Isabel's son Alfonso XII. In contrast to the political chaos of the preceding half dozen years, during which Spain was widely deemed "ungovernable," the Restoration ushered in an era of relative peace and stability lasting until the elections of 1931. Although the period was marked by the third Carlist War (a civil conflict occurring from 1872 to 1876 in Catalonia and the Basque country), labor unrest and bouts of anarchist violence in Andalusia and Catalonia, and colonial conflicts in the Caribbean, the Philippines, and North Africa, these upheavals were generally localized and had a limited effect on the central government, thus allowing the nation to turn toward capitalist enterprise and industrialization in "the first real economic boom in modern Spanish history" (Labanyi, *Galdós* 6).

In the realm of the arts, this period of general tranquility fostered the development of the Spanish novel, which Galdós played a pivotal role in shaping. Both the turbulence of the *sexenio revolucionario* and the comparative calm of the early Restoration period would be fictionalized in Galdós's *Episodios nacionales* (*National Episodes*), a collection of forty-six novels written between 1873 and 1912 that covered Spanish history from the Battle of Trafalgar in 1805 to the Bourbon Restoration. Recent Spanish history likewise played a major if less explicit role in the author's early *novelas de tesis* ("thesis novels") and later realist masterpieces, the *novelas contemporáneas* ("contemporary novels"), in the ways political, legal, and economic developments in Spain affect the lives of Galdós's multitude of characters, as in, for example, his best-known creation, *Fortunata y Jacinta* (*Fortunata and Jacinta*). The trajectory of Galdós's fiction, which evolved from early works with a markedly ideological bent to more complex explorations of psychology and society, influenced that of Spanish literature throughout the Restoration period, particularly with regard to the maturation of the national novel.

While not all of Galdós's works are set during the Restoration, the vast majority were written after Alfonso XII acceded in 1874, and the author is considered an emblematic literary figure and a public intellectual of Restoration culture. In his novels, plays, short stories, and articles, Galdós brings to life the social dynamics that characterized Restoration Spain, a period analogous to Victorian England for its reputation as the birthplace of Spanish modernity "both in terms of the political and social problems that came to the fore, and the scientific and technological advances that were implemented" (George and Tang 5). On the political front, the stability of the Restoration period was predicated on the *turno pacífico* ("peaceful turn"), a two-party system of power sharing through which election outcomes were predetermined so that political power continually alternated between the Conservative Party, led by Antonio Cánovas del Castillo, and the Liberal Party, under the leadership of Práxedes Mateo Sagasta. Political patronage and corruption, at the national level and particularly at the local one, is a constant theme in Galdós's work, as it is in that of contemporaries such as Leopoldo Alas, also known as "Clarín," and Emilia Pardo Bazán. Similarly worrisome to this generation of authors was Spain's irreversible decline as an imperial power, beginning with the loss of most American colonies between 1810 and 1825 and culminating in the so-called Desastre (Disaster) of 1898, in which Spain lost its final colonial holdings of Cuba, Puerto Rico, the Philippines, and Guam. Framed in hindsight as a national trauma, the loss of Spain's imperial status catalyzed a widespread crisis of national identity that permeates the literature of the period, such that "a central part of the national narrative involved a reckoning with Spain's colonial history" (Coffey 41). It is surprising, then, that Galdós's work has traditionally been judged to show "a lack of engagement with Spanish imperialism" (Coffey 3), although more recent scholarship has proven the author's works to be rife with references to and reflections on Spain's imperialist project and its failure, ranging from countless *indiano* characters (i.e., people made wealthy abroad in the colonies) to a direct engagement with Spanish American independence in the second series of *Episodios nacionales*.

Socially, late-nineteenth- and early-twentieth-century Spain was dominated by the fledgling bourgeois or middle classes, whose participation in the nation's political, legal, commercial, and academic arenas bolstered their cultural influence. In his 1870 essay "Observaciones sobre la novela contemporánea" ("Some Observations on the Contemporary Novel in Spain"), Galdós lays out the recipe for what will become the Spanish realist novel in the following decade, famously declaring the middle class to be "el gran modelo, la fuente inagotable. Ella es hoy la base del orden social: ella asume por su iniciativa y por su inteligencia la soberanía de las naciones y en ella está el hombre del siglo XIX con sus virtudes y sus vicios, su noble e insaciable aspiración, su afán de reformas, su actividad pasmosa" ("our model, our inexhaustible source. The social order nowadays is built on the middle class: through its initiative and intelligence, it has taken on the sovereign role in all nations; it is there that nineteenth-century man is to be found, with all his virtues and vices, his noble, insatiable aspirations, his passion for reforms, his frantic activity"; Galdós, "Observaciones" 130; "Some Observations" 33). Over the next half century, Galdós would become the great painter of Madrid's middle classes, capturing in detail their aspirations and failures. His characters desire to better themselves and their society but struggle against their own and others' hypocrisy, materialism, and corruption.

While deeply attuned to the sociopolitical reality of Restoration Spain, Galdós remained steadfastly engaged with transnational intellectual and artistic currents throughout his lifetime. An avid reader of Honoré de Balzac, Charles Dickens, and Émile Zola, Galdós shared those writers' positivist commitment to depicting the material realities of urban life. Unlike Zola, with his deterministic view of society, Galdós approached naturalism more cautiously, testing its principles in his 1881 novel *La desheredada* (*The Disinherited*). His interest in medicine, which underpinned this foray into naturalism, continued long after the movement's influence on him began to wane.

During the 1880s and early 1890s, the height of Spanish realism, Galdós's novels were populated with characters from across the social spectrum who evince a vast array of physical and psychic disturbances. His intellectual curiosity was fueled by developments in medicine, psychology, crime studies, and social reform from within Spain's borders and beyond. Galdós's close friendship with the novelist Emilia Pardo Bazán, who ignited intense debates over Zola's theories of literary naturalism in an 1881–82 forum at the Madrid Atheneum, also played a key role in shaping his ideas. A one-woman academy, Pardo Bazán kept discussions about international cultural developments alive, including Cesare Lombroso's theories of crime and the rise of the Russian novel, traces of all of which can be found in Galdós's works.

Despite his paean to the middle classes in his "Observaciones sobre la novela contemporánea" and his engagement with a range of scientific, sociopolitical, and artistic currents in his journalistic and other nonfiction writings, Galdós's ideology is often difficult to pin down, obliging scholars to look to his literary works for more nuanced evidence of his moral and philosophical stances. Like other writers of the group commonly referred to by scholars of nineteenth-century Spanish literature as the "Generation of 1868," Galdós's thinking was significantly influenced by the ideas of the German idealist philosopher Karl Christian Friedrich Krause, which were disseminated in Spain by the educator Francisco Giner de los Ríos. Galdós incorporated themes and concepts from Krausism, like pantheism, humanitarianism, spiritual self-realization, and moral reform, into many of his realist novels and gave sympathetic yet critical portrayals of Krausist characters, especially in his early works. By setting his contemporary novels against the backdrop of the *sexenio liberal* ("liberal sexennium," a reference to the politically progressive 1868–74 period), he tracks the evolution of the Krausists from intransigent proponents of rapid political change to reflective advocates of transformation through education (Gullón, "Lección" 69).

As Galdós's fiction illustrates, the bourgeois desire for reform often centered on two issues that dominated public debate during the Restoration period: *la cuestión femenina* ("the woman question"), concerning the state of women's rights, and *la cuestión social* ("the social question"), concerning the alleviation of poverty and improving the situation of the working classes. With respect to the first, Restoration society was marked by a rigid separation in acceptable gender roles for middle-class men and women; whereas men were to seek success in professional endeavors outside the home, women were tasked with seeking fulfillment through motherhood and household management in the role of the *ángel del hogar* ("angel in the house"). The limiting nature of this oppositional gender binary and the discontent that resulting gender norms unsurprisingly sowed are on full display across the spectrum of Galdós's works, as in the short novel *Tristana*, whose protagonist laments the dearth of professional opportunities for talented women of the time. Galdós's extensive treatment of gender and gendered deviance (as seen in figures such as the adulteress, the female prostitute, and the male dandy) is of a piece with Western European literature and culture generally in an age of radical social and economic change. At the same time, it is uniquely Spanish in the ways it served as a proxy for anxieties about national identity in an era of "imperial loss and . . . belated progress toward 'modernity' vis-à-vis the rest of Western Europe" (Tsuchiya, *Marginal Subjects* 6). This characteristic of harmonizing with broader European literary trends while also diverging from (and frequently enhancing) them is part of what makes Galdós's works such fascinating and complex objects of study.

Just as the debate surrounding *la cuestión femenina* was fueled by advancements in women's rights in Spain and elsewhere, *la cuestión social* grew increasingly pressing as the working classes agitated for rights at the century's end. The Restoration period saw a flourishing of labor movements with the founding of the Spanish Socialist Workers' Party in 1879 and the spread of anarchism (introduced into Spain in the late 1860s), particularly in Catalonia and Andalusia. Strikes and riots sprang up both in urban centers and agrarian contexts, with occasional bouts of anarchist terrorism, such as the 1893 attempted assassination of Arsenio Martínez Campos, the captain general of Catalonia, and the bombing of Barcelona's Liceu opera house. In this context of escalating class conflict, Galdós explored the plight of the urban poor through such memorable characters as the titular Fortunata. Despite publicly proclaiming that the answer to *la cuestión social* lay not in state intervention but in Catholic charity (Labanyi, *Galdós* 9–10), the author nevertheless presents an ambiguous depiction of the power of religion to remedy poverty and improve class relations in works like *Nazarín* and *Misericordia*. Such novels illustrate how the role of religion in Spanish society was itself a point of contention throughout the nineteenth and early twentieth centuries. Since the late 1700s, religious crisis had become "one of the defining features of emerging modernity in Spain" (Valis, *Sacred Realism* 2), and by the time of the Restoration, positivism had taken root in Spain, challenging the church's traditional hold, which was further weakened by a strong current of anticlericalism common to liberal intellectuals of the period. Many of Galdós's works are highly critical of the church, most notably the play *Electra*, whose premiere provoked anticlerical demonstrations and sparked a flurry of debate in the press. The heated reactions elicited by the drama attest to the ability of Galdós's writing both to reflect and reflect upon his social reality in a manner that resonated with and stirred the passions of his readers and viewers, a quality of his work that endures into the present day. Political drama, oppressive gender roles, class conflict, and spiritual crisis are recurrent themes across the chapters of this volume, attesting to the continued relevance of these topics for twenty-first-century students and scholars.

Getting to Know the Galdosian Oeuvre

Galdós had such a prolific and diverse career that it is difficult to categorize him as a writer in a way that is both satisfactory and succinct. We describe here his artistic trajectory in broad strokes for the purpose of introducing it to those unfamiliar with its general contours. As with the historical context of his life and times, we refer instructors who wish to learn more about his writing styles, genres, and subjects to the Materials section of this volume for further suggested reading.

While Galdós is widely recognized as the foremost representative of literary realism in Spain, to label him merely a realist writer is to shortchange him and elide the complexity of his work, its innovative and evolving nature, and the unique twist with which he imbues it by drawing on his Spanish cultural heritage. Galdós's compelling mix of traditional and transformational writing, his acute powers of observation as turned upon his social and political milieu, and the "inward turn" through which he plumbs the consciousness and conscience of his characters, in combination with his seemingly insatiable need to convey these to readers in ever more inventive ways, are qualities that merit the continued study of his work in today's classrooms and promise rich rewards for instructors and students alike.

Following the early phase of his so-called thesis novels of the 1870s, with their deceptively Manichean plots (e.g., the country versus the city and religion versus science in *Doña Perfecta*), Galdos's literary production takes on all the hallmarks of traditional, textbook realism. Like Balzac and Dickens before him, he reproduces broad swathes of the urban landscape in minute detail in an attempt to capture the changing nature of life in the modern city, a synecdoche for modernity itself. In his attention to the city, he is unique among the Spanish novelists of his time, such as José María de Pereda, Juan Valera, and Armando Palacio Valdés as well as the previously mentioned Pardo Bazán and Alas. Further, for Galdós, literary realism, premised as it was on empirical notions of comprehending reality and translating it to the page, was destined to become a plaything. He shared a comic sensibility and gift for mimicry with his American contemporary Mark Twain. The ludic quality of Galdós's writing, as evidenced in its unremitting irony, extensive self-reflexivity, and fickle, misleading narrators, is as evidently an homage to Cervantes as it is a subversive jab at the mimetic pretense of realism (Gilman, *Galdós and the Art* 154–86). In addition to being good fun, the many Cervantine manifestations in Galdós's writing signal a deeper kinship with his literary forbear: both writers participate in a sensitive and indulgent conception of the human condition as one comprising absurdity and wisdom, banality and sanctity, in equal measure.

Galdós's connection to the literary currents of his time and his technical prowess in reproducing them are in evidence throughout his oeuvre, even as he undercuts them. Jo Labanyi aptly notes the way in which the late development of Spanish realism endowed its practitioners with a "double focus, placing them simultaneously inside and outside realism." This ironic perspective is particularly evident in Galdós's works, where the texts "question the underlying tenets that make them possible in the first place" (Labanyi, *Galdós* 4). Galdós's sustained attention to international artistic and intellectual currents and his openness to exploring them in his own work throughout his lifetime demonstrated his commitment to evolving realism into a form capable of addressing the complexities of modern life. From Romantic writers, he inherits a penchant for melodrama, whose standard tropes of passionate excess and the predations of upper-class *señoritos* on penniless young women he brings to life in *Fortunata y Jacinta*. Yet the ubiquitous presence in that novel of José Ido del Sagrario, the somewhat deranged author of *folletines*, popular serialized novels rife with melodrama, serves as a funhouse mirror, mocking this commonplace plot. Moreover, Galdós fleshes out the storyline with an astonishingly detailed account of the rise of the bourgeois mercantile class to the seat of power. The realist project of *Fortunata y Jacinta* can be seen, for example, in the narrator's extended riff on the *mantón de Manila* ("Manila shawl") sold in the shops of the Santa Cruz family. At once contradictory and contemplative, Galdós thus invites readers to reflect upon the literary construct that is the world within the novel's pages while asking them to consider the web of economic and colonial interests that nourishes Spain's nascent middle class beyond the page. The latter consideration is both pithy and prescient, rendering as it does the uniquely Spanish dilemma of Galdós's time, which predicates modernity on a crumbling empire rather than on a robust industrial economy.

Even as Galdós embarked on developing the realist novel in Spain, which he deemed "la novela moderna de costumbres" ("the modern novel of manners"; "Observaciones" 130; "Some Observations" 33), his mature work of the 1880s and 1890s partakes of, without surrendering wholly to, naturalism and religious idealism, in that order. The former, inspired by his reading of Zola, draws upon a material conception of the world, in which the fate of his characters would seem to be foretold by the social and economic circumstances he conjures for them. A seasoned journalist and avid traveler, Galdós saturates his novels with objective facts and medical, juridical, and anthropological details. Yet even as he carefully constructs the outer attributes of his characters' world, he does not neglect their inner workings. A defining characteristic of Galdós's work, irrespective of its different phases, is his effort to show how his characters digest the world about them—literally, in his attention to quotidian matters such as the foods they eat, and figuratively, through his detailed representation of their dreams, neuroses, and delusions. In *La desheredada*, a novel whose naturalist resonances critics have long noted, Galdós initiates an experiment with free indirect style, the technique through which a character's thoughts are conveyed through the narrator's voice in the third person and the past tense. This tactic allows him to explore psychology—a burgeoning field of study popular among intellectuals of his era—while creatively portraying psychological depth in fictional characters.

In an analogy that draws upon the nineteenth-century urban milieu that Galdós so deftly depicts, the author has been likened to a ragpicker who spots writerly gems (techniques) amongst his progenitors and peers and repurposes them, piecing together his own eclectic, evolving style (Wolters). It seems fitting in a volume meant to help instructors pique an interest in Galdós amongst today's university students to describe him, as well, through the analogy of the rapper: Galdós was a writer who delighted in discovering and sampling the styles and genres of other writers and artists, remixing them so as to make them uniquely his own.

The Russian novel in particular left a deep imprint on Galdós, whose literary focus began to shift to more spiritual matters in the 1890s in novels such as *Ángel Guerra*, *Nazarín*, and *Halma*. These works, featuring religious reformers and latter-day saints, reflect Galdós's dialogue with Tolstoy's religious idealism. The character Nazarín, for example, at once a Christlike figure and modern-day Don Quijote, could be described, much like Cervantes's protagonist, as setting out to "andar por el mundo enderezando tuertos y desfaciendo agravios" ("roam the world righting wrongs and redressing injuries"; Cervantes, *Ingenioso hidalgo* 1.19; *Don Quixote* 185), in this case by ameliorating poverty and bringing aid to the sick. As with the failures of Don Quijote, those of Nazarín are both predictable and inspiring. *Tristana* is both a meditation on women's secondary status in Spain and a treatise on the relation of art to reality itself. In it, critics have found echoes of the playwright Henrik Ibsen. The theatrical asides in the narrative might be thought of as seeds that sprout first as hybrid *novelas dialogadas* ("novels in dialogue form"), such as *Realidad: Novela en cinco jornadas* and *El abuelo: Novela en cinco jornadas*, before flourishing in a full-fledged turn to drama with stage adaptations of these works alongside original plays like *La de San Quintín* (*The Duchess of San Quintín*) and the controversial *Electra*. Between those two plays, Galdós published the novel *Misericordia*, which takes a microscope to the urban poor in true realist fashion, even as it resolves the dramatic tension of the novel by means of an otherworldly turn to the spiritual and the fantastic. This novel engages a fictional mode in which Galdós demonstrated a sustained interest throughout his career, as evidenced in his consistent publication of fantastical short stories and novellas from the 1860s through the 1890s. This predilection for fantasy also runs through the final sequence of the historical *Episodios nacionales*, starting in 1898, as a testament to Galdós's intellectual curiosity and creative versatility and the diverse ways he continuously channeled them in his literary output. True to that diversity, the present volume endeavors to demonstrate through its assorted essays, as Galdós himself does through his multivalent and multifarious body of work, that the only limits—in this case, to engaging our students with his oeuvre—are those of the imagination.

Reading Galdós in Criticism and Theory

The historical trajectory of scholarship on Galdós's literature over the past century tracks the main trends shaping literary studies and their place in university curricula. Critical readings of his works also reflect Spain's political and cultural history in the twentieth century as it has been marked by colonial and civil wars, dictatorship and exile, and democratic transition and globalization. At the time of this writing, the search term *Pérez Galdós* in the *MLA International Bibliography* yields 2,659 results, including 179 dissertations and 160 books. The same inquiry on the Spanish academic search engine *Dialnet* produces 1,666 entries, with some 555 references in books and 72 dissertations. Both databases only go back as far as the 1920s, so neither includes reviews of his novels and theater or critical notes and introductions appended to translations published during his lifetime.

On the occasion of the fiftieth anniversary of Galdós's death in 1970, the journal *Hispania* published a special Galdós issue that includes a bibliographic essay by Hensley C. Woodbridge presenting a snapshot of the state of criticism up to that time. The detailed summary traces the emergence and consolidation of transcontinental interest in Galdós and his vast literary production from the turn of the twentieth century to that moment. Woodbridge notes that for scholars on both sides of the Atlantic, in North and South America, and around Europe, Galdós was widely considered to be the second-most-important Spanish writer after Cervantes. That same year, *Anales Galdosianos* (*Galdosian Annals*) published its fifth issue, bringing together papers presented at a centennial commemoration held at the University of Texas, Austin. The collection is a roster of pioneering figures in the field of Galdós studies in North America and signals the central role that the journal, founded in 1966 by Rodolfo Cardona, would continue to play as a reference point for criticism on the author in the following decades. The combination of scholars from the Spanish exile community in the Americas and those taught by them, especially at North American universities, captures the persistently transatlantic scope of Galdós studies. In 1973, the first Congreso Internacional de Estudios Galdosianos was held in the writer's birthplace of Las Palmas de Gran Canaria, and the collected proceedings were published in 1977. The event marks another watershed moment in the evolution of the field that launched a progressive restoration of Galdós in the Spanish academy in the waning years of the Francisco Franco dictatorship (1939–75) and the early stages of the transition to democracy (1975–78). The founding of the Asociación Internacional de Galdosistas at the 1980 Modern Language Association convention in Houston ushered in a period of intense publication and interest in Galdós that would continue through the end of the twentieth century.

The critical and pedagogical approaches outlined in the present volume respond to the dual challenge of teaching and researching Galdós in university settings in which, first, his cultural relevance and patrimonial or heritage status are points of contention rather than givens, and, second, his works are viewed as vehicles for both studying Spanish language and conveying historical and cultural understanding of Spanish society as well as that of the wider Spanish-speaking world. As such, the US- and UK-based scholars represented here partake of the common theoretical and critical apparatus of Galdós criticism that has evolved outside Spain over the last half century. In spite of the incorporation of more recent theoretical innovations, most of the approaches outlined are grounded in the practices of textual analysis pioneered by adherents of New Criticism and post-structuralism in the 1980s. The focus on reading Galdós's novels as closed systems of language and signification laid the groundwork for deeper reflections on the possibilities and limits of representation within the scope of European realism and helped frame the author's rich use of metacritical and self-reflexive commentary as a method of exploring his world. Studies in this vein necessarily opened the way for the incorporation of psychoanalytic and feminist approaches that further established the underpinnings for the subsequent explorations of gender across the breadth of the writer's work into the 1990s. Uncovering the inner workings of gender representation in Galdós casts light on the function of the novel as a harbinger and sounding board of social change in the emergence of a middle-class society in Spain. The resulting call to refocus more generally on the historicity of Galdós's literary texts through the critical lenses of new historicism and cultural studies drew attention to relationships of power in Spanish society and to questions surrounding Spain's position in the late-nineteenth-century world. Investigations in the latter area, especially after 2000, have advanced Galdós studies into the rich and fraught terrain of postcolonial studies, obliging scholars to reckon with Spain's colonial past and take into account questions of race alongside other previously ignored and marginalized identities. To be sure, the predominance of cultural studies and the further questioning of cultural categories spawned by the inherent cross-disciplinarity of this approach has led to work in a variety of emerging and interconnected fields, including ecocriticism, disability studies, media studies, and urban studies, among others.

As a primary source in the classroom, Galdós's oeuvre yields productive dialogue with multiple and varied critical approaches and speaks to the changing thematic interests of contemporary society. It is worth noting, however, that over the years, critical attention to the different fictional genres the author cultivated has waxed and waned, as has the popularity of certain titles. Since their time of publication, critics have demonstrated a sustained interest in the so-called contemporary novels, beginning with *La desheredada* in 1881 (evidenced by their canonical status as masterpieces of European literature): the *MLA International Bibliography* yields 251 entries for *Fortunata y Jacinta* and 105 for *La desheredada*. Both novels are likewise mainstays in graduate courses, although *La de*

Bringas (*That Bringas Woman*), *Tormento*, *Lo prohibido* (*The Forbidden*), *Miau* (*Meow*), and *Misericordia* are also common on such reading lists. In the undergraduate classroom, the four thesis novels written in the late 1870s and the works from the 1890s have pride of place, given their manageable length and contemporary themes; unsurprisingly, *Doña Perfecta*, *Marianela*, and *Tristana* are not only widely taught but have also been significantly studied, with 92, 34, and 105 *MLA Bibliography* hits respectively. The forty-six novels of the *Episodios nacionales* were "discovered" by scholars in the 1960s but have received scant critical attention and remain almost unknown to graduate and undergraduate students in spite of their short length and engaging plotlines that elucidate a variety of aspects of Spanish history. Likewise, Galdós's twenty-six plays are hardly studied or taught despite their accessibility; the *MLA Bibliography* gives only 64 hits, and only *Electra* and *La de San Quintín* stand out among the results, with one entry each. This is not surprising, since Spanish theater is a tiny subfield within Hispanic cultural studies, aside from works by authors of the seventeenth-century Golden Age or by Federico García Lorca in the twentieth. By contrast, Galdós's short fiction is continuously taught in the classroom, even though it is perhaps less representative of his literary opus. The development of his realist technique is readily evident in the stories and novellas, although experiments with other modes, particularly the fantastic, are equally, if not more, prevalent. For learners of Spanish, both "La novela en el tranvía" ("The Novel on the Tram") and *La sombra* (*The Shadow*) are highly accessible texts that have garnered a concomitant smattering of critical studies. Finally, scholars also occasionally bring into the classroom and comment critically on Galdós's nonfiction writings (e.g., "Observaciones"), but almost always as a supplement to readings of his novels. More recently, his essays on travel, social issues, and politics published in Spanish and Latin American periodicals have garnered increased attention as primary texts since they can be fruitfully read in the light of critical theories of race, gender, disability, and public health. The essays of the present volume focus on pedagogical approaches to a range of Galdós's works comprising his early and late novels, theater, short stories, and journalism, in recognition of the value of the entirety of his oeuvre and in hopes of enticing teacher-scholars to continue to examine and develop well-traveled critical pathways as well as lesser-known byways with their students.

Teaching Galdós: Challenges and Opportunities

Given the variety of potential approaches to teaching Galdós, we have chosen to include essays that address the needs of a wide range of instructors and students, confident that readers will find much that sparks their creativity and enthusiasm. Galdós's works are taught in a diverse array of educational settings to students who vary in their preparation and goals, and it would be fair to ask what challenges are shared by a professor at an elite institution in a university town teaching *Doña Perfecta* to advanced undergraduate and graduate students and a professor at a community college in a large city teaching this work to first-generation undergraduates. Moreover, the mode of instruction in these disparate settings varies from face-to-face to hybrid and fully online, each of which entails specific pedagogical benefits and drawbacks. Yet regardless of institutional profile, student demographic, or teaching aims or modality, MLA survey respondents and the contributors to this volume identified a remarkably uniform set of challenges in teaching the works of Galdós. These include unfamiliar vocabulary and cultural references, arcane nineteenth-century subject matter that appears to bear little relevance to students' twenty-first-century lives, the daunting length and complexity of many of Galdós's works for students who have grown up in an age of sound bites and tweets, and a general lack of familiarity with Galdós (as opposed to, say, Cervantes or Gabriel García Márquez). The present collection offers a sample of the innovative ways instructors have risen to meet these common challenges and explores avenues of research that derive from the turn toward cultural studies in the first two decades of the present century.

The development of digital tools and methodologies in the past twenty years, in combination with the ever-expanding range of critical and theoretical frameworks that have arisen following the advent of cultural studies in the late twentieth century, has generated a wealth of opportunities for instructors seeking to bring the relevance and import of Galdós's work home to a new generation of students. Rapidly advancing technologies have produced digital repositories and tools that facilitate the research and teaching of traditional humanistic questions, as well as an ever-growing archive of "born digital" cultural materials that have themselves become objects of study. There can be no doubt that technology has radically altered how instructors bridge the linguistic and cultural chasms that students find challenging when reading Galdós. Across the board, our essayists describe turning to digital repositories of nineteenth-century resources and cultural artifacts (detailed in part 1, "Materials": popular press, advertisements, art, etc.) to offer their students "real slices of nineteenth-century life" (as one contributor, Erika M. Sutherland, put it in the survey for the volume), while digitized film and video provide easy access to contemporary adaptations for screen and stage of Galdós's works. Moreover, online resources such as the *Nuevo Tesoro Lexicográfico de la Lengua Española* (the compendium of historical dictionaries of the Real Academia Española; www.rae.es/obras-academicas/diccionarios/nuevo-tesoro-lexicografico-0) and web-based tools for both distant reading and collaborative close reading put powerful, interactive tools for linguistic, literary, and cultural analyses of Galdós's works at students' fingertips. To give just one example, social annotation tools used for collaborative close reading (in this volume, see Cope; George; Payán and Miller), can ease the formidable and traditionally individual task of reading complex works by making it a collective endeavor. Social annotation tools allow individuals or groups of students to tackle discrete reading and analytical tasks while sharing the fruits of their labor through a single digital interface and within a collaborative document. Whether in a traditional classroom or an online one, students can use these tools to crowdsource information, seeking explanations from and conveying answers to one another in a dedicated forum. Their digital marginalia might include hyperlinks to resources such as online dictionaries, *Google Maps*, or digital museum exhibitions. By embracing technologies that enhance aspects of the traditional classroom, many of our contributors continue to transform the teaching of Galdós's works, revealing their worth to students by harnessing the media, applications, and platforms that inform their world.

Whereas technology has expanded the range of tools and resources through which to approach Galdós's works, cultural studies has broken down the distinction between high and low culture and emphasized the construction of cultural values, opening the door to the consideration of his oeuvre alongside a wide variety of cultural artifacts. These range from popular media to specialist journals, from advertisements to auteurist films, and from aesthetic masterpieces to mundane chronicles of everyday life. As befits these newly diverse objects of study, teacher-scholars of Galdós have broadened traditional philological and historical pedagogies to include insights and methodologies ranging from food to film studies, from gender to celebrity studies, and from critical media studies to the medical humanities. Many of the essays in the present volume represent these fresh approaches, which may in turn prepare the terrain for future avenues of teaching and research. It is helpful to recall, for instance, that official tributes to Galdós in Madrid in 2020, designated "El Año Galdós" ("The Year of Galdós") by the city to commemorate the centenary of the writer's death, were promoted using a wide variety of digital media and platforms. Digital phenomena such as these, in combination with the profusion of Galdós-related cultural works of recent years, have opened the door to new and expanded approaches to Galdós's writing that break down previously siloed categories, such as "the nineteenth-century novel," revealing a web of connections to modern-day artistic manifestations and cultural and social phenomena. More indirectly, the paradigm shifts that have occurred with the advent of cultural studies and evolving technologies are reflected in instructors' increasing openness to creative class activities and unconventional assignments that move beyond the confines of the traditional research paper. Indeed, our contributors describe innovative activities and assessments such as kinetic embodiment exercises, collaborative digital collections, and filmmaking, among others.

An abundance of contemporary phenomena can prime students to appreciate the depth and foresight of Galdós's works, even as students examine those works from an ever greater temporal remove. Cultural studies approaches to Galdós's works, which frequently emphasize difficult, intersecting issues of race, gender, and class, provide compelling topics of discussion for students who have experienced the Black Lives Matter and Me Too movements and the COVID-19 pandemic. Teacher-scholars of Galdós engage students through late-nineteenth-century issues of race and empire from a postcolonial point of view in dialogue with contemporary debates on social justice, critical race theory, nationalism, and immigration, among many other topics. Instructors develop courses around issues of disability, contagion, and health care in Galdós's works, drawing students pursuing degrees in public health and medicine to their classes and finding that these concerns resonate profoundly in a world shaken by a global pandemic. Others center their research and pedagogical practices on Galdós's charged representation of normative gender roles, a point of entry that enables them to connect with a receptive and sophisticated audience of students ever more accustomed to considering gender as a broad spectrum of identities and expressions. All these approaches are represented by essays in the present volume. One need only add to these foci any number of recent and present concerns (financial crises, rapidly expanding information and communications technologies, political polarization, ecological degradation, etc.) to envision how instructors might continue to probe apposite concerns in Galdós's works in ways that invigorate and captivate students while helping them to understand both Galdós's world and their own.

Essays in This Volume

The present volume comprises eighteen essays grouped into five thematically focused sections. Each teaching approach was evaluated on its effectiveness, its capacity to enhance student comprehension and appreciation of Galdós, his times, and his milieu, and its innovative character, although these elements are not weighted equally across all essays. Whereas some essays shine at providing clear guidance on how to break down the author's most familiar or accessible works (such as *Marianela* or *Tristana*) for students new to textual analysis, other essays stand out by introducing little-known Galdosian texts into the classroom within relatively novel theoretical frameworks. The volume contents thus reflect our commitment to addressing the learning needs of diverse student populations. Recognizing the humanistic value of Galdós's work across varied demographics, we have sought to include a range of approaches that might appeal to and best serve students with differing levels of language skills and previous exposure to literary studies. Given the particular challenges of teaching Galdós's works to undergraduate students, many of whom still struggle with fluency in the Spanish language, the essays focus on strategies for engaging and scaffolding student learning at the undergraduate level. Nevertheless, authors have indicated where certain approaches might be easily adapted for graduate students. The approaches described by Julia H. Chang, Sara Muñoz-Muriana, and Juan Jesús Payán and Robin R. Miller will prove particularly useful for those instructors looking to incorporate Galdós into graduate-level syllabi.

Given the plethora of factors shaping the contributions to this volume, the essays could be organized in any number of ways: by class type, by pedagogical approach, by works studied, or by sociohistorical, thematic, and aesthetic questions examined, for example. We have opted to group them according to what we perceive to be logical connections between essays, without the intent to establish any fixed reading order. The first section, "Galdós and His World," focuses on the ways in which Galdós's works dialogue with and facilitate student entry into the social and political context of late-nineteenth-century Spain. The essays examine how Galdós's depiction of material goods (George), food and its attendant cultures (Muñoz-Muriana), and medical beliefs and practices (Sutherland) paint a vivid picture of Spanish Restoration society that feels accessible to students. The second section, "Galdós and Gender," takes the historical thread a step further by focusing on how Galdós explored the limits of bourgeois femininity (Miller) and masculinity (McKinney), including the latter's most toxic variant (Cope). Essays in this section treat gender as an intersectional concern entwined with other social discourses, such as those of class (Miller), colonialism (McKinney), and disability (Chang). The preponderance of criticism over the last half century that approaches Galdós through the lens of gender studies speaks to the author's engagement with gender issues throughout his career, and a number of other contributions to this volume (Álvarez-Castro; Cueto; Davies; Davis; Lomask) likewise consider Galdós's treatment of gender, though not as a principal concern.

The next grouping, "Galdós beyond the Novel," recognizes the pedagogical value of Galdós's less-studied literary production, particularly his theater (Versteeg), short fiction (Tang), and journalistic pieces (Rodriguez), which have each proven to engage students from varied backgrounds. Elena Cueto Asín's examination of the afterimage of the author and his work in contemporary Spanish culture provides an interesting complement to Margot Versteeg's study of Galdós as a literary celebrity. In examining a graphic novel and a telefilm in which Galdós appears as a character, Cueto likewise provides an excellent transition to the volume's fourth section, "Galdós in Adaptation," which sheds light on the long and fruitful relationship between Galdós's writings and varied modes of visual and audiovisual production, such as film (Álvarez-Castro; Davies), television, and, more recently, comics (Willem). The final section, "Galdós in Practice," emphasizes classroom practices, both traditional and experimental, that have proven to enhance student comprehension of Galdós's texts at both the linguistic and thematic levels. Lennie Amores provides an excellent guide to teaching *Marianela* in a manner accessible to novices in literary studies, and Laurie Lomask describes the use of theater games as a pedagogical tool. Her essay, which centers on teaching Galdós's drama, could pair well with Versteeg's contribution in section 3, but we have placed it here to highlight its innovative teaching methodology. Engaging with new digital platforms, Payán and Miller describe their experience with creating an open educational resource on Galdós that allows students to explore and interact with the author's works in a purely virtual format. Instructors with less technical expertise who would like to experiment with connecting students to Galdós by means of online interactions can consult Stacy L. Davis's essay on the use of *Twitter*, now *X*, as a teaching modality.

Comparative literature or area studies instructors teaching Galdós in translation must contend with the inconsistent accessibility and availability of published translations. The Materials section outlines existing translations, and throughout this volume, authors reference and cite translations of the works they discuss, providing valuable resources for English-language instruction. Readers will notice that *Tristana* is a frequent focus and, thanks to Margaret Jull Costa's translation, an excellent choice for English-language courses. However, not all approaches to this novel or others align easily with themes typically explored outside the field of Hispanic studies. Essays focusing on specific aspects of Galdós's work—such as material culture in *Fortunata y Jacinta* (George), medical humanities in *La desheredada* and *Torquemada* (Sutherland), disability and visual culture in *Marianela* (Chang; Willem), and performance in *Electra* (Lomask)—are particularly relevant for interdisciplinary courses. These essays rely on readily available and often intriguing translations, making them valuable resources for instructors seeking to integrate Galdós's works into diverse academic contexts.

These groupings are intended to orient readers rather than to establish definitive categorizations. We recognize the limitations of any single organizational structure when considering such a breadth of material, and essays may be consulted selectively and in any order that might serve the instructor. Those who teach courses in the medical humanities, for instance, might be most interested in the chapters discussing nineteenth-century Spanish popular medicine (Sutherland) and dominant discourses of the period surrounding disability (Chang) and contagion (Rodríguez). Instructors seeking materials on Spanish culture in the age of imperialism could focus on George's discussion of Japonisme, Collin McKinney's account of "manliness" wrought overseas, and Wan Sonya Tang's take on gothic renderings of imperial decline. In essence, we ask readers to take a cue from the creative ingenuity of Galdós himself and mix and match the volume's contents in ways that serve their needs and those of their students so as to produce an approach in the classroom that is sui generis, edifying, and utterly captivating—in the best Galdosian fashion.

Part One

MATERIALS

Editions

The digital age, with its various modes and platforms for delivering texts, greatly enhances the possibilities for teaching Benito Pérez Galdós's works in different pedagogical contexts and expands the range of texts that might be included in course syllabi. Electronic publications offer many advantages for the twenty-first-century classroom: not only are they more accessible and affordable than print, but they are also adaptable to a variety of innovative and engaging activities. In this regard, ensuring the quality and reliability of the digital editions students are asked to consult and study is crucial. Instructors should rely mainly on three sites. First, the Galdós author portal on the *Biblioteca Virtual Miguel de Cervantes* (*Miguel de Cervantes Virtual Library*; www.cervantesvirtual.com/portales/benito_perez_galdos/) offers a complete collection of the author's novels, dramas, short stories, journalism, and miscellany that can be read online in facsimile and HTML versions or downloaded as PDFs. Users should note, however, that many of these online texts are first editions and not necessarily the definitive versions of the works. In addition to the primary sources, the Spanish-language portal also contains introductory materials, a selection of classic critical studies of Galdós's writing, and access to the dedicated peer-reviewed journal *Anales Galdosianos* (*Galdosian Annals*) and a bank of audiovisual materials from the Televisión Española archive. Second, the Galdós page maintained by the Casa Museo Pérez Galdós (perezgaldos.grancanaria.com/obra-completa-en-epub) provides open access to the author's complete works in EPUB format and digital editions of three of his most popular short stories, "La novela en el tranvía" ("The Novel on the Tram"), "La conjuración de las palabras" ("The Conspiracy of Words"), and "¿Dónde está mi cabeza?" ("Where's My Head?"). The site also includes biographical notes, an overview of Galdós's literary works, and an image gallery. Third, the University of Pennsylvania's *The Online Books Page* (onlinebooks.library.upenn.edu) offers linked digitized editions of many of Galdós's works available on *Project Gutenberg* and *HathiTrust*; of particular note here is access to out-of-print English translations alongside various first editions.

Even if students are assigned digital editions, most instructors will want a hard copy for their own use in or outside the classroom. Over the past century, hundreds of editions of Galdós's novels have been published in Spain, Latin America, and the United States, and among these are numerous critical or didactic editions designed for students and scholars. Apart from the Aguilar edition of the complete works, which first appeared in 1958, the list of titles available to readers over the years has varied in accordance with the changing sociopolitical landscape and Galdós's perceived place in the Spanish national literary canon, which has determined how his works figure in high school and university curricula in Spain and globally. Since Spain's return to democracy in 1978, certain novels, such as *Marianela*, *Misericordia*, or the *Episodios nacionales Trafalgar* and *Zaragoza*, have been mainstays for students in Spain. Where Spanish is taught as a second language, *Doña Perfecta* and *Tristana* are the most popular choices for undergraduate courses, and *La desheredada* (*The Disinherited*) is most commonly selected for graduate syllabi.

The collection of Galdós's novels published by Alianza is one of the most complete and readily available in both new and used copies. However, the Alianza editions include neither notes nor introductions and may be of little use to instructors, especially those unfamiliar with the works. We have asked contributors to the volume to cite, when available, the Cátedra Letras Hispánicas editions of novels or plays they use. The collection includes sophisticated introductions, concise bibliographies, and extensive annotations, which, although aimed at academic readers, can be valuable supplements for students in upper-level undergraduate and graduate courses. These include *El abuelo* (*The Grandfather*), *La desheredada*, *Doña Perfecta*, *Fortunata y Jacinta* (*Fortunata and Jacinta*), *Marianela*, *Miau* (*Meow*), *Misericordia*, *Tristana*, the series of four *Torquemada* novels (*Torquemada*), and *La de San Quintín; Electra* (*The Duchess of San Quintín; Electra*). Where no Cátedra exists, we suggest the Crítica edition of *Tormento* and the Alianza edition of *Nazarín*.

For instructors who choose to assign physical books for classroom use, the Alianza editions might be an appropriate choice for the reasons already mentioned. However, excellent alternatives, especially for advanced and intermediate undergraduate courses, are the Cervantes & Co. editions of *Doña Perfecta*, *Tormento*, and *Tristana*, which include English-language introductions to the novels and their time, a Spanish-English glossary of words annotated in the text, and cultural notes that facilitate reading comprehension.

Translations

Unlike the French novelists of the nineteenth century, Galdós is not well known to contemporary readers outside the Spanish-speaking world. This situation is primarily due to the shortage of translations. A complete English translation of Honoré de Balzac's *Human Comedy* first appeared in 1897, but no similar translation exists of Galdós's contemporary novels, for example. Even so, during his lifetime, a handful of works were translated and published in the United States, including an 1895 translation of *Doña Perfecta* by Mary J. Serrano (Harper) and an unattributed 1911 translation of *Electra* (Dramatic Publishing). Of particular interest for their historical value are the 1879 translation of *Gloria*, by Nathan Wetherell (Remington), published only two years after the original Spanish (J. M. Perez); the 1886 *León Roch*, translated by Clara Bell; and the 1910 stage adaptation of *El abuelo*, *The Grandfather*, translated by Elizabeth Wallace). In the century after Galdós's death, some twenty additional titles have been translated into English, sometimes more than once.

To make Galdós's fiction accessible to instructors and students in fields beyond Hispanic studies, we have requested that contributors quote from the most recent translations in their essays. Contributors' essays on *Marianela* cite the 1923 version (Translation Publishing). Elsewhere, when available, more up-to-date editions have been used, including *Doña Perfecta*, translated by Graham Whittaker (Oxbow Books); *The Disinherited*, translated by Lester Clark; *Fortunata and Jacinta: Two Stories of Married Women*, translated by Agnes Moncy Gullón; and *Tristana*, translated by Margaret Jull Costa (New York Review Books). Unfortunately, except for Jull Costa's *Tristana*, most translations of Galdós's works are out of print. Many are available digitally, while others can be accessed by interlibrary loan or purchased through rare booksellers online.

Apart from those cited above, other notable translations include *A Royalist Volunteer*, translated by Lila Wells Guzmán; *Compassion*, translated by Toby Talbot; *That Bringas Woman*, translated by Catherine Jagoe; *The Duchess of San Quintín: A Play in Three Acts*, translated by Robert M. Fedorchek; *The Forbidden*, translated by Robert S. Rudder and Gloria Chacón Arjona; *The Golden Fountain Café*, translated by Walter M. Rubin; *Meow*, translated by Ruth Katz Crispin; *Miau*, translated by J. M. Cohen; *Misericordia*, translated by Charles de Salis (Dedalus); *Nazarín*, translated by Jo Labanyi (Oxford UP); "The Novel on the Tram" in *Madrid Tales*, translated by Margaret Jull Costa and Helen Constantine; *Our Friend Manso*, translated by Robert Russell; *The Shadow*, translated by Karen Austin; *Torment*, translated by J. M. Cohen; and *Torquemada*, translated by Frances M. López-Morillas.

Instructor Resources

We suggest three kinds of secondary resources for use by veteran Galdós scholars as well as those new to teaching the writer's oeuvre. The first includes histories of nineteenth-century Spain. Raymond Carr's classic account of Spanish history, *Spain, 1808–1939* (covering the period from the Madrid uprising against Napoleon's armies in May 1808 to the victory of Francisco Franco in November 1939), Adrian Shubert's *A Social History of Modern Spain*, José Álvarez Junco's *Mater dolorosa: La idea de Espana en el siglo XIX* (*Mater Dolorosa: The Idea of Spain in the Nineteenth Century*), and Jesús Cruz's study *The Rise of Middle-Class Culture in Nineteenth-Century Spain* provide accessible overviews of the era that includes Galdós's literary career. Carr explains the broad contours of events that shaped the nation. Álvarez Junco offers a more detailed reflection on the ebbs and flows of Spanish nationalism over the course of the century. Shubert analyzes the social conflicts that have determined the course of Spanish history from 1800 to the present. Finally, Cruz's study of the emergence and consolidation of middle-class society provides insights into the society that Galdós portrays in his works. These historians give helpful background on Spanish society of Galdós's time.

Second, to get a clearer picture of Galdós himself, instructors can consult two recent biographies: Yolanda Arencibia's *Galdós: Una biografía* and Germán

Gullón's *Galdós: Maestro de las letras modernas*. Whereas Arencibia takes a classic approach to the biographical genre, allowing the personal to drive reflection on the literary, Gullón is academic, organizing the life story around the main phases of Galdós's literary career. Alongside these two works, Hyman Chonon Berkowitz's classic *Pérez Galdós, Spanish Liberal Crusader* gives English-language readers a reliable, albeit quaintly old-fashioned, account of the author's life.

Finally, a third category of resources includes the vast body of literary criticism of Galdós's work. Joaquín Casalduero's *Vida y obra de Galdós* and José F. Montesinos's three-volume study *Galdós* offer extensive, comprehensive analyses of Galdós's writings and their biographical context. Another foundational text is Stephen Gilman's *Galdós y el arte de la novela europea: 1867–1887* (*Galdós and the Art of the European Novel: 1867–1887*), which situates Galdós's novels in the context of the broader development of the realist novel in Europe and argues for his influence on the genre. For more contemporary perspectives, Jo Labanyi's critical overview *Galdós* explores themes like gender, class, politics, and aesthetics in Galdós's works, situating the author in his cultural moment. Rounding out introductory materials is Harriet Turner's essay "Benito Pérez Galdós" in *The Cambridge History of Spanish Literature*, which serves as an essential orientation to Galdós's novels and his significance in Spanish literary history. Another valuable resource for instructors and students navigating Galdós's literary world is Federico Carlos Sáinz de Robles's "Ensayo de un censo de los personajes galdosianos comprendidos en novelas, cuentos y teatro" ("An Attempt at a Census of Galdós's Characters in Novels, Short Stories, and Plays"). The census of characters provides brief biographical sketches along with a cross-referenced list of the novels, plays, and stories in which the characters appear. Together, these titles provide classic foundational studies and more recent critical lenses.

The *MLA International Bibliography* is an excellent tool for discovering essential analyses of specific works by Galdós that have appeared in various academic journals. When executing such searches, students and instructors might narrow their results by examining the collection of articles published in *Anales Galdosianos*. The peer-reviewed journal, published since 1966, contains a comprehensive selection of studies by the most prominent figures in Galdós studies written in English and Spanish.

Multimedia Resources

Surprisingly, many Galdós scholars approach television and film adaptations and other transpositions of the author's works produced over the years with skepticism, disdain, or a certain trepidation. Nonetheless, few would deny that such resources can be invaluable tools for undergraduate and graduate classrooms. They can aid in comprehending complicated and lengthy texts read in Spanish but also open alternative avenues for engaging with Galdós's literary universe and the historical periods in which his works are set. The use of such materials as supplements to course readings, furthermore, helps connect the realist novel to other forms of mass media storytelling that emerged in the nineteenth century and have persisted into the present.

Here, we list three categories of items selected for their relevance, pedagogical potential, and availability. Many film and television adaptations are available on *RTVE Play*, on *YouTube*, or on DVD. All videos recommended include closed-captioning in Spanish, and some also offer English subtitles. Essential film and television adaptations that bring Galdós's works to life include *Fortunata y Jacinta*, directed by Mario Camus; *Tormento*, directed by Pedro Olea; *Marianela*, directed by Angelino Fons; *El abuelo*, directed by José Luis Garci; *La de San Quintín*, directed by Juan Antonio Hormigó; *Miau*, directed by José Luis Borau; *Nazarín*, directed by Luis Buñuel; *Tristana*, directed by Luis Buñuel; *Doña Perfecta*, directed by Alejandro Galindo; and *Sangre de mayo*, directed by José Luis Garci.

The radio dramas produced by Radiotelevisión Española in the 1970s, available on the public broadcaster's *RTVE Play* site (www.rtve.es/play), and audiobook versions offer an additional way for students to engage with Galdós's storytelling. Moreover, these resources hold attractive pedagogical potential and facilitate inclusive teaching practices by providing an alternative mode of accessibility. Notable audio adaptations include the 1973–75 Radiotelevisión Española radio dramas adapting the *Episodios nacionales* (first and second series), by Carlos Muñiz, as well as recent Penguin audiobook recordings of *Fortunata y Jacinta*, narrated by Paula Iwasaki; *Doña Perfecta*, narrated by Israel Elejalde; *Misericordia*, narrated by Elejalde; and *Marianela*, narrated by Elsa Veiga.

Finally, comics, graphic novels, and illustrated editions, as visual reinterpretations of Galdós's novels, also merit instructors' attention as supplements to the works upon which they are based. Relevant among such items is the Reino de Cordelia edition of *Fortunata y Jacinta* with illustrations by Toño Benavides; Rayco Pulido Rodríguez's graphic novel *Nela*, adapting *Marianela*; and Juan Pablo García's graphic retelling of the 2 May 1808 uprising in *El 2 de mayo* (Pérez Galdós and García).

Part Two

APPROACHES

GALDÓS AND HIS WORLD

"¿Dónde vas con el mantón de Manila?": A Material Culture Approach to *Fortunata y Jacinta*

David R. George, Jr.

Nineteenth-century European novels are filled with things that reflect the rise of a new political, social, and economic order based on the tastes and values of the urban middle classes. Objects represent the consumer revolution, spurred by global flows of knowledge and capital, that enabled far-flung colonial empires and interconnected the burgeoning metropolises of Europe. Things lost and found, collected and accumulated, bought and sold, discarded and stolen, can tell a great deal about a novel's characters and their fictional world. At the same time, they uncover the transformations of public and private spaces and processes of cultural assimilation in which realist novels were written, circulated, and read.

The categories of stuff that populate the works of Benito Pérez Galdós are innumerable and provide a rich ground for cultivating students' critical analytical skills and cultural awareness in various classroom scenarios. In this essay, I draw attention to a collection of objects from Asia found in *Fortunata y Jacinta* (*Fortunata and Jacinta*) to illustrate how a material culture approach might be designed and executed in an undergraduate or graduate class. My chosen things from China and Japan are undoubtedly obscure and perhaps even unimportant; they reflect my interests and expertise and serve as examples of what might be gained from this approach. The apparent randomness of my selection, though, effectively draws attention to material culture as a strategy adaptable to various course themes and combinable with almost any of the approaches described in this volume. Likewise, the tactic can be applied to any of Galdós's novels, plays, and short stories. Here, I suggest the method be used to teach *Fortunata y Jacinta* for two reasons: the sheer amount of stuff the novel contains gives instructors a multitude of options, and choosing from this cornucopia can make an otherwise unwieldy novel accessible in the undergraduate classroom (or feasible to include on a tightly packed graduate course syllabus).

Understood as material culture, stuff represents everything that involves the design, manufacture, and use of the material world. Things describe and narrate the past and present through their very condition as objects desired, traded, consumed, wasted, or cast off. Material culture studies is an interdisciplinary field whose methodologies intersect with literary and cultural studies, social history, and art history. It partakes of the traditional research methods germane to all these disciplines as it simultaneously relies on digital humanities techniques to mine an ever-growing electronic archive of artifacts and texts.

Scholars of Victorian and Gilded Age literature have done much foundational work on nineteenth-century material culture. Essential background readings for instructors wishing to implement the present approach should include Bill Brown's *The Material Unconscious* and Elaine Freedgood's *The Idea in Things*. Both describe a method of "strong metonymic reading" by which, as Freedgood notes, first, "the material characteristics of objects are sought out beyond the immediate context in which they appear" (5). Then they are returned to their "novelistic homes" and allowed to "inhabit them with a radiance or resonance of meaning they have not possessed or have not legitimately possessed" (6).

Practices of reading realist fiction have long privileged the analysis of subjects and plots, whereas objects have been deemed mostly inconsequential beyond what they suggest about the characters who own or use them. Freedgood enjoins, however, "But each of these objects, if we investigate them in their 'objectness,' was highly consequential in the world in which the text was produced" (2). Much can be learned by taking things literally rather than only figuratively: a material studies approach expands the possibilities of interpretation by considering not only what realist novels invite readers to look at, but also what they overlook in the configuration of what Roland Barthes called the "reality effect" (*Rustle* 139).

Attention to objects that seem meaningless because they appear to be nothing more than what they are allows readers a temporary break from the literary confines of novels to venture out into the world that produced them. The process involves investigating things to uncover the full range of their possible meanings in the light of their histories and properties and the social significance assigned to them at the time the text was produced. The practice opens tears in the narrative screen through which readers can catch glimpses of the play of history operating outside the novel. Traced out in this fashion, the study of objects reveals histories that, while not fully narrated in the text, nonetheless inform its meaning and undergird the metaphors and allegories that shape subjects and plots.

Concern with material culture has, not surprisingly, influenced nineteenth-century Spanish studies and enriched readings of Galdós's work and that of his contemporaries. The historian Jesús Cruz's observations on the emergence of liberal identities and middle-class culture in Spain, as reflected in things enumerated in household inventories, provide fundamental references for instructors and students. Notably, in the context of Galdós's literature, Noël Valis and Jo Labanyi have underscored the importance of things and the fluctuations over time of their possible meaning. Valis argues that material culture is a site where social and economic inequalities are constructed and contested and where objects mediate social and psychological identity (*Culture* 44). Labanyi, too, has identified how things reveal the underlying social and economic relations that shape characters' lives; however, she emphasizes more explicitly how the production and exchange of commodities involved in them are obscured by the apparent value of the objects themselves ("Things"). Both critics allude to *Fortunata y Jacinta*, among other novels, in this light, calling attention to how references to material culture construct notions of domesticity, gender, and class.

By and large, Valis's and Labanyi's analyses offer metaphoric readings of objects, drawing out what they convey or reveal about Galdós's characters and their circumstances and actions. However, neither explicitly undertakes the kind of metonymic reading outlined by Freedgood, where objects are first taken literally as they are embedded in the cultural practices of a more extensive network of things existing within and beyond the text. Metaphors can be rich sources of meaning, but in the classroom, they can be misleading if students ignore the literal or surface-level meanings of words and images in a text. Focusing exclusively on abstract, metaphorical readings can lead to the neglect of other vital aspects of the text. Students are especially prone to forcing symbolic interpretations onto objects, resulting in strained or unconvincing interpretations that may not accurately reflect the cultural context in which the text was created.

A material culture approach grounded in metonymic reading addresses this problem and offers many potential benefits for the hybrid language-literature classroom where Galdós's novels are most often taught in the United States. Metonymic reading encourages close attention to the details of objects in a text and emphasizes their interconnectedness. It can help students develop critical thinking skills by training them to notice the relationships and associations between different things and to use these connections to form interpretations and analyses. This can be especially useful for teaching students how to read complex texts in another language, since it allows them to break readings down into smaller, more manageable parts anchored by objects and to examine them closely for meaning.

A material culture approach focused on things from Asia might be used to analyze various novels in any number of teaching scenarios. In the present essay, I describe the strategy I have used in two different advanced undergraduate courses at a small liberal arts college. One is a seminar on realism in Spain that is conducted in Spanish and covers novels by Galdós and his contemporaries. The other is a course on the nineteenth-century fashion for things Japanese, known as Japonisme, in Spain, taught in English and cross-listed between Hispanic studies, European studies, and Asian studies. In each case, students are assigned three parts of *Fortunata y Jacinta*: part 1, chapter 2, "Santa Cruz y Arnaíz: Vistazo histórico sobre el comercio matritense" ("Santa Cruz and Arnáiz: A Historical View of Madrid's Business World"; Pérez Galdós, *Fortunata y Jacinta* 217–62; *Fortunata and Jacinta* 30–32); part 2, chapter 5, "Las Micaelas por fuera" ("The Micaelas, from Without"; *Fortunata y Jacinta* 729–43; *Fortunata and Jacinta* 330–38); and part 2, chapter 6, "Las Micaelas por dentro" ("The Micaelas, from Within"; *Fortunata y Jacinta* 744–801; *Fortunata and Jacinta* 339–79).[1]

Delivering course readings through a social or collaborative annotation tool, such as *Perusall* or *Hypothesis*, dramatically facilitates engagement with material culture. The general guidelines for annotation posted on the course syllabus prompt students to pay special attention to the objects they encounter in the readings. Students are advised to annotate not only things that seem significant and symbolic but also those that appear ordinary and mundane to accumulate a collection.

In the course on realism, the first reading exercise provides an entry point into the novel by connecting the world of commerce presented in the early chapters to the global flows of goods that passed through nineteenth-century Madrid. In the course on Japonisme, it establishes a framework for a broader exploration of cultural relations between Spain and Japan, which originated in the fifteenth century and extends into the twenty-first. Rather than front-loading the lesson with background information about the fashions for chinoiseries and japonaiseries in Spain in the eighteenth and nineteenth centuries, respectively, I use references to the "manton de Manila" ("Manila shawl") that appear in part 1, chapter 2 ("Santa Cruz y Arnáiz"), of the novel as points of departure for a student-led inquiry into the cultural phenomenon.

Using the annotation tool, I highlight the following passage in the reading for students to comment on:

> Creció Bárbara en una atmósfera saturada de olor de sándalo, y las fragancias orientales, juntamente con los vivos colores de la pañolería chinesca, dieron acento poderoso a las impresiones de su niñez. . . . Mal conocido es en España el nombre de este peregrino artista, aunque sus obras han estado y están a la vista de todo el mundo, y nos son familiares como si fueran obra nuestra. Es el ingenio bordador de los pañuelos de Manila, el inventor del tipo de rameado más vistoso y elegante, el poeta fecundísimo de esos madrigales de crespón compuestos con flores y rimados con pájaros. A este ilustre chino deben las españolas el hermosísimo y característico chal que tanto favorece su belleza, el mantón de Manila, al mismo tiempo señoril y popular, pues lo han llevado en sus hombros la gran señora y la gitana. (*Fortunata y Jacinta* 225)
>
> Barbarita grew up in an atmosphere redolent of sandalwood and Oriental fragrances and saturated with the vivid colors of Chinese shawls, all of which strongly influenced her childhood impressions. . . . In Spain this foreign artist's name is not well known, although his works have been and still are in plain sight, as familiar to us as works by our own artists. He is the genius of embroidery in Manila shawls, the inventor of the most

> striking and elegant type of branched flower designs, the extremely fertile poet of those madrigals of crêpe de chine composed in flowers and rhymed in birds. Spanish women owe to this illustrious Chinaman the very handsome, characteristic shawl that suits their beauty so well, and also the embroidered silk Manila shawl, as majestic as it is common, worn by great ladies and gypsies alike. (*Fortunata and Jacinta* 13–14)[2]

Many instructors might start the discussion of the passage by asking students to consider the symbolism of the overstock of Manila shawls mentioned in the description of Barbarita Arnaiz's childhood in the family store. Instead, I begin by asking them to think about the possible categories of merchandise such items might belong to or represent, centering the discussion on the Manila shawl. The Asian origin of the emblematic item is easily discerned from the narrator's descriptions. Still, students are encouraged to offer other taxonomies such as textiles, clothing, decoration, handicraft, luxury goods, and imports. Delaying further explanation beyond the narrator's remarks, I ask students to work in groups and use the list of descriptors in conjunction with Galdós's words to search for images and additional information about the objects. While a traditional search engine like *Google* or *Bing* may uncover visual representations and encyclopedia references, I instruct the class to use an online antique auction site like *1stDibs*, *Todocoleccion*, *Bonhams*, *Sotheby's*, and others, since these typically render a more comprehensive array of objects associated with the category.

As students share what they have discovered in their searches, the next step is to call attention to how the narrator's presentation of the Manila shawl marks it ironically as out of fashion by connecting the emblematic accessory to certain types of consumers. I ask what this association suggests about the item's market value and how this might also relate to its Asian origin. Twenty-first-century students quickly apprehend the specific association of China with inexpensive goods. Still, the question also prompts them to think more deeply about other aspects of the history of trade between Europe and Asia hidden in the object and now visualized through their electronic searches. The information to be gleaned from the auction sites is helpful here since, along with photos, item descriptions typically include origin, manufacturer, current location, and an estimated or actual price. The value of shawls in today's market for antiques, collectibles, and curiosities is crucial in discussing how they circulate in and around the novel, intersecting with the desires and aspirations of Galdós's characters and those of nineteenth-century Spanish society (as well as of contemporary consumers).

Before students read the two selections from part 2 of the novel, I ask them to suspend the impulse to attach symbolic meaning to the other things from Asia they will now encounter in the text. Instead, I instruct them to proceed as collectors of objects whose significance is derived from their accumulation and classification. In preparation for this task outside of class, students should become familiar with Walter Benjamin's concepts of the collector and allegorist described in his fragmented essay "The Collector." The instructor might introduce this essay in the classroom to wrap up the discussion of the Manila shawl or assign key passages from Benjamin's text along with the assigned chapters from *Fortunata y Jacinta*. In either case, for the purposes of the exercise, it is vital to note that whereas the collector gathers and owns objects of value for the pleasure of owning them, the allegorist sees objects not as possessions but as symbols with hidden meanings (Benjamin 211). The distinction guides students to realize that the work of attaching importance to objects in the world and in texts always involves a process of inquiry and research. In other words, students come to understand that both collectors and allegorists, despite their divergent goals, proceed in ways that are similar in accumulating things that further elucidate and substantiate their understandings and interpretations of objects (211).

In the second reading, students annotate references to items from Asia found in the novel using the taxonomies established in class. They uncover two things from Japan: a parasol and a mask. Once students have discovered these objects, I instruct them to identify and classify both according to their form, material, and origin using the previously mentioned online resources. I ask students to consider the newly found things alongside the Manila shawl (and Chinese silks) collected and discussed in the previous class. As students consider the connections between things as objects, they draw out deeper meanings and interpretations than if they were to consider the items as only symbolically connected. At the next class meeting, I divide the class into small groups and ask them to research the literal meanings and values attached to the objects in the context of nineteenth-century European culture. I ask them to pay attention to references that elucidate how the items connect to trends in fashion and allude to a taste for things Japanese, what images of Asia and Asians emerge on the surface of the things, and how the objects might be tied to larger social, political, economic issues and events of the period.

In the final step, with the results of this conversation fresh in students' minds, the objects are returned to the novel and examined in the light of their possible functions as structural and symbolic elements. I ask the groups to perform a close reading of the passages in which their items appear:

> El inmenso disco, semejante a una sombrilla japonesa a la que se hubiera quitado la convexidad, daba vueltas sobre su eje pausada o rápidamente, según la fuerza del aire. (Pérez Galdós, *Fortunata y Jacinta* 740)
>
> The immense disk, rather like a Japanese parasol without convexity, revolved on its axis, either slowly or rapidly, depending on the force of the wind. (*Fortunata and Jacinta* 337)

> Era Sor Marcela, una monja vieja, coja y casi enana. . . . Su cara, parecía de cartón, era morena, dura, chata, de tipo mongólico. . . . Su rostro, tan parecido a una máscara japonesa, continuaba imperturbable. (*Fortunata y Jacinta* 754)

> It was Sor Marcela, a lame old nun, practically a dwarf. . . . Her face (which looked as if it were made of cardboard) was dark, hard, flat, almost Mongolian. . . . Her face, whose resemblance to a Japanese mask was so marked, remained imperturbable. (*Fortunata and Jacinta* 346–47)

With the information gathered in the preceding activities, students should now be equipped to formulate and venture their own metaphorical readings. The discussion can be modeled by returning to the first reading selection and looking at how the presentation of the Manila shawl functions as a metaphor in the characterizations of Barbarita Arnaiz and, by extension, her ne'er-do-well son Juanito Santa Cruz in the middle-class world of commerce of mid-nineteenth-century Madrid. Here, instructors should take advantage of the opportunity to cite readings by Galdós scholars such as Mary Coffey and Lisa Surwillo, as well as other cultural critics and historians, that find in this passage evidence of the undercurrents of angst caused by Spain's waning imperial domination in the Philippines and the Caribbean that course through *Fortunata y Jacinta.*

When taking account of the things collected in the second reading, discussion questions will vary depending on the interests of the instructor and students. In the course on realism, I focus on notions of gender and class and delve into issues of race, imperialism, and national identity that emerge in the evocation of the Japanese mask as a vehicle for visualizing Sor Marcela, further expanding the previous discussion. The conversation then turns to complex aesthetic questions of how similes are used to produce mental images of things not existing in the text that facilitate readers' comprehension. Through the preceding activities, students became aware of the market value and symbolic relevance of the Japanese mask and parasol in the world outside the novel such that they might then consider why Galdós uses them to decorate his fictional world.

In the course on Japonisme, similar topics might be discussed to flesh out the geopolitical and economic trends that defined Europe's cultural relations and imaginations of Japan in the nineteenth century. However, in this context, I emphasize Galdós's aesthetic choices uncovered through the selection of items and how they suggest his awareness of the fashion for things Japanese that raged in Europe in the second half of the nineteenth century. The simile of the parasol provides an opportunity to introduce the impact of Japanese prints on Western artists. At the same time, the mask opens the way for discussions of encounters with other aspects of Japanese culture, such as religion and the performing arts, that served as touchstones for artistic innovation and experimentation in the European fin de siècle.

The title of this essay refers tongue-in-cheek to the famous tune "¿Dónde vas con el mantón de Manila?" ("Where are you going with a shawl from Manila?"), from Tomás Bretón's 1894 zarzuela *La verbena de la Paloma* (*The Festival of Our Lady of the Dove*), as a warning not to get carried away when interpreting the possible symbolism of objects in Galdós's literature. No doubt, the Manila shawl refers to a material culture marked, but not wholly determined, by colonial relations and their corresponding ideologies. Encouraging students to think first about the ubiquitous accessory literally rather than figuratively and in relation to other objects of similar origin and taste does not undermine such interpretations. Rather, it complicates them.

In conclusion, a material culture approach to *Fortunata y Jacinta* leads to the discovery of new connections and insights. It ultimately helps reveal the underlying themes and meanings of the text. Through the tactic of prioritizing metonymic over metaphoric readings of objects, students engage in active and interdisciplinary learning through inquiry and research. Ultimately, they better understand how material culture enriches interpretations of literature through individual and group exploration. The skills acquired in the sequence of activities described here can be applied to subsequent readings or form the basis of research projects on other categories of things students discover in Galdós's works.

NOTES

1. This essay cites the Cátedra edition of *Fortunata y Jacinta.*

2. The translator's choice of what are now considered antiquated terms—*Chinaman* and *gypsy* as equivalents of the Spanish words *chino* and *gitana*—might merit discussion of the trends of Orientalism and exoticism in the context of nineteenth-century Spain; for further background on this topic, see George, "Playing Japanese"; Charnon-Deutsch, *Spanish Gypsy.*

A Food Studies Approach to Social Class in Galdós

Sara Muñoz-Muriana

Food creates a powerful connection between the experiences of readers 150 years ago and those of readers today. A striking number of characters in the works of Benito Pérez Galdós talk about food, fantasize about it, indulge in it, and sometimes refuse it. Readers and scholars are drawn to the scene in which Fortunata slurps a raw egg in *Fortunata y Jacinta* (*Fortunata and Jacinta*, 285), they thrill to Francisco de Torquemada's excessive final feast in *Torquemada en la hoguera* (*Torquemada at the Stake*; 564–71), they react to the image of oranges sold by an itinerant vendor and devoured minutes later by Isidora Rufete in *La desheredada* (*The Disinherited*; 130–31), and they frown at the overwhelming stench of onions emitted by the girls of *El abuelo* (*The Grandfather*; 293). Food provokes strong emotional reactions in students, who soon realize, if they haven't before, that, although literary characters do not need to eat to stay alive, as Mervyn Nicholson notes, they do eat. And eating is something students can relate to, no matter their linguistic or cultural background. This essay therefore proposes to make nineteenth-century Spanish literature in general and the works of Galdós in particular more accessible and stimulating for students by approaching them through the lens of one of the most important cultural artifacts in every society: food.

A food studies approach works well with a large variety of graduate and undergraduate courses, ranging from introductory offerings on modern Spanish cultures to classes on critical and literary analysis and more advanced seminars that explore multidisciplinary connections with fields such as sociology, anthropology, gastronomy, human rights, and gender studies. Here, I focus on my upper-level course titled Is Spain a Modern Country? The Nineteenth Century Responds, in which I examine Spain's complex process of modernization from different perspectives that are highly relevant to understanding the way nineteenth-century Spanish literature articulated a discourse of modernity, including the emergence of marginal identities as political subjects, the role of fashion, discourses of subordination and rebellion, industrial development, urban space, visual art through the lens of food studies, and food studies itself. My motivation to bring food to the classroom is grounded in questions of class identity, a central organizing principle of modern life, as Robert Nisbet and Ulrich Beck, respectively, have made clear. In this context, I teach the novel *Torquemada y San Pedro* (*Torquemada and Saint Peter*) along with a selection of passages from *Tristana*, *Miau* (*Meow*), *Fortunata y Jacinta*, *Misericordia*, and *La desheredada* as well as a group of visual works that bring food to center stage and frame the food-identity connection that guides our discussions. Connecting food and class identity opens up multiple fields of debate. It introduces students to food as a powerful cultural signifier and symbolic marker of identity and social difference, since certain foods in these texts are rich with associations with a privileged middle class as well as a dispossessed working class. This encourages students to read foods as bearers of meaning that are highly relevant to understanding the way nineteenth-century Spanish literature articulated a discourse of modernity—from the chocolate devoured by Nicolás Rubín in order to satisfy his repressed libidinal appetite to the raw egg, symbolizing the most primal instincts, associated with Fortunata; from the taste for *cocido* (a traditional Madrilenian stew featuring chickpeas, potatoes, and a variety of vegetables and meats) acquired by Don Lope in *Tristana*, denoting his adaptation to his new underprivileged social situation—the same *cocido* that Doña Paca rejects as "comida de pobres" in *Misericordia* ("poor people's food"; 382)—to the unpleasant "olor de fiambre" ("smell of cold cuts") that dominates the Villaamil household in *Miau* as a metonymy of the desperation brought about by Ramón's *cesantía* ("unemployment"; 171).[1]

A close reading of these texts helps students understand what Gian-Paolo Biasin calls the "connotative function" of food (15), used to define the characters at the social, psychological, and affective levels. Francisco de Torquemada's obsession with amassing wealth and climbing the social ladder is materialized in the interclass marriage with Fidela del Águila. This "twisted" ascent, as one student described it, translates into an invasion of different social, economic, political, and spatial fields but is made evident in the novel mostly by the foods Torquemada chooses to ingest and, most importantly, those he rejects. His refusal to eat fresh fish and fruit, his extreme thirst for cheap wine, and his love for *garbanzos* ("chickpeas"), *pucheros* ("stews"), *salchichas crudas* ("raw sausages"), and *pan seco* ("stale bread"), along with the voraciousness with which he eats, reveal a brute, barbarian, uncultured and uncultivated self. Similarly, Isidora, in her aversion to onion-smelling foods and marinated dishes and her longing for hake and *besugo* ("red sea bream"), reveals an ambitious and fanciful character, her food preferences symbolizing the economic, social, and moral abyss into which she has let herself fall. These analyses lead to fruitful class debates about social mobility—undoubtedly a symptom of modernity—and the anxieties these metaphorical displacements generated among the middle and upper classes. Following Mikhail Bakhtin's conception of the novel as the hegemonic form of modernity (12), I discuss how literature examines human experience—an experience carried out in part through foods. Because the discourse on food inevitably becomes a discourse on pleasure and power, authority and rebellion, scarcity and excess, the individual and the community, it is in effect a discourse on the world. Students connect with the text, with Galdós, and with the nineteenth century when they discover the novel as a powerful cognitive vehicle where the discourse on food is, to borrow a phrase from Hans Blumenberg, an indispensable tool for *la legibilidad del mundo*, or "the readability of the world."

Students come to the first class on food having read the introduction to the book *The Flavors of Modernity: Food and the Novel*, which describes the representation of food in literature as a bearer of meanings that have to do with human experience (Biasin 3–28). This reading provides multiple examples of works that unite gastronomy and literature, offering students comparative contexts that are useful for studying Galdós's novels. I bring to class a list of quotations by cultural studies scholars who have written about food. Discussing these maxims, which identify food as a subject to think with and as a key ingredient in literature, gives students a taste of important relationships—not only between food and identity but also between food and word, or food and literary interpretation—that will guide our subsequent conversations. The list includes the following:

> "Some books are to be tasted, others to be swallowed, and some few to be chewed and digested" (Bacon 11).
>
> "If there is one sure thing about food, it is that it is never just food . . . food is endlessly interpretable" (Eagleton 25).
>
> "For what is food? It is not only a collection of products. . . . It is also, and at the same time, a system of communication, a body of images, a protocol of usages, situations, and behavior" (Barthes, "Toward" 24).
>
> "Tell me what you eat: I will tell you what you are" (Brillat-Savarin 1).
>
> "It is important to ask why and how we read, write, work and play with food in the gastronomically obsessed twenty-first century" (Gilbert xv).

These last words speak directly to the rationale behind our class meetings, where we search for the meanings of food in a literary text and try to understand how food is good to think with, as Lévi-Strauss suggests. This leads to an enriching class discussion about the omnipresence of food and how it connects us across centuries, geographies, races, and religions. At the same time, we comment on how food acts as a marker of selfhood since what we eat makes us different and gives us authenticity. In the light of the increased politicization of food, the increased awareness of food consumption and production, and the expansion of social movements associated with food, food today links the personal and the political, the material and the symbolic.

To complement this first discussion, I introduce the notion of taste as a model and value functioning powerfully on social classes by giving students a section of chapter 3 (169–201) of Pierre Bourdieu's *Distinction: A Social Critique of the Judgement of Taste*, where the sociologist discusses tastes as a practical affirmation of an inevitable social difference. I ask students what Bourdieu means when he states that taste is "a class culture turned into nature" (190) and to consider why and how the social definition of appropriate foods is established. For that purpose, we discuss the "taste of necessity" among the working classes (173) and what tastes in food depend on (for example, the dominant ideas within each social class of the body and the effects of food on physical strength and health). Following up on the different foods that Bourdieu associates with the working classes, I ask students to consider what dishes and ingredients would acquire a social connotation in nineteenth-century Spain and why. To tease out the social identity of foods, I assign Mariano José de Larra's short essay "El castellano viejo" ("The Old Castilian"), where a group of middle-class characters shows a lack of etiquette in devouring "un cocido surtido de todas las sabrosas impertinencias de este engorrosísimo plato" ("a well-stocked *cocido* with all the delicious impertinences of this difficult dish"; 107); Emilia Pardo Bazán's prologue to her cookbook *La cocina española antigua* (*Traditional Spanish Cuisine*; i–viii);[2] and the chapter "Unas palabras previas" ("Preliminary Words") from Vicente Palacio Atard's *La alimentación de Madrid en el siglo XVIII* (*Foods in Madrid in the Eighteenth Century*; 7–8). These readings identify food as a field of cultural production and focus on the role of typical ingredients and dishes of the working classes, like *garbanzos*, *escabechados* ("marinades"), garlic, and onions. The advice that Pardo Bazán gives to *señoras* ("ladies") at the end of her prologue stems from the social association of onion and garlic with underprivileged groups: readers using these ingredients should let the cook handle them so they will not be impregnated with an "avillanado rastro cebollero" ("crude onion trace"; viii). A close reading of these texts elicits a broader debate on Spanish modernization wrought in culinary terms, where the presence of the *pueblo* ("common people") and the rustic *cocido* is fundamental, as implied by the centrality given to this main dish, which has gained an identity as Spain's national dish in contemporary times. "¿Qué sería el mundo sin cocido?" ("What would the world be without *cocido*?"), the narrator of *Miau* wonders (Pérez Galdós, *Miau* [Cátedra] 250). It is worth reminding the students of the meaning of the word *garbancero*—a vulgar and ordinary person or thing—a definition that, once again, metaphorizes the relevance of the common people in building a Spanish national identity.

At this point, I assign the students a food scene from *Fortunata y Jacinta* (part 1, ch. 10, scene 5; 523–29) in which aristocrats and cardinals meet at the Santa Cruz dinner table to enjoy a sumptuous and copious banquet. In the light of Bourdieu's distinction between tastes of necessity and tastes of luxury or freedom, I invite students to identify food tastes as symbolic markers of social difference present in this scene. They recognize how the dominant class—distinguished, delicate, and concerned with appearances—tends to prioritize foodways that capture a privileged relationship to the social world where they enjoy benefits stemming from the possession of capital: freedom of choice, exemption from labor, leisure, and time. Finally, we closely analyze the chapters 8–11 of the second part of *Torquemada y San Pedro* (*Novelas* 557–74), in which a sick and starving Francisco, in an attempt to affirm his identity and, by extension, the relevance and centrality of the proletariat, decides to reclaim his agency by taking a walk through the western margins of the city, a physical place associated with his past identity as *pueblo*. While sitting at a bounteous banquet, he gives in to temptation, and after devouring the substances that define his plebeian social origins—*sopas de ajo* ("garlic soup"), *callos* ("tripe"), *magras con tomate* ("lean pork with crushed tomatoes"), *judías* ("beans"), and *aluvias y chorizos* ("pork sausages")—Torquemada suffers serious indigestion that causes him to lose his balance, regurgitate, and defecate in the middle of the tavern in a highly grotesque episode that elicits all kinds of reactions from students. The questions I propose below stem from productive conversations and conclusions that students reach when close-reading this chapter:

What substances does Torquemada consume, and how do these speak to the character's social trajectory throughout the novel?

What is Torquemada really saying when he refuses food (fish or succulent soups) or cannot digest it (chocolate)?

How does the imaginary banquet anticipate the subsequent real one?

How is the working class from Madrid's periphery defined in terms of substance and form?

How do hunger and gluttony connect geographical, corporal, and social spaces?

How do you interpret Torquemada's return to his social origins through food, only to be expelled and returned to the (geographical and social) center? Might this centripetal movement point to a revalidation of the still-empowering presence of the old ruling classes in nineteenth-century society?

When discussing these questions in groups, students bring Bourdieu back to the classroom to analyze how Torquemada embraces a taste of necessity and turns it into a taste of freedom, gobbling down everything that is heavy and fattening. But this choice of destiny only reveals his true nature, allowing students to identify the primacy of food and taste as classifying principles that chain the individual to his physical and social territory.

In commenting on Torquemada's social ascent, I call students' attention to the anthropologist David Howes's assertion that "social revolutions are always sensory revolutions" (11). Times of crisis are times of social revolutions (a maxim in which this whole seminar is grounded), and by giving cultural centrality to tastes of necessity, students comprehend how Galdós conceived of food as a key ingredient in the modern project, bringing forward the working classes as main cultural and political subjects and calling for a revision of traditional categories, such as clearly delimited and separated social spaces and a hierarchical system in which the lower classes are powerless and underrepresented in the social and symbolic order. In this conversation, one student once aptly asked whether the behavior exhibited by Torquemada in his final banquet—agitation, haste, rebellion, gesticulation, lack of restraint, use of hands instead of silverware—might be a metaphor for the escalating forms of social conflict in the late nineteenth century in western Europe, where the working class, fueled by the growing familiarity with basic industrial conditions and a greater tolerance to labor organizations, developed more active protest modes in the form of general strikes and street demonstrations. This idea is reinforced by the role of food as formative of community, which, on a small campus like Dartmouth's, where students do not have much to do socially other than eat together, serves to strengthen the verisimilitude of the fictional scene. "¡Es como la vida misma!" ("It is like real life!"), students have said about Torquemada's binge eating, his surrender to a world of culinary pleasures, and his subsequent evacuation: "Who has not suffered from indigestion in their lives?" These comments prompted me to seek other opportunities to move students beyond the words on the page and draw them into imagined worlds. I soon found my answer in visual literacy as a powerful complement to reader development, a means of encouraging communication and exchange of ideas, and a tool for increasing students' critical thinking skills. This approach is especially apt in today's world, where learners rely on images more than ever before, as research shows (Brumberger 19–22).

To introduce the idea that images are complex texts to be evaluated in a similar way to written texts, I bring to class a set of paintings contemporary with Galdós's work that are framed within the food-identity connection. These images serve as material for group presentations at the end of the course, where students draw from what they have learned, incorporating Galdós's texts into the discussion and offering meaningful comparative contexts between the written and visual texts. For instance, Pierre-Auguste Renoir's *Luncheon of the Boating Party* shows a group of men and women eating fruit and drinking wine at a restaurant along the Seine. Despite the numerous figures, it is the meal itself and the absence of ordering forms—expressed in the lack of etiquette governing posture and gesture, ways of serving oneself, the seating plan, or the arrangement of dishes, and in the primacy of quantity over quality in the substances consumed—that are the true subject of the painting. The presentation of this visual text sparks a class discussion of how the contestation of the established order boils down to a contesting of forms—those of established etiquette, politics, or art. Vincent Van Gogh's *The Potato Eaters* is concerned with portraying the dark atmosphere and primitive nature of the arduous peasant life. Examined in the light of questions of food and identity, the five figures with coarse faces and bony, work-worn hands are painted in earth tones, resembling the color "of a really dusty, unpeeled potato," a student once noted. The image serves as an invitation for research into the cultural tradition and sustainability of potatoes—a cheap, heavy taste of necessity—and the class discussion focuses on possible social interpretations of Van Gogh's canvas: might it be a rebuke of the harsh reality of the life of the working class along with a call for an endorsement of a simple, hearty lifestyle? Another powerful example is Joaquín Sorolla's *La comida en la barca* (*Lunch on the Boat*), which shows a group of Valencian men and boys eating an improvised lunch under the awning on their fishing boat. The image connects with Renoir's in the vulgar manners these hungry men display, devouring their bread and eating with their hands from a common bowl. A student cleverly commented on the irony exhibited in the painting in that the high price of fish, a controversial issue of public debate at the time, meant that only the wealthy classes could afford the products of the fishermen's labor, so the workers lunch on cheaper foods.

A food studies approach equips students with a few valuable lessons about the literary text: that food is never just food, as Eagleton would say; that food is embedded in all kinds of works, even those that are not, strictly speaking, about food; and that food bridges the gap between the nineteenth and the twenty-first centuries, providing an entry point to the fictional world whose characters and experiences express enduring themes to which we can all relate. More than a century later, Galdós is still nourishing the mind. And no matter how studied he continues to be, food gives us the chance to rediscover him, with delight, with each new class.

NOTES

1. Translations in this essay are my own.
2. I was introduced to Pardo Bazán's cookbooks by Rebecca Ingram's illustrative essay "National Identity and Class Conflict in Pardo Bazán's Cookbooks."

Medical Knowledge and Debate in the Novels of Galdós

Erika M. Sutherland

The nineteenth century saw the formalization of modern medicine: reforms in the system of medical education, new professional organizations, and a scientific approach to life more generally all contributed to this process. With significant numbers of students combining their language and culture studies with preparation for careers in the health professions, connecting medical issues with literature—bringing Spanish to the emerging field of medical humanities—is a strategic and rewarding choice for Spanish programs. In what follows, I propose approaching the texts of Benito Pérez Galdós more specifically through the study of popular expressions of public health and medicine in his works.

Galdós's novels feature medicine and medical doctors so prominently that they have been called a *colegio medico*, a medical association (Granjel 656). Their detailed descriptions of croup and the inner workings of a contemporary hospital for psychiatric patients merited inclusion in specialized medical journals. Galdós possessed more than two dozen medical texts and counted prominent physicians among his closest friends. For a century now, critics and scholars have parsed his use of medical imagery to see where it fails and how it succeeds in capturing contemporary realities.

Galdós was not, however, a doctor, a scientist, or even a scholar of medical practices. He was, instead, "un *curioso* de toda clase de conocimientos, capaz de penetrar en lo más hondo de muchos de ellos, si le importa y se lo propone" ("*curious* about all kinds of knowledge, able to penetrate the deepest aspects of many, if it matters to him and if he so decides"; Alas, "Benito Pérez Galdós" 22).[1] The students in our Spanish classes, who may one day become health care providers, are not specialists either, but they are generally curious. The approach I propose here is an invitation to engage with basic questions of what constitutes real medicine, who determines the validity of treatments, and how these ideas are disseminated. It is an approach that is accessible to undergraduates and calculated to inspire that curiosity using thoughtfully scaffolded activities and digitized resources from the period.

Galdós documented the evolution of medicine and medical practices across his *novelas contemporáneas* ("contemporary novels"), but several stand out for their extended focus on matters of health and disease. *Fortunata y Jacinta* (*Fortunata and Jacinta*) is in many ways a compendium of nineteenth-century medicine; an advanced undergraduate or graduate course could easily be designed around this novel's encyclopedic portrayal of the evolving discourses of public health and hygiene. Such a course would be structured around the literary, scientific, and periodical evidence documenting changes in medical education and practices, the rapid proliferation of patent medicines, and the open questioning of medical authority. However, and despite the compelling possibilities suggested by *Fortunata y Jacinta*'s representation of contemporary medicine, the sheer length of the novel can overwhelm less advanced students even before they begin.

I propose instead to use shorter novels as a jumping-off point. Read together, *La desheredada* (*The Disinherited*) and *Torquemada en la hoguera* (*Torquemada at the Stake*) show the interconnectedness of the Galdosian world. Both are accessible for undergraduate readers in a single-semester Spanish literature class or, with their English translations, in world literature classes. The two novels also provide excellent models for my approach to teaching through the lens of popular medicine.

For either monographic or survey courses, initial primary and critical readings help situate medicine within the humanities. The opening chapter of Claude Bernard's *Introduction to the Study of Experimental Medicine* outlines the basic principles guiding the thinking of contemporary physicians that would inspire Emile Zola and many of the naturalist writers who would follow (5–26). Michel Foucault's chapters "Spaces and Classes" and "Seeing and Knowing" from *The Birth of the Clinic* introduce the fundamental concept of the medical gaze (3–21, 107–23), while Lilian Furst offers a more focused pedagogy of medical humanities in "Medical History and Literary Texts." Michèle Respaut's essay "The Nineteenth Century's Obsession with Medicine: Flaubert's *Madame Bovary*" is an excellent introduction to the intersection of nineteenth-century literature and medicine. The toolbox I present in *Approaches to Teaching Emilia Pardo Bazán* can be applied more broadly to explore medicine in other texts, authors, and contexts (Sutherland, "Naturalism").

Focusing more specifically on Galdós, Michael Gordon's "The Medical Background in Galdós' *La desheredada*" and the opening chapter of Michael Stannard's monograph *Galdós and Medicine* provide a solid overview of how Don Benito interacted with medical science and its practitioners (1–36). Where Stannard observes that "Galdós possessed a singularly penetrating mind that enabled him to master many more contemporary medical ideas than have been recognized" (35), I invite readers to ask what it means for a nonspecialist to master medical ideas. It is here that the notion of popular medicine, medical knowledge accessible to the general public, takes on importance. To what extent did Galdós master popular medicine, and how might today's students do the same? Finally, what might inspire our students to want to do so?

I start this approach by appealing to students' emotions with a multimedia presentation inspired by an image from the second chapter of *La desheredada*: the leech (Sutherland, "Sanguijuelas"). When Isidora arrives at her aunt's shop, she recognizes the business by its distinctive logo: "la redoma pintada, en cuyo círculo aparecían nadando unas culebrillas, o curvas negras de todas formas, que servían de insignia industrial a Encarnación Guillén, conocida en distintos barrios con el nombre de la *Sanguijuelera*" ("the painted flask, and inside the circular outline little snakes, or black curves in various forms, seemed to be swimming. These curved lines served as the industrial insignia of Encarnación

Guillén, known in various quarters of the city as the *Leech woman*"; Pérez Galdós, *Desheredada* 96; *Disinherited* 21). The images of the leech and the practices related to its cultivation, harvesting, and use are guaranteed to capture students' attention. The initial and generally inevitable reaction of disgust quickly turns to curiosity as we explore ads for leech purveyors in period newspapers, scan articles addressing the science and business of the annelids, and see how different medical practitioners embraced or rejected their use. The entry for leeches in the *Farmacopea oficial española* (*Official Spanish Pharmacopeia*) serves to confirm that leeches were indeed used for a variety of purposes ("Sanguijuela"; see also Sutherland, "Industria"). This presentation foregrounds the issue of what constituted popular medicine in nineteenth-century Spain: How did the working classes perceive modern medical practices, learn about health and treatments, and access medical care? This presentation also models the use of the *Hemeroteca Digital* (*Digital Periodical Archive*) at the Biblioteca Nacional de España and the Biblioteca Virtual de Prensa Histórica. Each of these resources allows users to navigate their sites in Spanish or English, but the articles themselves are in Spanish. To help students navigate unfamiliar medical vocabulary in the texts, I direct them to the digital dictionaries of the Real Academia de la Lengua Española (Royal Academy of the Spanish Language; dle.rae.es) and the Real Academia Nacional de Medicina (Royal Academy of Medicine; dtme.ranm.es/index.aspx). Used in conjunction with English-language or bilingual medical glossaries, these guide students to identify the elements of health and illness found in the texts they read.

Using the scaffold and model of this initial presentation, students then work in small groups to create presentations on a treatment from *La desheredada*: they choose from the hydrotherapy or drugs mentioned in the opening chapter, set in the mental hospital at Leganés; the orthopedics crafted and sold by Emilia and Juan José; or the ipecac jokingly prescribed by Miquis in the second half of the novel. Presented in class over two days, the group project allows students to explore the medical resources and tools available while also digging more deeply into the novel.

Individual students then use the same tools and techniques to explore a disease or condition represented in either *La desheredada* or *Torquemada en la hoguera*, this time bringing nineteenth-century science into dialogue with the medical practices of today. Students are invited to choose from the different manifestations of mental illness seen in the first chapter of *La desheredada* and Mariano Rufete's epilepsy as it evolves over chapters 14–16 of the second part, or, from *Torquemada en la hoguera*, the symptoms of Valentín's meningitis, heartbreakingly described in chapters 3–5 and 9, or tuberculosis, introduced in chapters 7–8.

These two projects, detailed as part of the leech presentation, require that students consult a wide range of digital resources. Indeed, one of the most attractive aspects of using popular medicine as a point of entry into Galdós's Madrid is the extraordinary accessibility of realia from the period. For the group presentations, which must include a graphic component, students turn to ads for medical doctors, services, and medications from the period press. As noted above, these can be searched through the digital archives of the Biblioteca Nacional de España, the Biblioteca Virtual de Prensa Histórica, and Madrid's *Hemeroteca Municipal* (*Municipal Periodical Archive*). It bears noting that while many newspapers were financed through subscriptions, others published ads that both attracted readers and provided financial support for the publication. The final pages of *El Imparcial* and *La Correspondencia de España* include dozens of classified ads; as they are limited to the final pages of each weekly, it is easy for professors and students alike to get a sense of the scope of medicine's presence in daily life. By the 1890s, two new weeklies, *Blanco y Negro* and *Nuevo Mundo*, took the lead in advertising, with ads that featured additional, bolder graphics and were scattered throughout the publication. Medical advertising figured heavily in late-nineteenth-century papers: in a review of advertising from 1891 to 1899 in *Blanco y Negro*, nearly thirty-five percent of the ads were for medical products and services (Fernández Poyatos 114). In addition to providing images, the ads name contemporary practitioners and include vocabulary and cognate products and services that help students dig more deeply into the language and practices at hand: students tend to react to and remember ads featuring cocaine or alcohol or selling cures for the still-incurable syphilis and other *enfermedades secretas*, venereal diseases, mixed in with ads for piano lessons, movers, and books.

It may be tempting for students to assume that ads in these popular magazines and newspapers were for quacks and the patent medicines they hawked, but the digital tools in the Biblioteca Nacional de España's *Hemeroteca Digital* allow for easy and quick cross-referencing with the medical press. Indeed, the categories listed on the left side of the archive's site allow researchers to limit their search to specific *colecciones* ("collections"), including medical, public health, or women's periodicals.

Additional journals and hundreds of nineteenth-century medical texts are freely available in digital format, both through *Google Books* and a variety of other archival sources. Since there is no shortage of period sources, it is helpful to guide students to texts either exceptionally popular or familiar to Galdós. The *Libro médico azul* (*Blue Book of Medicine*), one of the books in the personal library of Galdós, is available in digital format in the Wellcome Collection, the London-based museum and library of health and the human experience. Like the *Farmacopea oficial española*, also available online, it is a fascinating compendium of period medicines and pharmacological practices. The journal *Anfiteatro Anatómico Español* (*Spanish Anatomical Amphitheater*), written for both the professional and the more dedicated amateur, is available through *Google Books* and includes a wide range of topics. From the private library of Galdós, all three volumes of Sigismond Jaccoud's *Tratado de patología interna* (*Treatise on Internal Pathology*) can also be found on *Google Books*. Jaccoud's detailed descriptions of meningitis, for example, can be seen in the suffering of Torquemada's beloved son, Valentin, "sofocado, echando lumbre de su piel, los ojos atónitos y chispeantes, el habla insegura, las ideas desenhebradas" ("choked up, his skin emitting heat, his eyes astonished and sparkling, his speech unsteady, his thoughts disorganized"; Pérez Galdós, *Torquemada en la hoguera* 98; *Torquemada at the Stake* 35). The minutiae of Valentín's treatments, including *calomelanos* ("calomels"), *revulsivos* ("counterirritants"), *sinapismos* ("mustard plasters"), *embrocaciones* ("liniments"), and *yodoformo* ("iodoform"; 109; Appelbaum 55), can again be checked against period recommendations.

Luis Granjel wrote that "[e]ntre las convicciones ideológicas que alimentan la vida intelectual del médico galdosiano, destaca, en primer término, su admiración, sin reservas, ante las conquistas de la ciencia" ("[a]mong the ideological convictions sustaining the intellectual life of the Galdosian doctor, what stands out more than anything else is his unreserved admiration of the progress of science"; Granjel 663). Nonetheless, in *La desheredada* and *Torquemada en la hoguera*, medicine is presented as a science very much up for debate, where more traditional practices and practitioners stand in opposition to modern techniques and younger doctors, and patients and their families turn to patent and folk remedies even as they consider or receive professional care. The fluid interplay between "real" medicine and out-of-date medicine or quackery was a staple of the professional medical and popular press of Galdós's Spain. Students see these tensions in the first chapter of *La desheredada*, set in the hospital at Leganés, and in the problematic relationship that develops between Augusto Miquis and Isidora in the second part of the novel, notably in chapter 17, when Augusto counsels Isidora that "valdría mil veces más que te murieras" ("it would be far better if you were to die"; Pérez Galdós, *Desheredada* 489; *Disinherited* 323). Torquemada's endless criticism of Dr. Quevedo and questioning of his methods and skills are summed up in chapter 4, when the distraught father cries out, "¿Para qué sirven los médicos?" ("What good are doctors?"; *Torquemada en la hoguera* 98; *Torquemada at the Stake* 35).

This question introduces a final motivation behind this pedagogy: not only is medicine a source of interest in a literature class, but the role of literature in the education of medical practitioners is also compelling. Literature offers unique insight that complements the specialized language training in a medical Spanish course, a first step toward the more intentional and reflective inclusion of the humanities in medicine advocated by Caroline Wellbery. In the British medical journal *The Lancet*, Wellbery explains that "[a]rt can demonstrate the interpretive process that leads to resolution of uncertainty: first, by defining its precise nature; second, by identifying which information is lacking; third, by recognising that interpretation is a process that occurs over time; and finally, by knowing the contributions of various aspects of the context" (1687). In practice, literature guides doctors and nurses "a recuperar el lenguaje que permite entendernos y respetar al enfermo" ("to recoup the language that allows us to understand each other and respect the patient"; Barbado Hernández 198).

Nearly a century and a half earlier, Bernard closed his *Introduction to the Study of Experimental Medicine* with a thought for teachers: "The true scientific method confines the mind without suffocating it, leaves it as far as possible face to face with itself, and guides it, while respecting the creative originality and the spontaneity which are its most precious qualities. Science goes forward only through new ideas and through creative or original power of thought" (Bernard 226). Bringing to life the vital tensions of health science, creativity, accessibility, information, and acceptance in a relevant and accessible way, Galdós's novels offer new inspiration for our Spanish students headed to professions in health care and fresh insight on the many ways we all connect with medicine.

NOTE

1. All translations are by the author unless otherwise attributed.

GALDÓS AND GENDER

Teaching the Woman Question through Selections from Galdós's *Tristana*

Gabrielle Miller

As in Victorian England, where men and women hotly debated what was widely known as "the woman question," in contemporaneous Spain what was often called *la cuestión femenina* became something of an obsession within the newly dominant middle classes. Unlike England and the United States, however, Spain did not experience a consolidated feminist movement centered on female suffrage and emancipation until the early twentieth century. Nevertheless, as Spain grappled with modernization and industrialization in the second half of the nineteenth century, issues central to the woman question—particularly, the perceived need to define both the nature of women and their role within Spain's rapidly changing society—seemed increasingly urgent. Indeed, in January 1892, Emilia Pardo Bazán—a leading Spanish feminist, renowned realist author, and close friend of Benito Pérez Galdós—opined, "Es la llamada *cuestión de la mujer* acaso la más seria entre las que hoy se agitan" ("The so-called *woman question* is perhaps the most serious issue debated today"; "Opinión" 72).[1]

As both a keen observer of Spanish society and a key player in the cultural processes of Spanish nation building, Galdós consistently dialogued with the issues and anxieties surrounding the woman question in his realist fiction.[2] Yet Galdós is often left out of discussions of gender and feminism in intermediate-level Spanish language, literature, and culture classes because of the considerable length of his novels. This essay draws from my experience teaching selections from Galdós's novel *Tristana* alongside writings by contemporaneous social commentators who hotly debated Spain's woman question. Of course, there are disadvantages to not reading a work in its entirety; however, analyzing strategic portions of Galdós's novel exposes students to his unique realist style and, perhaps more importantly, facilitates their critical engagement with the text (in this case, through a gendered lens) and contextualizes their analysis in the work's particular sociohistorical moment. As we will see, students also learn about the emergence of feminist thought, both in Spain and in England, and begin to make connections between nineteenth-century gender issues and those that remain unresolved in the United States today.

This essay will outline a two-to-three-day unit that I have taught in "traditional" intermediate courses for Spanish minors and majors, such as Spanish Civilization, Introduction to Hispanic Literature, and Spanish Composition, as well as more advanced classes on nineteenth-century Spanish cultural topics or Iberian feminisms. Since Margaret Jull Costa has published an excellent translation of *Tristana*, this lesson plan could also be adapted for inclusion in English-language courses that, for example, focus on the emergence of Western feminism or modern world literature. In the first section of this essay, I detail nineteenth-century Spanish and Victorian-era texts that describe the feminine ideal of the *ángel del hogar* ("angel in the house") prevalent in both countries. This middle-class ideal emerged as "an emblem of bourgeois hegemony" not only in Spain but throughout Western Europe, replacing aristocratic codes of conduct associated with the *ancien régime* (Jagoe, *Ambiguous Angels* 7). The latter part of this essay details specific narrative moments in *Tristana* that students analyze in my courses. I suggest productive lines of classroom debate that encourage students to contextualize their literary analysis in the nineteenth-century primary documents discussed in previous days. Finally, I briefly consider the pedagogical possibilities afforded by reading *Tristana* alongside Luis Buñuel's film adaptation of the novel, drawing from my experience teaching both at the undergraduate and graduate levels.

A brief summary of Galdós's novel illustrates why *Tristana* lends itself particularly well to discussions of Spanish protofeminism as it relates to the woman question. The eponymous protagonist of *Tristana* is a high-spirited young woman who is determined to overcome her precarious socioeconomic situation and limited education to pursue a vocation that will grant her both self-fulfillment and financial independence. These aspirations are truncated both by her personal situation—an orphan without an inheritance, Tristana has also been seduced by her elderly guardian, Lope Garrido—and by the expectations of Spain's patriarchal society. Tristana falls in love with Horacio, a young artist of means who asks for her hand in marriage. Yet Tristana repeatedly refuses to marry him, radically insisting on chasing her highest ideal instead: "ser libre . . . y honrada" ("to be free—and honest"; Pérez Galdós, *Tristana* [Cátedra] 139; *Tristana* [New York Review Books] 23). While Horacio is away from Madrid caring for an ailing aunt, Tristana suffers a grave illness that culminates in the amputation of her leg. Tristana's disability leaves her permanently in Lope's care, and in the end, guardian and ward are married.

Reading *Tristana* alongside nineteenth-century social commentaries contextualizes the titular protagonist's predicament, helping students understand why Tristana could not simply "get a job" or resist masculine authority by abandoning her abusive, aging guardian. Before analyzing *Tristana*, students first study mainstream discourses of femininity that emerged in the mid–nineteenth century, with the concomitant rise of Spain's bourgeois, or middle, class. The idealized model of femininity was the aforementioned *ángel del hogar*, the virtuous wife and mother who transformed the home into a refuge that safeguarded her husband and children from corrupting forces outside.[3] What Catherine Jagoe has called "la obsesión burguesa con la moralidad" ("the bourgeois obsession with morality"; "Misión" 27) is thereby guaranteed by the angelic wife and mother, whose "misión santa," or "saintly mission," elevates her stature within the bourgeois family, which came to be viewed as a sacred cornerstone of Spanish society. On the one hand, nineteenth-century gendered discourses of domesticity represent a welcome departure from misogynistic cultural attitudes that historically assumed and even insisted on women's physical, mental, and moral inferiority to men with few exceptions (25). In a country where, as late as 1877, only twenty percent of women could read and write, the fact that the angelic ideal tasked middle-class mothers with the early education of their children galvanized a concerted push for women's education (Jagoe, "Enseñanza" 104). On the other hand, however, in identifying women exclusively as wives and mothers, mainstream views of gender espoused by the emergent middle class all but guaranteed female exclusion from the labor market, perpetuating women's financial reliance on men, be they husbands, fathers, or brothers. Moreover, even as women were no longer considered inferior to men—morally, they were often considered superior—in practice women's value was predicated on gendered expectations of self-sacrifice and abnegation rather than self-realization, as we will see in Pardo Bazán's complaint below.

Students weigh these tensions as they analyze texts by Spanish commentators—many of them women—that discuss the *ángel del hogar* model and feminine nature more generally. While there was not a widely organized political feminist movement in Spain until the early twentieth century, in the final decades of the nineteenth century several Spanish women writers expressed what Alda Blanco has called a "conciencia feminista" (feminist consciousness), that is, the realization that women's subordinate position in society was socially rather than naturally ordained ("Teóricas" 447, 462–65). Undergraduates who read selections of Ángela Grassi's article, aptly named "La misión de la mujer" ("The Woman's Mission"), observe the religious and almost bombastic rhetoric she employs to exalt women's domestic role. Given the exaggeratedly laudatory tone, employed by Grassi in all earnestness, students often assume either that the author is a man or that the piece is a satire. At this point, I introduce students to the concept of protofeminism and offer them the opportunity to reflect on why Grassi feels the need to insist so vehemently on the inherent value of women's domestic role in the first place. Reading Grassi as a protofeminist suggests to students both the considerable cultural prevalence of misogyny in Spain up to this point in history and the uphill battle to be fought by future Spanish feminists at the turn of the century and beyond. Students may also read selections such as "El Ateneo de Señoras" ("The Women's Athenaeum"), by Faustina Sáez de Melgar, and "Un libro para las damas" ("A Book for Ladies"), by María del Pilar Sinués de Marco. Both authors argue that greater educational opportunities will help women become better wives and mothers. Nevertheless, as observers of growing feminist movements elsewhere, they vehemently express their opposition to women's emancipation.

Students may also read a selection from Francisco Alonso y Rubio's treatise *La mujer* (*Women*), which provides a particularly useful example of complementarianism, a central tenet of bourgeois gendered discourses: "Los sexos han nacido el uno para el otro. . . . Son dos seres que se completan" ("The sexes were born for each other. . . . They are two beings that complement each other"; 66). After reading what from our twenty-first-century perspective is a decidedly nonscientific text, students are routinely surprised to learn that Alonso y Rubio was a physician. This may open conversations about the ways in which even today, women's medical needs may be minimalized or misunderstood, particularly by male doctors. While students often respond with indignation to this text, it is worth reminding them—especially at a Christian school like Baylor University, where I teach—that complementarianism remains an important theological concept in some evangelical circles.

Students may also be surprised to learn that at the time of *Tristana*'s publication, Catholic thought exercised a profound influence on the writings of prominent feminist authors such as Concepción Arenal and Concepción Gimeno de Flaquer. Students may read selections of Arenal's "La mujer de su casa" ("The Woman in Her House"), which strongly critiques the "angel of the hearth" model for discouraging women from contributing to "el bien público" ("the public good") through charitable (rather than remunerated) work (496). In Gimeno's "El problema feminista" ("The Feminist Problem"), meanwhile, the self-proclaimed "feminista conservadora" ("conservative feminist") defends women's right to an advanced education and even a salaried profession (531–34); yet her essay "La mujer intelectual" ("The Intellectual Women") declares that "la mujer moderna . . . tiene una maternidad moral, ilimitada e infinita" ("the modern woman . . . has a moral, unlimited, and infinite maternity"; qtd. and trans. in Bieder, "First-Wave Feminisms" 171). Analyzing such texts stimulates student debate on the ambivalences and contradictions inherent to early feminist thought in Spain by underlining how arguments in favor of improving women's social conditions, and their education in particular, were consistently tied to their perceived maternal identity. To further contextualize this debate in the graduate classroom, I introduce Karen Offen's oft-cited article, "Defining Feminism," which differentiates between "relational" and "individual" feminism in the nineteenth-century European context (134–53).[4]

Although these works were published two to three decades before Galdós penned *Tristana*, the original "angel of the hearth" model expressed by the Isabelline-era authors Grassi, Sinués de Marco, and Sáez de Melgar remained extremely influential at century's end. Indeed, Sinués de Marco's *El ángel del hogar* underwent eight editions published between 1857 and 1904, a bestseller among an avid reading public of chiefly middle-class, female readers (Blanco, "Domesticity" 373). Albeit that the "angel of the hearth" model emerged in England as a central tenet of Victorian bourgeois ideology as well, we should not think of the Spanish *ángel del hogar* as a mere copy of the English version but rather as a similar ideology that emerged contemporaneously as a result of shared processes of modernization, despite the material differences between both countries.[5] Therefore, a comparative examination of women's roles in the nineteenth century further enriches student comprehension of Tristana's plight. Students in the Spanish classroom as well as those reading *Tristana* in translation may benefit from reading Coventry Patmore's 1854–56 poem "The Angel in the House."[6] An ode to Patmore's first wife, the poem describes the eponymous feminine ideal in Victorian middle-class society, exemplifying the so-called separate spheres ideology also dominant in Spain. A more extreme example of the absolute cultural identification of women with domesticity is evidenced in William R. Greg's essay "Why Are Women Redundant?," which laments the growing number of unmarried, "superfluous" women in England. Owing to a gender disparity in the population during this time, women vastly outnumbered men (Liggans 18). Greg's solution is to ship England's unpartnered women to Australia and the other British colonies to find husbands. For students reading *Tristana* in translation, these Victorian texts both elucidate the radicality of Tristana's desire to eschew marriage and emphasize the transnational nature of such gendered paradigms. Instructors might also contrast Galdós's *Tristana* with George Gissing's *The Odd Women* to compare the limited opportunities afforded single women in both countries during this period. Students could identify similarities between Rhoda Nunn, the spirited "New Woman" protagonist of Gissing's novel, and Tristana to consider to what extent each achieves her respective ideal.

Although the movement for women's political emancipation was virtually nonexistent in Spain in the 1890s, by the final decades of the nineteenth century, progressive Spanish voices advocating for women's greater access to education had become mainstream (Jagoe, "Enseñanza" 127–32).[7] Spain's most radical feminist—and a close friend of Galdós's—was Emilia Pardo Bazán, whose feminist thought in the 1880s and 1890s more directly reflected Tristana's demands for educational and professional opportunities outside the realm of motherhood. Students in the Spanish-language classroom may read excerpts of Pardo Bazán's decidedly feminist article "Una opinión sobre la mujer" ("An Opinion about Women"), cited earlier in this essay. Unlike Sinués de Marco, Sáez de Melgar, and even Gimeno de Flaquer, who would advance women's education for the benefit of their husbands and children, Pardo Bazán insists that women, like men, possess the right to self-determination. At the same time, she condemns the lack of labor opportunities afforded women, critiquing bourgeois discourses that censure prostitution while denying women professional training. Pardo Bazán not only argues that women should not be exclusively defined as wives and mothers but also states that they have the right to celibacy—that is, the right not to marry and bear children. As students will see, Tristana goes one step further, claiming that sexual relations with Horacio outside of marriage do not impinge on her honor.

Reading these myriad texts before analyzing Galdós's text not only contextualizes *Tristana* but also enables students to see the radicality of the protagonist's claims to autonomy and independence. I then provide students with a document containing a detailed synopsis of the novel as a whole and the excerpts from *Tristana* that they will analyze in class, which include passages from chapters 5 (Pérez Galdós, *Tristana* [Cátedra] 137–41), 13 (180–84), 14 (185–89), 17 (204–08), 28 (267–69), and 29 (270–72). Group work, including close reading and answering discussion questions, precedes class-wide discussion. Initially, students identify contrasts between the gendered expectations put forth in the primary texts they have read and Tristana's own aspirations. Analyzing one of the protagonist's early conversations with Horacio, from chapter 5, illustrates Tristana's radical desire for self-realization and financial security outside of marriage: "Si nos hicieran médicas, abogadas, siquiera boticarias o escribanas, ya que no ministras y senadoras, vamos, podríamos. . . . [Y]o quiero vivir y ser libre" ("If they'd let us be doctors, lawyers, even pharmacists, or scribes, if not government ministers or senators, then we would be able to manage. . . . I want to live and be free"; *Tristana* [Cátedra] 139; *Tristana* [New York Review Books] 23). In the same chapter, Tristana's servant and confidant, Saturna, similarly describes what she views as the only three professions open to women: marriage, the theater, or prostitution. In their analysis of this section, students may compare Saturna's attitude toward prostitution—she refuses to even name it—with that of Pardo Bazán in "An Opinion about Women."

Students particularly enjoy discussing Tristana's aversion to marriage, which she explains in no uncertain terms to Horacio in chapter 9. I remind students that Tristana's antinuptial positioning is in fact an idea inherited from her corrupt guardian, Lope, who himself is an aged Don Juan claiming marriage to be repugnant. Students observe that Lope manipulates seemingly progressive ideals to maintain control of his ward: her refusal to marry Horacio in fact strengthens her dependence on Lope, whose belated support of her education—which students analyze in chapter 17—all but guarantees her unwillingness to leave him. Despite their apparent unorthodoxy, Lope and Horacio, whose lifestyle in Madrid initially suggests a more open-minded bohemianism, both ultimately subscribe to gendered bourgeois values: as we have seen, Lope ultimately marries Tristana while Horacio, students read in chapter 14, secretly hopes that over time his future wife will become "más mujer, más doméstica, más corriente y útil" ("more feminine, more domestic, more ordinary and useful"; *Tristana* [Cátedra] 186; *Tristana* [New York Review Books] 75). Students perceive the extent to which patriarchal, gendered expectations, and the angelic ideal in particular, were ingrained in Spain's middle-class society.

Finally, students read the final two, short chapters of the novel that detail Tristana's physical decline, her newfound spirituality, and her eventual marriage to Lope. The novel closes with one of Galdós's most enigmatic conclusions: "¿Eran felices uno y otro? . . . Tal vez" ("Were they happy, the two of them? Perhaps"; *Tristana* [Cátedra] 272; *Tristana* [New York Review Books] 169). While the conclusion's ambiguity tends to provoke considerable indignation in class, it also generates animated conversation as students debate whether Tristana's fate represents a punishment for her feminist ambition, so ahead of its time, or a condemnation of Spain's patriarchal society and the shortcomings of the "angel of the hearth" model. If time permits, students should also read the review of *Tristana* in which Pardo Bazán, as a self-declared feminist, takes serious issue with the novel's conclusion. They might also watch Luis Buñuel's film adaptation of the novel, starring Catherine Deneuve, which radically changes the denouement: Tristana is made responsible for Lope's death in an unprecedented if hair-raising assertion of feminine agency.

Buñuel sets his adaptation of *Tristana* in 1930s Toledo during the Second Spanish Republic, a progressive government that granted women the vote in 1933 but was subsequently toppled by Spain's bloody civil war (1936–39) and Francisco Franco's ensuing, decades-long dictatorship. By the Second Spanish Republic, feminist activism in Spain, though far from homogenous, was increasingly recognized as endemic to the modern world (Johnson and Castro 221).[8] Thus Tristana's emancipatory ambitions in the film would have been seen as less radical for the period and perhaps even indicative of a certain nostalgia on the director's part for the Second Spanish Republic. Don Lope's control of his ward, meanwhile, seems still more despotic. Students enjoy debating Buñuel's alternative ending: Is Tristana's decision to not intervene in Lope's heart attack defensible, or is she an accomplice to his death? At the graduate level, students with an introduction to disability studies may also debate Buñuel's sexualization of Tristana following the amputation of her leg. Does Tristana's decision to show her naked body to Saturna's deaf son constitute a form of agency? Is Tristana objectified by the camera? To what extent are we as spectators implicated as voyeurs? Are both characters somehow united in their disability? And to what extent is that identification problematic?[9]

In the final decades of the nineteenth century, Spanish society would become increasingly polarized along political and cultural lines in ways not dissimilar to the so-called culture wars dividing the United States today.[10] It is not difficult for undergraduates in the United States to identify parallels between Spain's nineteenth-century woman question and the myriad social and political debates bound up in the rights, identities, and cultural expectations of those who identify as women in US society. Our conversations may turn to a discussion of the desirability of marriage today—and the often-gendered societal pressures to find, and marry, a partner—in which some students critique and others defend the institution of marriage. Students also readily identify with the myriad issues in the United States surrounding access to affordable education and, while recognizing women's progress in the workplace, reflect on both the gender wage gap and the mounting pressures on women to perfectly embody professional and maternal identities, often simultaneously. That Tristana at first refuses and then is unable to leave her abusive guardian also generates discussions about the cyclical and persistent nature of gender violence. Finally, students may learn more about contemporary feminist activism in Spain and Latin America by, for example, reading social media posts and newspaper reports about the worldwide demonstrations traditionally held on International Women's Day. Galdós's realism represents an interrogation of the Madrilenian society he lived and breathed. So too might *Tristana* provide students the opportunity to interrogate gender issues in their own twenty-first-century society.

NOTES

1. All translations from Spanish to English not otherwise attributed are my own.

2. Catherine Jagoe's groundbreaking study, *Ambiguous Angels: Gender in the Novels of Galdós*, is mandatory reading for teachers and researchers new to this topic. Chapter 5 in particular provides a fantastic overview of feminism in fin de siècle Spain as well as a thought-provoking analysis of *Tristana* (120–55).

3. This gendered model emerged more or less contemporaneously in England and Spain and should be understood as part of a wider, shared paradigm of modernization and industrialization in the West, with the concomitant rise of the middle class (Jagoe, *Ambiguous Angels* 6–9, 14).

4. For a class in translation, the study of *Tristana* should be paired with Maryellen Bieder's twin essays in the English-language volume *A New History of Iberian Feminisms*, both of which provide excellent historical context for the disparate threads of feminist activity and thought that characterize Spain's long nineteenth century ("Women Authors"; "First-Wave Feminisms").

5. For more on the transatlantic discussion on this topic, see Jagoe, *Ambiguous Angels* 15.

6. Jagoe situates Sinués de Marco's "domestic novel-conduct manual," *El ángel del hogar*, as emerging in roughly the same period as, but not in imitation of, Coventry Patmore's poem (*Ambiguous Angels* 14–15).

7. According to the historian Pamela Radcliff, although the "angel in the house" ideal is a middle-class construction, aristocratic and "elite" bourgeois families also "embraced" this gendered ideology throughout nineteenth-century Spain (126). News of political feminist activism abroad permeated Spanish borders and created considerable anxiety amongst the middle classes (Tolliver, *Cigar Smoke* 44–45). For more context on Spain's more limited political feminist movement in the late nineteenth century, see Arkinstall.

8. Prominent Spanish feminists in the early decades of the twentieth century include Carmen de Burgos, Margarita Nelken, and María (Gregorio) Martínez Sierra. Disparate strands of feminist thought also broke through during this time period: Martínez Sierra, for example, was a Catholic feminist, and Nelken was a socialist feminist. For a useful overview of Spanish feminism in the early decades of the twentieth century through the Second Spanish Republic, see Johnson and Castro.

9. For an excellent comparative analysis of Galdós's novel and Buñuel's film in English, see Sara Muñoz-Muriana.

10. Jennifer Smith compellingly made this observation in her presentation at the XII Congreso Internacional Galdosiano.

Galdós's Portrayals of Masculinity in *Tormento*

Collin McKinney

College students are constantly doing gender: when they choose their outfits in the morning, share their pronouns on the first day of class, or post on social media. In each of these mundane moments and a hundred more, they participate in the performativity of gender identities. Yet, however deftly they may navigate this process, it does not necessarily mean that they are able to translate these lived experiences into an academic conversation or apply them to the study of masculinity in literary works, since they may lack the language and theoretical concepts provided by gender studies or are unfamiliar with the author's cultural milieu. The central purpose of this brief essay is to provide suggestions on how to bridge this gap in the classroom. As an example, I describe my approach to teaching *Tormento* (*Torment*), by Benito Pérez Galdós, which I use in undergraduate literature and culture classes.[1] Galdós's work, and *Tormento* in particular, provides an ideal way to study Spanish masculinities because, on the one hand, it was in the nineteenth century that many contemporary gender norms were codified, and, furthermore, Galdós's depiction of Spanish society includes vignettes that creatively illustrate a variety of masculine identities. By introducing the general concepts of masculinity studies and providing some context for reading Galdós, I scaffold student discussions of the diverse masculine identities portrayed in the author's work. The goal is to prepare students to evaluate Galdós's representations of gender with a more critical eye and to consider what connections these particular formulations of masculinity from the past may have with the gender norms of today.

I begin by introducing some basic concepts from the field of gender studies, such as the fact that masculinity is both plural and culturally variable. Present-day readers of *Tormento* will have an easier time recognizing and thinking critically about how medical theories, the Catholic Church, and various societal forces influenced the author's depictions of masculinity if they first understand that discursive fields shape identities. However, rather than diving straight into a dense text by Michel Foucault or Judith Butler, I find it best to begin with an informal discussion highlighting the variability of masculinity across time and cultures. What does manliness look like? This seemingly simple question is a good starting point because it usually generates lively conversations and can segue into additional questions. Students respond by highlighting the behaviors and markers of masculinity they see daily: fashion trends, music or food preferences, body language, grooming routines, gym habits, pastimes, professions, and so on. I follow up by asking whether these things are learned or innate. I ask if this is what manliness looks like for their parents' or grandparents' generation. If they got in a time machine and traveled to the 1800s or earlier, what would masculinity look like across social or racial groups? What would masculinity look like in different countries? The answers to this line of questioning allow us to see that gender norms change over time and across cultures. In other words, students arrive at the same conclusion as prominent scholars of masculinity studies, like Michael Kimmel, who explains that masculinity is not a monolith:

> Manhood is neither static nor timeless. Manhood is not the manifestation of an inner essence; it's socially constructed. Manhood does not bubble up to consciousness from our biological constitution; it is created in our culture. . . . What it means to be a man in America depends heavily on one's class, race, ethnicity, age, sexuality, region of the country. To acknowledge these differences among men, we must speak of *masculinities*. (4)

At this point, students are primed for a crash course in masculinity studies. Depending on the level of the class and their familiarity with the basic tenets of gender studies, I may assign a handful of essays, or I may simply prepare a collection of shorter excerpts from key scholars such as Kimmel (211–37), Judith Butler (10–17, 183–93), R. W. Connell (67–86), Jeff Hearn, Michael Messner, Jack Halberstam, Arthur Brittan, and Michelle Adams and Scott Coltrane. This is an important step because it provides the language and theories needed to examine masculinities as products of sociocultural pressures and to see why nineteenth-century Spanish masculinities were distinct from yet related to expressions of masculinity today. It introduces terms like *discourse*, *performativity*, *essentialism*, *intersectionality*, and *hegemonic masculinity*, which are necessary tools for a robust examination of gender in *Tormento*.

After establishing a basic theoretical framework, I prepare students for reading *Tormento* by highlighting some features of the novel's cultural context. Galdós's writing can be linguistically challenging for nonnative speakers of Spanish, so in courses taught in the target language, I find that a bit of context can help. Even when the work is taught in translation, it can be hard for a student who might never have visited Spain to visualize the story's setting. Some information about the social and political realities of the period is important, but so too is imparting a feel for nineteenth-century Madrid. A few carefully chosen slides with photographs, newspaper illustrations, and paintings from the period will help students imagine life in Madrid and the characters that populate Galdós's novelistic world.[2] For instance, images of residents making their way down the Calle de Alcalá by foot and coach, *tertulias*—artistic or literary gatherings—in crowded cafes, or portraits of wealthy Spaniards painted by Raimundo de Madrazo y Garreta all provide examples of people doing gender, or what Judith Butler calls gender performativity:

> acts, gestures, and desire produce the effect of an internal core or substance, but produce this on the surface of the body. . . . Such acts, gestures, and enactments, generally construed, are performative in that the essence or

> identity they otherwise purport to express are fabrications manufactured and sustained through corporeal signs and other discursive means. (185)

In other words, a glimpse into the lives of the affluent bourgeoisie provides important visual clues to the ways that individuals communicate class, gender, and power to the world. Given their high level of visual literacy, students tend to enjoy seeing these images and are quick to notice a stark gender binary. These images also provide a useful touchpoint when we want to discuss gender performativity in popular culture today

The social landscape of nineteenth-century Spain comes into sharper focus when these images are paired with contemporary texts. A conduct manual, such as Mariano de Rementería y Fica's *El hombre fino al gusto del día* (*Today's Refined Man*), can provide insights into what behaviors were expected of men. Similarly, the popular *Higiene del matrimonio* (*Hygiene of Marriage*), by the leading medical expert Pedro Felipe Monlau, shaped views about gender by combining biology with middle-class values. To paraphrase Monlau, man is bold, hard, rational, rugged, and commanding, while woman is meek, soft, emotional, delicate, and nurturing (389–90). It was believed that the roles of men and women were simply natural to their sex—that is, an extension of biological differences that made them opposite but complementary. Such ideas were used as evidence that the natural habitat of women was the domestic sphere whereas that of men was the public sphere. I usually end this part of the discussion by asking if such views still have currency today. It is one of many opportunities I take to draw comparisons between Galdós's Madrid and our own social landscape, a technique that helps draw in students and makes Galdós's work feel more relevant to their lives.

Against this backdrop, it becomes easier for students to appreciate Galdós's portrayals of masculinity in *Tormento*, which not only reflect nineteenth-century Spanish gender norms but also offer a commentary on these norms. While many of Galdós's novels would work well for an examination of masculinities in Spanish culture, there are a few reasons why *Tormento* is a good choice for an undergraduate classroom. First, at around three hundred pages, it fits into a syllabus more easily than some of Galdós's other works, such as his better-known *Fortunata y Jacinta*, whose length is challenging for many students. Second, many of the novel's motifs and themes, such as sex, family dynamics, fashion, and status, are highly relevant to a discussion of gender. And, finally, the variety of male characters lends itself to a comparative examination of Spanish masculinities.

Originally published in 1884, *Tormento* is set in Madrid during the months prior to the revolution of 1868. It tells the story of the penniless Amparo Sánchez Emperador, a recently orphaned woman who lives with her sister and helps out in the home of her distant relatives, Francisco de Bringas and his wife, Rosalía. Amparo is kind, generous, and humble, and students find it easy to root for her, even when they discover a secret from her past that threatens to make her a social outcast and derail her engagement to the wealthy *indiano*—a man who amassed wealth while living in the colonies—Agustín Caballero. And while femininity is clearly a central focus of the novel, the question of masculinity is prominent as well. To examine this topic with students, I like to lead them through a series of close readings of certain passages that spotlight the leading male characters: Bringas, Caballero, and Amparo's former lover, Pedro Polo. When discussing each character, it helps to highlight their physical appearance, behavior, and personality to see how each one embodies a different model of masculinity.

We begin with Bringas, who is introduced in the opening paragraphs of chapter 2. Working together as a class, we make a list of his physical attributes and character traits. Students often point out passages that signal his "temperamento sociable, aquel decir ameno, aquella voluntad obsequiosa, aquella cortesanía servicial" ("sociable by nature, so pleasant in speech, so over anxious to be obliging, so courteous and so helpful"; Pérez Galdós, *Tormento* 16; *Torment* 18). They also note that he is clean-shaven and does not smoke (*Tormento* 17; *Torment* 21). If nobody else mentions the references to his penny-pinching, docility, domesticity, and lack of professional ambition, I make sure to bring them up (*Tormento* 16; *Torment* 18). Once our list is compiled, we go through the attributes and discuss whether or not Bringas fits the conventional image of Spanish masculinity. If students have trouble viewing Bringas from any vantage point other than their own cultural perspective, I make an effort to point out how today's masculine ideals differ from those of the nineteenth century. For instance, Bringas's domestic qualities may be viewed positively by today's standards but were not in Galdós's day. I also ask students to pay close attention to the narrator's tone, which seems to suggest that he has a soft spot for Bringas even when the text gently mocks some of his behaviors as being more in line with period ideals of femininity than with those of masculinity. Highlighting changes in the narrator's tone in reference to particular characters helps students begin to see how the text not only reflects the gender norms of its time but critiques them as well.

For our subsequent discussion, I ask students to work in groups and make and evaluate a list of attributes and traits for Caballero, paying special attention to chapter 5, which contains passages about his difficulty assimilating into Madrid's so-called "afeminada sociedad" ("effeminate society"; *Tormento* 40; *Torment* 42). After the group discussions, we reconvene to discuss some of the key passages in greater detail. We discuss Caballero's behavior as well as his physical qualities, which more closely reflect popular descriptions of manliness than is the case for Bringas. Students note that his hair and beard are thick, dark, and neatly trimmed, with a few strands of gray, and that his skin is weathered from a life spent outdoors (*Tormento* 39; *Torment* 41). I ask students to find passages that reveal how the narrator views Caballero and how the other characters view him. For instance, the narrator describes "una fuerte salud gastada en mil pruebas; una hermosura tostada al sol" ("a vigorous physical constitution, half destroyed in the bitter tussle with Nature and men; great health expended in countless hardships, and good looks burnt away by the sun"; *Tormento* 40; *Torment* 42), whereas Rosalía thinks of him as a "pedazo de bárbaro" ("the boor"; *Tormento* 48; *Torment* 50). I use the Goldilocks story as an analogy for the types of masculinities that we might find in Galdós's novels: some are too soft for the norms of the time, others are too hard, and some are just right. Caballero's coarseness is assuaged by his discipline and humility. He is wilder than Bringas, to be sure, but his roughness provokes affinity and admiration from the narrator rather than fear, which we find later in the descriptions of Pedro Polo. Similarly, the description of Caballero as a serious and successful businessman more closely matches the popular view of male comportment than that of Bringas, who is seen scurrying around the house making paella and coffee.

Students are especially interested in discussing Caballero's interactions with other characters. Caballero is well aware of his deficiencies, namely his ineptitude in social situations, which he attributes to his life at the frontier: "El hombre nace, y la Naturaleza y la vida le hacen. . . . A mí me han hecho como soy el trabajo, la soledad, la fiebre, la constancia, los descalabros, el miedo y el arrojo, el caballo y el libro mayor, la sierra de Monterrey, el río del Norte y la pútrida costa de Matamoros" ("A man is born, and Nature and life create him. . . . I have been made what I am by hard work, solitude, fever, steadfastness, misfortunes, fear and boldness, the horse and the ledger, the mountains of Monterrey, the Río del Norte and the fever coast of Matamoros"; *Tormento* 42–43; *Torment* 45). We note that even this shortcoming is a plus for the narrator, who mocks the pretentious customs of Madrilenians who can tie a tie but offer little else to society. Caballero may be rough around the edges—"revelando una sutil agudeza, más propia del salvaje que del cortesano" ("revealing a subtle cleverness more characteristic of a savage than of a courtier"; *Tormento* 41; *Torment* 43)—but when compared to Bringas, who embodies the "afeminada sociedad" mentioned above, it is clear which of them is seen by the narrator in a more favorable light. The same is true when we compare Caballero to Polo, who is so unruly as to pose a threat to the social order. Caballero occupies an ideal middle ground, neither too refined nor too rough. This may explain why our classroom discussions about Caballero tend to run longer than our discussions of the other characters. Comments in class suggest that many students identify with the challenge of trying to strike the right balance between hard and soft masculinities in their personal lives.

Overall, students have varying reactions to Caballero. They frame many of their comments within the nature-versus-nurture debate, which can be an excellent opportunity to remind students that biology and circumstances may create differences, but it is society that assigns value to those differences. It is also possible to bring in concepts like hegemony and symbolic capital in order to explore why certain traits become elevated while others are diminished. Some students joke that Caballero "lowkey gives off dad vibes," while others say his awkward behavior around Amparo is "cringey." Some are bothered by the age difference, as well as the gulf in economic standing, between Caballero and Amparo. But plenty of others admire Caballero's trajectory as a self-made man and his rejection of social norms. Indeed, some students even open up and say that they find social pressures unbearable at times and wish they could be free of them. Because gender is a part of everyone's lives, it is not uncommon for students to identify with different aspects of the novel.

Our discussion of Caballero provides a good opportunity to play devil's advocate and point out both positive and negative attributes of the character to ensure a balanced exchange. I point out that nobody can truly embody all the gender ideals, because gender ideals are inherently contradictory. In an effort to remind students that gender norms were different in the nineteenth century, I ask how well Caballero would fit into our own society. This typically inspires a lively exchange in which most students declare that he is clearly a product of his time and place and would not do well in twenty-first-century America. They argue that his treatment of Amparo is generous and well-intentioned, if somewhat clumsy, but that ultimately his hopes and expectations are antiquated. Others argue that it depends on which social circles we are looking at. They see corollaries between the characters and people they know. For instance, one student discussed examples of "sugar daddies" who marry young, beautiful women. They lament that the fundamental inequities built into the gender discourse of the nineteenth century, which severely limited women's opportunities for financial independence, have not entirely disappeared in our own time.

Pedro Polo's transformation from a feeble and despondent priest into a brutal savage provides a final portrait of masculinity for students to consider. For this discussion, I like to prepare my class with a homework assignment, asking them to perform a close reading of the letter that starts chapter 25 and to write a short response about the sort of masculinity embodied by Polo before the next class.[3] After a conversation about their short essays, we have a group discussion of chapters 28 and 29. Students are invariably (and justly) harsh critics of Polo. When Polo makes his initial appearance in the novel, he provokes repulsion rather than sympathy. He is apathetic and wallows in self-pity, and his lingering infatuation with Amparo is a liability because he threatens to expose their secret past to Caballero and others. As a class, we read about Polo's drastic transformation after a stint living in the countryside (*Tormento* 217; *Torment* 221). His thick beard, powerful physique, and rugged attire set him apart from the *hombre fino* ("refined man") found in conduct manuals. Polo himself describes his newfound manliness in the following terms: "Estoy hecho un salvaje, un verdadero hombre primitivo, un troglodita sin cuevas y un anacoreta sin cilicio" ("I've become a savage, a real primitive man, a troglodyte without a cave and an anchorite without a hair-shirt"; *Tormento* 188; *Torment* 191).

Students acknowledge that Polo's appearance includes many of the physical characteristics that we associate with traditional masculinity, but they also easily see past this and comment on the aspects of his personality that, in today's parlance, we equate with toxic masculinity. For example, the text repeatedly uses "bárbaro" ("savage") to refer to Polo and his actions, as well as terms like "fiera" ("wild beast") and "bestia" ("beast"), and describes his "salvaje ímpetu de amor" ("savage excess of passion") and "insano furor espasmódico" ("lunatic's spasm of fury"; *Tormento* 217–33; *Torment* 219–32). His savagery is most notable when he assaults Amparo, hoisting her into the air, blocking her way when she tries to leave, dragging her violently from the door, and holding her in his apartment against her will for hours. Whereas Caballero's exposure to the rough conditions of life at the frontier gives him an air of toughness and resolve, in the case of Polo, it turns him into a menace, and students are quick to call out this abuse as yet another example of the links between violence and traditional masculinity.

Students' reactions to these three characters reveal in the novel a subtle commentary on nineteenth-century Spanish gender norms. Which of these men gets the most generous treatment by the narrator, and which the least? What class or ideological vantage point does the narrator represent, and how might his perspective influence our opinion of the characters? What do our reactions say about contemporary gender norms and our own biases? Students tend to feel ambivalent about Bringas. They appreciate his kindness toward Amparo but are frustrated by his weakness. Caballero is more likable, both for his unpretentious ways but also because of his generosity toward others. Polo tends to provoke the most robust dislike. He is a selfish bully, and in a post–Me Too era students have little patience for men who use coercion or force to get their way. As one student commented, "You just want to punch him in the face."

In order to better appreciate the way Spanish masculinities were formed and hierarchized, and how Galdós's depictions of masculinities dialogue with current forms of masculinity, I find it useful to consider examples that are a little closer to home. Students show great interest when the conversation turns to examples of gender performativity in contemporary culture, something we can exploit for pedagogical purposes. I conclude our unit on *Tormento* by asking students to imagine that they are a modern-day Galdós and to write their own narrative about contemporary society in order to represent the diverse masculine identities they encounter. They might write a short piece on the campus social scene, a story inspired by the social media accounts of celebrities, or an alternative storyline for their favorite show in which manliness figures prominently. In these types of assignments, students can think about where they are most likely to find examples of traditional masculinity and where they are likely to find people who challenge or transgress that model. What sources tend to celebrate or denigrate alternative models of masculinity, and how might these sources condition our own behaviors? Such assignments allow students to appreciate how an author like Galdós portrays the norms of his day with a critical eye and also consider how they might be caught in the grip of cultural norms or how they might free themselves from its grasp. Furthermore, these exercises can help collapse the distance between Galdós's world and our own. After all, one reason Galdós's readers enjoyed his stories so much was that they were familiar. Nineteenth-century Spaniards saw themselves, or perhaps their friends and neighbors, in his characters. By centering gender, past and present, in our reading of *Tormento*, our students can have a similar experience. Galdós's novels are entertaining, but they can be (and always have been) much more than that. These stories can change the way students think about their own cultural milieu and might even move us all one step closer to a more just and equitable society.

NOTES

1. Although I use the Spanish edition from Alianza Editorial when teaching, there are two good English translations of the novel: *Torment*, by J. M. Cohen, and *Inferno*, by Abigail Lee Six. For English quotations in this essay I have used Cohen's translation.

2. By way of example, a photo of Galdós reading at a *tertulia* offers a glimpse of men's and women's fashions at the end of the century (upload.wikimedia.org/wikipedia/commons/6/6e/Gald%C3%B3s_por_Franzen_Tertulia_literaria_1897.jpg?uselang=es). Similarly, the paintings of Ramón de Errazu and his sister, Manuela de Errazu, by the artist Raimundo de Madrazo y Garreta provide an interesting contrast between representations of middle-class masculinity and femininity during the period in question. Images from newspapers, which can be found by searching the Biblioteca Nacional's *Hemeroteca Digital* (*Digital Periodical Archive*), are also useful in showing Madrid in Galdós's time. For additional images, and an in-depth study of their significance, see Vanesa Rodríguez-Galindo's *Madrid on the Move: Feeling Modern and Visually Aware in the Nineteenth Century*.

3. This short writing assignment and the subsequent class discussion of Polo often bring to the fore popular terminology from outside academe that relates to gender and its performance, such as *cottagecore*, *manosphere*, *down bad*, *revenge porn*, and *man box*.

The Rebranding of Don Juan Tenorio as Social Misfit in *Tristana*

Brian Cope

Of the several novels written by Benito Pérez Galdós that feature a Don Juan character, *Tristana* stands out for the way in which it positions its two main characters—Tristana and Don Juan López Garrido, aka Don Lope—at the center of a social critique related to the subjugation of women that has the potential to resonate deeply with twenty-first-century readers. *Tristana* can work especially well in courses that examine topics related to sexual violence, patriarchy, misogyny, male entitlement, sexism, and toxic masculinity. Its treatment of these themes makes it a groundbreaking work in the modern Spanish literary canon and an excellent candidate for inclusion in courses that explore the adversities faced by women in patriarchal societies. Because *Tristana* focuses deliberately on the harm done to Tristana by Don Lope—who is portrayed as Tristana's seducer and abuser—it can also serve as a point of departure for surveying a selection of modern and contemporary texts that explore the condition of women through stories about abusive men.

I teach *Tristana* in an undergraduate seminar on the figure of Don Juan Tenorio in Spanish literature. The course examines a selection of literary and cinematic texts featuring a protagonist whose behavior elicits association with Don Juan Tenorio and who functions as a vehicle to explore themes related to male privilege, toxic masculinity, and the objectification of women. I prepare students to analyze the pertinent layers of each text by assigning the first three chapters of Kate Manne's *Entitled: How Male Privilege Hurts Women* (3–55) at the beginning of the course. These chapters serve as a touchstone for reading *Tristana* and other works in which men perpetrate heinous acts against women within a patriarchal system that favors and empowers them. Because Don Lope exhibits the tendencies and patterns that Manne describes in her study, utilizing *Entitled* as a point of reference while reading *Tristana* can help encourage students to pay attention to the novel's layered and nuanced portrayal of sexual wrongdoing. The definitions of sexism, misogyny, and gaslighting found in *Entitled*, along with the accompanying case studies, furthermore provide a conceptual scaffold apt for probing the sometimes explicit, other times subtle representations of toxic masculinity in *Tristana* and the other cultural artifacts used in the course.

To draw attention to the pertinent layers of each assigned literary text, I require students to read them on *Perusall*, which has a communal annotation tool that allows me to flag specific passages and embed strategic homework questions. In class, I often open the discussion by sharing a selection of the students' answers in the form of screenshots that I incorporate into my *PowerPoint* presentation. I use the selected comments to acknowledge the students' original observations and to help set up the subsequent group activity. Methodologically, I employ a conversation-based approach in which students receive a brief contextualization of the day's topic before being asked to break into groups, analyze passages, answer interrelated questions, and report back to the class.

Although the realist genre contains numerous examples of characters inspired by Don Juan Tenorio, *Tristana* stands apart in its use of a main character, Don Lope, to overtly condemn the social phenomenon of *donjuanismo* ("Don Juanism"). The Don Juan Tenorio archetype functions in tandem with two other literary and artistic referents in the novel to endow Don Lope with a human psychology apt for carrying out sexual conquests with egotism and a conspicuous lack of social consciousness. The narrator describes Don Lope as a man who bears a physical resemblance to the central figure of Diego Velázquez's *La rendición de Breda* (*The Surrender of Breda*), implying that he is a man of conviction and tactical skill who belongs more to the seventeenth century than to his own day. His militaristic competence in the art of seduction is tempered by a quixotic idealism, moreover, that governs his daily life and gives him a higher sense of purpose. Like Don Quixote, Don Lope belongs to the lowest caste of Spanish nobility and lives in accordance with a subjective understanding of the code of *caballería* ("chivalric order"). Although his womanizing behavior casts a dark shadow over him, Don Lope has one redeeming quality: he never turns his back on a friend in need despite the heavy toll it takes on his personal finances. In effect, the quixotic and bellicose traits that Galdós bestows on Don Lope add complexity to the psychological profile of the character as a committed bachelor and libertine whose values deviate markedly from the dominant social norms of the late nineteenth century. Don Lope represents entitlement, machismo, and fanaticism that stem from his social class, his military background, and his steadfast commitment to a worldview that affords him immense latitude in his sexual exploits.

Tristana's omniscient narrator, who functions as an implicit character in the novel, periodically expresses disapproval of Don Lope's reprehensible behavior toward women. The first and perhaps most significant instance appears in chapter 4, where the narrator focuses on Don Lope's limited restraint and limitless sense of entitlement when pursuing his romantic conquests:

> Era que don Lope, por añejo dogma de su caballería sedentaria, no admitía crimen ni falta ni responsabilidad en cuestiones de faldas. Fuera del caso de cortejar a la dama, esposa o manceba de un amigo íntimo, en amor todo lo tenía por lícito. Los hombres como él, hijitos mimados de Adán, habían recibido del Cielo una tácita bula que los dispensaba de toda moral. (Pérez Galdós, *Tristana* [Cátedra] 133)
>
> In accordance with the fusty old dogma of a knight sedentary, Don Lope accepted neither guilt nor responsibility when it came to anything involving the ladies. While he would never have courted the wife, spouse, or mistress of a close friend, he considered that, otherwise, everything was permitted in matters of love. Men like him, Adam's spoiled brats, had

> received from heaven a tacit [papal] bull that allowed them to dispense with all morality. (*Tristana* [New York Review Books] 17)

In analyzing this passage with students, I ask them to identify at least two ways in which it illustrates male entitlement and to speculate about what might fall into the realm of the permissible based on the limited information given. Subsequently, I draw their attention to the phrase "Men like him" in order to establish that the narrator sees Don Lope as fitting a particular social mold that he finds categorically deplorable. The ire Don Lope inspires in the narrator leads him to proclaim, "Si no hubiera infierno, sólo para don Lope habría que crear uno, a fin de que en él eternamente purgase sus burlas de la moral" ("If hell did not exist, it would be necessary to create one just for Don Lope, so that he could spend eternity doing penance for his mockery of morality"; *Tristana* [Cátedra] 134; *Tristana* [New York Review Books] 18). The narrator's deliberate and unambiguous condemnation of Don Lope's deceitful behavior toward women in this passage implies the unbounded nature of the permissible in Don Lope's womanizing ventures and effectively amplifies the theme of *donjuanismo* in the novel.

Students read José Zorrilla's *Don Juan Tenorio* before *Tristana* and subsequent texts in preparation for engaging with the theme of *donjuanismo* in the course. My objective in assigning the play is to probe how potently it glorifies male sexual prowess and promotes the prerogative of men to take possession of women's bodies through manipulation and premeditated deceit. In order to prepare students to follow the thread of *donjuanismo* in *Tristana* after having read *Don Juan Tenorio*, I ask them to conduct keyword searches on *donjuanismo* in academic databases, read article synopses, and come to class prepared to give a brief report on what they have discovered. My students have encountered studies on *donjuanismo* as a recognized social pathology, as a behavior linked to machismo and narcissism, as a focal point in philosophical meditations on national identity, and as a recurring theme in the work of Spanish and Latin American authors. Although the course I teach focuses on Spain, I encourage students to excavate the concept without regard for national borders and to use *Google* to probe how *donjuanismo* persists more broadly in the social imaginary of Spain and Latin America. These exercises prepare students to examine Don Lope as a representation of a social type that exists in the real world and not just as a character belonging to the fictional milieu of the novel.[1]

Don Juan Tenorio's popularity as a play performed annually on All Souls' Day contributed to keeping the figure of the seducer alive in the popular imagination during the second half of the nineteenth century. Novelists during this period often found inspiration in the play for characters who transgressed social norms and engaged in womanizing behavior. Several novels written by Galdós prior to the publication of *Tristana*, in fact, contain characters who exhibit traits associated with the social phenomenon of *donjuanismo*. A few include Joaquín Pez from *La desheredada*, D. Manuel María José del Pez from *La de Bringas*, and Pepe Serrano Morentín from *Torquemada en el Purgatorio*.[2] It is not surprising, therefore, that throughout *Tristana* Galdós draws direct associations between Don Lope and Don Juan Tenorio in the psychological portrait of the unscrupulous libertine that he constructs. He does so, moreover, in ways that recast the deeds of the romanticized seducer in a negative light. One noteworthy example arises when Tristana echoes Don Juan's famous soliloquy as she describes Don Lope as a man who indiscriminately victimizes women:

> Sus conquistas son tantas que no se pueden contar. ¡Si tú supieras . . . ! Aristocracia, clase media, pueblo . . . , en todas partes dejó memoria triste, como don Juan Tenorio. En palacios y cabañas se coló, y no respetó nada el muy trasto, ni la virtud, ni la paz doméstica, ni la santísima religión. Hasta con monjas y beatas ha tenido amores el maldito, y sus éxitos parecen obra del Demonio. (Pérez Galdós, *Tristana* [Cátedra] 171)

> You see, he was an inveterate womanizer in his time, and his conquests, too many to count. You can't imagine! Like Don Juan, he left sad memories behind him everywhere, from the aristocracy to the middle classes to the peasantry. He wormed his way into palaces and hovels alike, and the rogue showed no respect for anything, be it virtue, domestic peace, or religion. The wretch has even seduced nuns and other saintly women; indeed, his successes appear to be the work of the Devil.
> (*Tristana* [New York Review Books] 58)

The tenor of Tristana's remarks contrasts dramatically with that of Don Juan Tenorio in the play when he proudly boasts of his sexual conquests to a captive audience of male admirers (Zorrilla, *Don Juan Tenorio* 96–112; act 1, scene 12). Prompting students to consider this passage alongside the corresponding scene from the play gives them an opportunity to discuss how Galdós reframes it in the novel and helps them see the intentionality with which he depicts Don Lope as a real-life Don Juan Tenorio. The condemnation of Don Lope's *donjuanismo* intensifies when Tristana reflects on what he did to her. In one especially poignant moment, she recounts: "Recogióme cuando me quedé huérfana. Él fue, justo es decirlo, muy generoso con mis padres. Yo le respetaba y le quería; no sospechaba lo que me iba a pasar. La sorpresa no me permitió resistir. Era yo entonces un poco más tonta que ahora, y ese maldito hombre me dominaba, haciendo de mí lo que quería" ("He took me in when I was orphaned. He was, it must be said, very generous to my parents. I respected and loved him; I had not the slightest suspicion of what was going to happen. I was too surprised to resist. I was rather more foolish then than I am now, and that wretched man dominated me entirely and dealt with me as he wished"; Pérez Galdós, *Tristana* [Cátedra] 170; *Tristana* [New York Review Books] 57). The words spoken here by Tristana insinuate an absence of consent and open the door to examining Don Lope's behavior in relation to the examples of gaslighting, coercion, and sexual assault that Manne offers in *Entitled.*

Reading *Tristana* in conjunction with the first three chapters of Manne's *Entitled* can further help students focus their attention on the topic of sexual assault in the novel and analyze the complex narrative of patriarchal authority that unfolds around it. Students can use Manne's definitions and case studies as points of reference when analyzing the asymmetrical power relationship on display or when interrogating the viewpoint of the narrator, who, in addition to repeatedly and unequivocally condemning Don Lope's behavior toward women, also defends him, asserting that "[c]asos había en la vida de este sujeto que le enaltecían en sumo grado, y si algún ocioso escribiera su historia, aquellos resplandores de generosidad y abnegación harían olvidar, hasta cierto punto, las oscuridades de su carácter y su conducta" ("[t]here had been episodes in this man's life that would have exalted him in a high degree, and had anyone—with nothing better to do—decided to write his biography, those glowing examples of generosity and self-denial would have helped obscure, up to a point, the darker side of his character and conduct"; Pérez Galdós, *Tristana* [Cátedra] 126; *Tristana* [New York Review Books] 10). Here, the narrator's stance invites reflection on attitudes toward male perpetrators of sexual harm, especially those of other men, and connects to one case study used by Manne in *Entitled* to illustrate her argument on male privilege. The case is that of Brock Turner, a collegiate swimmer convicted of rape in 2016, who received a scandalously light sentence from a male judge who referenced evidence of his good character as among the mitigating factors (37–38). Using this case study as a point of reference, the following questions can be directed toward students: Does Galdós draw attention, through the position taken above by the narrator, to a moral relativism at work in male psychology in situations involving the sexual misconduct of other men? If so, how does it compare to that of the judge in the Turner case? If not, what other purpose might the narrator's statement serve? Is it possible that it serves more than one purpose?

The critical vocabulary presented in *Entitled* also prepares students to focus on details in the story that support understanding Tristana as living in a continuous state of exploitation, sometimes requiring reading against the grain and connecting disparate dots. Chapter 4 can be used to center an exercise of this nature. In one instance, for example, the narrator describes a phase of mutual reciprocity between Tristana and Don Lope and attributes it to the latter's charm. Yet, the narrator also discloses that "Tristana aceptó aquella manera de vivir casi sin darse cuenta de su gravedad" ("Tristana accepted this way of life almost without realizing the gravity of her situation"; Pérez Galdós, *Tristana* [Cátedra] 135; *Tristana* [New York Review Books] 19) and that Don Lope saw Tristana as his earned possession, "bien me la he ganado" ("I've earned her"; *Tristana* [Cátedra] 135; *Tristana* [New York Review Books] 18). Students can be asked to interrogate the narrator's assertion of mutual reciprocity with these details in mind and to craft a paragraph (to later read aloud in groups) that recasts it through the lens of Manne's definitions of entitlement and gaslighting. After reading more of the text, including Tristana's denunciation of her abuser from chapter 11, quoted earlier, students can be assigned a short paper in which they are tasked with connecting more disparate dots that support understanding Tristana as living in a normalized state of subjugation to her abuser, retelling her story for a twenty-first-century audience using the conceptual framework provided by Manne.

In the context of my course, *Tristana* comes first in a series of assigned texts that explore the themes of toxic masculinity and misogyny through a character inspired by Don Juan Tenorio, with the goal of examining a broad selection of works that draw attention to *donjuanismo* as a destructive and persistent social problem. Emilia Pardo Bazán's "Sor Aparición" follows *Tristana* in the sequence of assignments. Published four years later, it kindles antipathy for the figure of the sexual predator and is loosely based on a revolting deed allegedly perpetrated by the Romantic poet José de Espronceda against a young woman with whom he pretended to be in love.[3] The main character persuades an adoring young acquaintance to come to his apartment, where they end up having sex. Afterward, the man's friends emerge from behind a curtain in the bedroom and ridicule the woman as she quickly gets dressed and flees. The men follow her out of the house and continue to deride her mercilessly in public for several blocks. Her fate is to enter a convent and spend the rest of her life praying for the man who callously stole her dignity and purposely humiliated her. Prior to assigning this story, I ask students to read Pardo Bazán's review of *Tristana*, in which she lamented the minimal development given to the social themes related to women in the novel.[4] The review exposes students to an unflattering contemporaneous perspective on *Tristana,* held by an equally accomplished female novelist who also happened to be Galdós's friend. The review can serve as a model of critical analysis for students to study before completing an in-class writing assignment in which they attempt to articulate their own original critique of *Tristana*'s depiction of the challenges women encountered and the risks they faced in late-nineteenth-century Spanish society, which can then form the basis of a longer paper assignment. The work students do to understand Pardo Bazán's objections to *Tristana* and the task of the literary critic will equip them to better situate "Sor Aparición" on a continuum with *Tristana* and appreciate Pardo Bazan's implicit motivations for creating, through a story about the heartless victimization of a young woman and how it changed the course of her life, an unambiguous and forceful denunciation of *donjuanismo.*

Antonio Bardem's *Calle Mayor* (*Main Street*) follows "Sor Aparición" in the sequence of assignments. I use the film in my course to continue examining representations of misogyny and portrayals of *donjuanismo.* The main character, Juan, feigns interest in a single woman over thirty, ostensibly destined for spinsterhood, so as to amuse his friends. One such friend objects to the public humiliation planned for Isabel and informs her that she is being pranked. Devastated, she stands strong and continues to live her life, knowing that she is now a social pariah and her prospects for marriage have been ruined. The film offers a glimpse into a social dynamic in which dehumanizing outcomes are ruthlessly orchestrated by entitled men without regard for the dignity of their victims. Various points of comparison arise with *Tristana,* including the portrayal of a patriarchal social order that tolerates the misdeeds of men, the inclusion of a female protagonist whose situation prompts reflection on the condition of women, and a parallel focus on the ruinous manipulations needlessly enacted by men against women. Other texts I have used in the course include Ramón del Valle-Inclán's *Sonata de invierno* (*Winter Sonata*), Concha Espina's *La esfinge maragata* (*The Maragata Sphinx*), Miguel de Unamuno's "Nada menos que todo un hombre" ("Every Inch a Man"), Luis Buñuel's *Viridiana*, Pedro Almodóvar's *Átame* (*Tie Me Up, Tie Me Down*), and José Ángel Mañas's *Historias del Kronen* (*Stories of the Kronen*), all of which present thought-provoking points of comparison with *Tristana* through their portrayal of misogyny, male sexual entitlement, and patriarchal privilege.

The archive of early-twentieth-century Spanish women writers contains several other novels to consider reading as companion pieces to *Tristana*. The possibilities include María Martínez Sierra's *Tú eres la paz* (*You Are Peace*), Blanca de los Ríos's *Las hijas de Don Juan* (*Don Juan's Daughters*), Concha Espina's *La niña Luzmela* (*A Girl Called Luzmela*), Sofía Casanova's *Princesa del amor hermoso* (*Princess of Beautiful Love*), and Carmen de Burgos's *La entrometida* (*The Busybody*). Roberta Johnson's analysis of these works in the chapter entitled "The Domestication of a Modernist Don Juan" in *Gender and Nation in the Spanish Modernist Novel* (111–44) can be a helpful reference point during the selection process. Johnson argues that the Don Juan characters in these novels frequently parody the main character of Valle-Inclán's *Sonatas*, the Marqués de Bradomín (Marquis of Bradomín), who ironically reflects on his past sexual exploits with sentimentality in his memoir. She affirms that "[w]omen novelists rejected Valle-Inclán's narratorial positioning of the Don Juan figure" and opted to depict him "in more real, contemporary settings that undermine his image as a positive national symbol" (122). This aspect of the aforementioned novels connects them to *Tristana* and, moreover, situates it as their thematic precursor. A graduate seminar could be designed to offer a more concentrated examination of the figure of Don Juan in the realist and modernist periods, framing *Tristana* as a pioneering work and further extending the path of inquiry previously described in relation to Pardo Bazán's review of *Tristana* and her short story "Sor Aparición."

Because my course is designed for undergraduates, I include a mix of shorter and longer texts along with a selection of digital media in order to construct a broad chronology of assignments. In the final unit, I shift attention to the contemporary cultural milieu and assign readings and viewings that offer constructive voices on the fight for gender equality and sexual respect. One assignment is to listen to a podcast in which the Mexican social activist and feminist Jessica Fernández García interviews the Spanish author Nicko Nogués, whose self-help book *Hackea a tu macho: Diez acciones para hombres que se atreven a desafiar una masculinidad tóxica* (*Hack Your Inner Macho: Ten Actions for Men Who Dare to Defy Toxic Masculinity*) offers advice to men on examining and overcoming their socially conditioned harmful attitudes and behaviors toward women. Another assignment is to research and report on the different social movements in Spanish-speaking countries that stand in opposition to violence against women and the patriarchal social order that enables it. One that has received attention in my course is Un Violador en Tu Camino (A Rapist in Your Path), which was started in Chile by the feminist group Las Tesis and has spread to numerous other countries, including Spain.[5] I also assign a selection of music videos by women artists from across the Spanish-speaking world that condemn the behaviors associated with machismo and deliver empowering messages to women. These songs include Ana Tijoux's "Antipatriarca" ("Antipatriarch"), Bebé's "Malo" ("Bad"), and Paquita la del Barrio's "Rata de dos patas" ("Two-Hoofed Rat"). Each features the voice of a woman who confronts, rebukes, or reviles her male partner for the abuse and denigration that she has experienced from him. "Antipatriarca" also includes a stanza that conveys a forceful call for women's liberation and affirms the ability of women to make a positive difference both at home and in the world. These songs, along with the other assigned materials, exhibit points of thematic intersection with chapters 5 and 11 of *Tristana*, in which the protagonist expresses her desire for freedom, her conviction that women should receive opportunities to work and enter the professions, and her truth about the harm done to her by Don Lope. These chapters can be used to help frame a broad conversation on the role of literature and the arts in drawing attention to social problems, eliciting empathy for victims, and advocating for social change. The final unit of my course is designed to encourage students to recognize and value the agency women exercise today and to reflect on the persistence of the same cluster of problems across time and cultural geographies. *Tristana* can thus play a valuable role in establishing continuity with the past and in serving as a point of reference in discussions centered on the progress that has been made in fostering respect for women, normalizing female autonomy, and affording women access to the workplace, while also acknowledging the immense unfinished work that remains.

NOTES

1. This exercise can easily be tailored to a graduate seminar and serve as the starting point for a research project designed by the student in consultation with the instructor.

2. Morales and Matallana-Abril provide lucid analyses of the Don Juan social type in Galdós. For an examination of a larger sample of donjuanesque characters across a wide range of authors that include, in addition to Galdós, Leopoldo Alas (also known as Clarín), Ramón del Valle-Inclán, Pío Baroja, and Miguel de Unamuno, see Ignacio Javier López's *Caballero de novela: Ensayo sobre el donjuanismo en la novela española moderna, 1880–1930*.

3. See Tolliver for a careful contextualization and rich examination of "Sor Aparición" as a critical and gendered response to Promethean Romanticism, which originated in

Lord Byron and continued in the poetry and persona of José de Espronceda. Tolliver also makes a strong case for understanding the story as based on an episode in the life of Espronceda ("Sor Aparición").

4. See Ewald for an enlightening analysis of *Tristana* carefully anchored in Pardo Bazán's review of it. See also Gabrielle Miller's essay in the present volume for a discussion of the social themes related to women in the novel.

5. Other movements students can research include Me Too, #Miracomonosponemos (based in Argentina), Ni Una Más (based in Mexico), and Comisión8M (based in Spain).

Marianela and *Tristana*: Lessons on Disability, Medicine, and Gender

Julia Haeyoon Chang

The broad and burgeoning field of disability studies has recently gained traction among scholars of Iberian literatures, spurring much-needed conversations on historical and literary representations of disabled bodyminds.[1] Benito Pérez Galdós's narrative fiction is replete with characters that diverge from normative notions of health and embodiment. My essay, however, treats disability not only as a theme but also as method[2]—one that offers unique insights into narrative fiction by providing a frame that helps readers assess not only the cultural bounds of bodily and psychic normativity but also the mechanics of fiction itself. Attending to the latter helps orient students to different ways of reading and analyzing the nineteenth-century Spanish novel, which co-emerges alongside the institutionalization of medicine.

In what follows, I delineate how I teach two of Galdós's novels—*Marianela* and *Tristana*—with a few key works from disability studies. These examples are derived from my advanced Spanish literature course titled Reading the Body in Medicine and Fiction, of which thirty percent of the material is focused on Galdós. The course also surveys novels by Emilia Pardo Bazán and Eduardo López Bago alongside nineteenth-century medical texts. This class typically brings in a mix of undergraduate and graduate students from both literature and STEM fields. Most of the undergraduate students aspire to a career in medicine as either physicians, veterinarians, or researchers. The graduate students all come from doctoral programs in literature or language. Seldom (if ever) has either group studied the history of medicine or been asked to consider disability beyond the so-called medical model, which treats disability as a defect that is inherently pathological and requires medical intervention. Consequently, this course is usually students' first opportunity to think critically about medicine and disability from the perspective of the humanities and literary studies. My approach draws both from the social model of disability, which views an individual's impairments in conjunction with social and physical barriers that ultimately create a disabling environment, and from critical disability studies. This subfield scrutinizes the social norms that define certain human attributes as impairments or aberrations.

Over the course of the semester, we study medical and literary representations of the human body; medical and lay notions of normalcy, disease, disability, and beauty; and the intersection of those concepts with gender. Two of the central learning outcomes of the course are to explore feminist approaches to disability and to examine medicine from a literary-humanist perspective. In addition to these broader goals, my aim is to orient students to the practice of close reading and the use of disability studies as a critical tool. Course assignments consist of short reflection papers and student-led discussions, culminating in a research-driven project that delves more deeply into a text or topic explored in the course. The final project may be either a traditional research paper or a creative endeavor such as a painting or podcast. Graduate students are given the opportunity to write comparative papers (when coming from other linguistic traditions or regional literary expertise) or to prepare their research paper with a potential conference or publication venue in mind. For the purposes of this essay, I set out to illustrate how teaching Galdós's depictions of disability offers more complex and nuanced understandings of disabled embodiment that unsettle the dominant culture of ableism.

Get Lost: Vision, Knowledge, and Beauty in Marianela

Marianela is a novel that easily lends itself to contemporary debates within disability studies, engaging the contemporary reader in ways that the Canarian author might never have imagined. At the outset, it destabilizes the ocularcentric order of things, which positions vision as the superior mode of apprehending the world. On the first day discussing the novel, we spend time unpacking the opening lines in which Galdós asks his sighted reader to get lost, so to speak; the first chapter is titled "Perdido" ("Gone Astray"), and the opening line is "Se puso el sol" ("The sun had set"; Pérez Galdós, *Marianela* [Cátedra] 69; *Marianela* [William S. Gottsberger] 2). Thus, the novel starts with temporal inversion and closure. It is dusk and the end of the workday in the rural mining town dubbed Socartes, an oblique nod to Socrates, a reference that has served as an invitation to engage with Galdós's exploration of Platonic idealism (see Ruiz; Dendle, *Galdós* and "Shipwreck"). Uncertain of his surroundings, Dr. Teodoro Golfín fumbles his way through the darkness as he navigates a particularly dangerous part of the mines—a zone known as La Terrible (The Terrible). Vision becomes paradoxically futile for the renowned ophthalmologist who built his career in the Americas. However, rather than simply equate darkness (and by extension blindness) with ignorance—a move that would uphold "ocularnormativism," or "the perpetuation of the conclusion that the supreme means of perception is necessarily visual" (Bolt 14)—the novel orients the doctor and the reader toward a different sensorial apprehension of the world.

Students are likely to miss such details at first, so I invite them to return to the text. I ask, "What verb does the narrator use to tell us that Golfín notices a voice in the distance?" Golfín, blinded by the absence of sunlight, *feels* the voice of Marianela—"sintió una voz" ("*felt* a voice"; Pérez Galdós, *Marianela* [Cátedra] 72; my trans.)—and *senses* the distant footsteps—"creyó sentir pasos lejanos" ("believed he *sensed* distant footsteps"; 73; my trans.)—of the visually impaired Pablo, who together with Marianela will guide him to safety.[3] To feel is not the same as to hear. These examples of questions that may seem tedious at first help students quickly begin to grasp the purpose and value of close reading. This exercise helps the class get attuned to the value of precision in language.

Attention to language in conjunction with theoretical concepts from disability studies, moreover, allows for a different readerly assessment of the text.

I teach the first chapter of *Marianela* alongside David Bolt's *The Metanarrative of Blindness*, a foundational text for blindness studies, in order to equip students with critical tools that help them make sense of the formal aspects of fiction and the politics that often subtend them. This pairing serves as a particularly useful springboard to train students not only in disability studies but in literary analysis as well. I have observed that most undergraduate students in my classes, even those with previous coursework in literature, are typically "reading for plot," to appropriate Peter Brooks's words; that is, their questions tend to probe characters' motives, interpret the cause of their ill-fated trajectories, or predict their next moves. Driven by plot, their orientation vis-à-vis the novel tends toward linearity, futurity, action, and causality. Galdós's prose, however, invites a reader to linger, to feel, and to ponder; and Bolt's work in turn gives students the tools to be reflexive about the intersection of knowledge, language, and ableism. From Bolt's book, I assign chapter 1, "Community, Controversy, and Compromise: The Terminology of Visual Impairment" (16–34). Because most theoretical texts I assign are in English, I provide students with list of key terms for disability studies with Spanish translations at the start of class (see appendix). In this chapter, Bolt advances the term *ocularnormativism*, defined above. By way of introducing this concept in class, we examine the ableist ideology that subtends everyday expressions such as "blind trust," or, in Spanish, "hacer algo a ciegas." After some time for silent reflection, students generate their own lists of terms like "Está claro" ("It's clear") and "¿Ves?" ("You see?"). Becoming attentive to the ordinary forms of ocularnormativism—in this case, equating blindness with ignorance or irrationality—allows for a generative conversation on the mechanics of the novel, which we so closely align with visual mastery in this period.

Such is the case of *Marianela*'s opening chapter, "Perdido," which temporarily upends the utility of sight—disorienting, momentarily, the eye doctor, and by extension challenging the potency of what Michel Foucault in *The Birth of the Clinic* would term the "medical gaze." With this initial lesson, students start to become cognizant of the symbolic force of vision—and the epistemic shifts that buttress it—in both clinical medicine (as Foucault has argued)[4] and narrative fiction. From a methodological standpoint, they also, crucially, become reoriented to fiction—paying attention not only to plot and characters but also to the novel's form, its affective contours, synesthesia, and aurality, to cite a few examples. It is the disability studies framework, in particular, that readily facilitates this reorientation.

Among my students, probing the visuality of the novel necessitates an examination of perhaps the most commonly discussed topic in regard to *Marianela*: beauty. The two central characters—Marianela and Pablo—share an intimate bond and simultaneously remain diametrically opposed according to bourgeois societal norms. Unlike most women protagonists of the modern Spanish novel, whose enticing beauty drives the plot, Marianela is impoverished, rickety, and unsightly. Pablo, by contrast, is handsome—like chiseled marble—physically robust and belongs to the upper middle class. The juxtaposition of beauty and blindness in the case of Pablo renders him an oddity for a man of his social stature. The narrator coarsely describes him as "hermoso como un hombre y ciego como un vegetal" ("to have all the faculties of a man and be as blind as a vegetable"; Pérez Galdós, *Marianela* [Cátedra] 110; *Marianela* [William S. Gottsberger] 60). Perhaps the even greater offense to bourgeois society is the fact that Pablo calls Marianela—deemed monstrous by Pablo's father—beautiful. This alone necessitates the curing of Pablo's visual impairment—not so that he may navigate his surroundings with greater independence or even enter the workforce but so that he may properly comprehend the dominant canon of feminine beauty and marry his classically beautiful and moneyed cousin Florentina. At this point, the students, who have grown rather fond of Marianela, feel betrayed by Pablo. To help them assess the relationship between gender, sexuality, and disability, we turn to two theoretical texts. The first is *Crip Theory*, where Robert McRuer advances the precept of compulsory able-bodiedness: a properly heterosexual man is also free of physical and cognitive impairments. This medically induced transition from blind man to sighted (and therefore eligible) bachelor upholds this normative ideal.

The narrative focus on Marianela's purported ugliness, which is difficult to disentangle from her sickliness, provides a window into Rosemarie Garland-Thomson's assertion that beauty and normalcy are "twin ideologies" (11). That is, Marianela's purported ugliness also operates as a sign of her disability. Other disability studies scholars have made similar claims, noting the ways in which ableism hinges on a notion of aesthetic normativism (see Mitchell and Snyder, *Narrative Prothesis*). Many students, I have noted, struggle to grasp the relationship between beauty standards and ableism. Susan Schweik's book *The Ugly Laws: Disability in Public* is particularly poignant in this context and brilliant for understanding how the impoverished disabled body has historically been legislated out of public spaces. The danger here is that students may be tempted to think that such laws and discriminatory beliefs are no longer operative, siloed to the late nineteenth and early twentieth centuries. In countering this, I ask them to reflect on what kinds of social events require dress codes or which social organizations (e.g., fraternities and sororities) explicitly and implicitly subscribe to certain beauty norms. Students are particularly eager to discuss these matters in pairs or small groups, drawing from personal experiences, and they also notice how beauty requirements align not only with ableist ideals but also with racism, classism, and misogyny. The discussion on gender and class in particular is a useful way to bring the conversation back to the novel.

Pablo's fate is redirected by the technologies of modern medicine, making this beautiful man now a useful one too.[5] This example of rehabilitation from the novel helps students retroactively make sense of McRuer's claims about compulsory heterosexuality. No longer disabled, Pablo can be a proper bourgeois man and marry. Meanwhile, Marianela is forever consigned to the realm of inutility, not only because she is impoverished and sick and deviates from conventional notions of feminine beauty but also because Pablo—once sighted—swiftly deems her monstrous. If there was any doubt about the novel's scrutiny of the medical-male gaze, Galdós heavy-handedly titles the chapter in question "Ojos que matan" ("The Eyes Kill"). "Who or what kills Marianela?" I ask my students. A debate ensues. At this point, if anyone struggles to come up with a confident answer, I give them time to return to the chapter in question and highlight key phrases surrounding Marianela's death. There is more to Marianela's death than her poverty-stricken condition or her impoverished health, I hint. "A broken heart?" some conjecture. Indeed, Marianela is broken by the cruelty of the ableist bourgeoisie. Doctor Golfín says as much when he speaks of Pablo regaining his sight: "¡La ha visto [a Marianela]!, lo cual es como un asesinato" ("he has seen her—seen her! The shock was a death-blow"; Pérez Galdós, *Marianela* [Cátedra] 237; *Marianela* [William S. Gottsberger] 257). The class is generally surprised to see the lack of medical certainty in this instance. If the novel started with ocular futility—the ophthalmologist finding his way through sound and touch—it ends with an even clearer critique of clinical medicine writ large. When Golfín is unable to discern the medical cause of Marianela's sudden death, he—somewhat ashamed—retreats to a position of humility to say that he is but a mere carpenter of the eyes (*Marianela* [Cátedra] 238; *Marianela* [William S. Gottsberger] 236). This pivotal moment (in which the novel diminishes the power of clinical medicine) lands particularly well with my students. Here they start to grasp how fiction does not merely "reflect" the medical discourse of the time but also intervenes in said discourse.

How to Treat a Lady: The Medical Theater of Tristana

Tristana takes readers on a different route to explore the aesthetics of the disabled feminine body—linking the erotics of reading and epistemophilia with the masculine clinical medical gaze. In the discussion of *Tristana*, we examine how the novel centers feminine beauty, but rather than equating it with youth, vibrancy, and health, it relates Tristana's apparent allure to an imagery of sickness and death—a sharp departure from the case of Marianela. The narrator notes over and over the paleness of Tristana's skin, calling her "una muerta hermosísima" ("a very beautiful dead girl"; Pérez Galdós, *Tristana* [Cátedra] 173; *Tristana* [New York Review Books] 60). While at first shocking students, a more in-depth look at contemporary and historical fashion ads allows students to see familiar images anew, like the "smoky eye" makeup technique trending once again and reminiscent of Kate Moss's iconic "heroin chic" look. While Marianela's sickliness is a source of repugnance, Tristana is highly aestheticized as a cadaverous beauty. Lou Charnon-Deutsch's essay "Death Becomes Her" is particularly productive here. It opens with a close reading of Tom Petty and the Heartbreakers's "Last Dance with Mary Jane"—a music video that plays on the fantasy of necrophilia with Kim Basinger playing the beautiful corpse—before looping back to nineteenth-century paintings and illustrations that romanticize the female corpse, particularly in the medical context. In class, we watch the music video in full and spend time in pairs discussing it alongside the nineteenth-century paintings.

In my experience, students like to weigh in on the debate of whether or not *Tristana* can be considered a feminist novel, and again, their answers tend to use plot to justify their claims. They question whether or not Tristana makes the right decision by refusing Horacio as a husband. They are keen on determining whether or not Tristana's choices are feminist. These questions are certainly worth pondering, but to further advance the debate, I press students on how we come to know what we know about Tristana: "What kind of access does the novel give or deny us?" The conversation shifts when I ask how Tristana as a character is built aesthetically and discursively: "When does the narrator first mention Tristana's name? What imagery does the narrator use to describe her beauty?" With these sorts of questions, students come to understand the uncertainty around Tristana and her gendered objectification. Early in the novel we are slow to learn her name and precisely what role she plays in Don Lope's home. She is beautiful, but her beauty derives from a fantasy of a highly aestheticized, corpse-like passivity. The narrator renders her a paper doll and objet d'art. "Thingified" from the outset, she is, in a way, ontologically dead.

Crucially, the moment at which Tristana's material body becomes fleshly and lifelike is when she starts to feel pain in her leg, which is later amputated. Hers is a transition from paper to violated flesh. Through a close reading of the amputation scene—a rarity in Galdosian fiction—our class discussions drift toward questions of informed consent and the violent erotics of the medical gaze. (It is productive here to loop back to the imagery from Charnon-Deutsch's essay.) As I have already noted, at the outset, Tristana is not ill but is aestheticized as sickly. Over the course of the novel, when she actually does grow sick, her pathology is a source of erotic inspiration that can be easily overlooked. In class, I invite students to analyze the tone of the following love letter Tristana writes to Horacio:

> No quiero decirte dónde: ya sabes que una señorita, inglesa por añadidura, *miss Restitute*, no puede nombrar decorosamente, delante de un hombre, otras partes del cuerpo que la cara y las manos. Pero, en fin, grandísimo poca vergüenza, yo tengo confianza contigo, y quiero decírtelo claro: me duele una pierna. ¡Ay, ay, ay! ¿Sabes dónde? Junto a la rodilla, *do* existe aquel lunar . . . ¡Vamos, que si esto no es confianza . . . !
>
> (Pérez Galdós, *Tristana* [Cátedra] 217)

> I can't tell you where exactly because, as you know, a young lady, and an English young lady to boot, Miss Restitute, cannot in the presence of a man, decorously name any parts of her body other than her face and hands. But I trust you, shameless creature that you are, and want to speak openly:

> My leg hurts. Ay, ay, ay! Do you know where? Just by my knee, where that mole be . . . Well, if that isn't trust, I don't know what is.
>
> (*Tristana* [New York Review Books] 107–08)

Tristana playfully exploits her sickness as an opportunity to taunt Horacio, coquettishly describing intimate parts of her body with great specificity—"*do* existe aquel lunar" ("where that mole be")—while feigning a desire to remain chaste. Reading the passage aloud helps students more readily pick up on the coquettish tone. We might presume that it is not only Horacio (and the reader) but Tristana herself who derives pleasure from this play of epistolary peekaboo occasioned by her real, material pain. But as Tristana's health further declines, the ludic, coquettish discussions about her illness fade away.

Tristana's illness, as I have noted, culminates in the amputation of her leg. I approach this conversation with care, warning students of the gender violence it entails and the discomforting conversations we may have around doctor-patient relations.[6] Before the amputation, Dr. Miquis administers ether. "Does Tristana consent to this?" I ask students. Tristana appears not to have consented to ether, they conclude. "Does she resist in any way?" Here the students mostly look puzzled until I invite them to return to the text. *Tristana* resists with her eyes: "Tristana se puso lívida, clavando en el médico una mirada medrosa, infantil, suplicante" ("Tristana turned deathly pale, fixing the doctor with a look that was at once fearful, childish, and pleading"; *Tristana* [Cátedra] 241; *Tristana* [New York Review Books] 134). Once the ether takes effect, the narrator notes, "Mas no era fácil engañarla. La pobre señorita comprendió las intenciones de Augusto, y le dijo, esforzándose en sonreír: '—Es que quiere usted dormirme . . .'" ("She was not easy to deceive however. The poor young woman knew what his intentions were and, trying very hard to smile, she said, 'You want to send me to sleep, don't you?'"; *Tristana* [Cátedra] 242; *Tristana* [New York Review Books] 134).

Here, by providing a brief overview of the belated entry of women into the medical profession, I prompt students to explore the gendered dynamics of the doctor-patient relationship as one that is subtended by hetero-patriarchal culture. We reflect on the fact that medicine in the nineteenth century (not only in Spain) was male-dominated and particularly fascinated with the pathologies of the female body.[7] (My premed students are quick to note that even though women now regularly work in medicine, there is documented gender bias in the field.) We read excerpts of nineteenth-century medical texts, including Pedro Felipe Monlau's *Higiene del Matrimonio*, to get a glimpse of the gendered bias in medicine in Galdós's time. Charnon-Deutsch's aforementioned essay surveys a host of visual images that depict the female corpse in the so-called medical theater—on display and opened up for the masculine medical gaze. Even as the ether takes hold, Tristana, in her hallucinatory state, manages to say to her doctor, "Miquis, usted no es caballero, ni lo ha sido nunca, ni sabe tratar con señoras" ("You are no gentleman, Miquis, you never have been, you don't even know how to treat a lady"; Pérez Galdós, *Tristana* [Cátedra] 242; *Tristana* [New York Review Books] 135). Here

Tristana, I suggest, likens Miquis to a vulgar suitor, seducing her against her will. That is, he does not know how to *treat a lady*, in the dual sense of *treatment*: both in terms of medicine and in terms of courtship. Following this line of reasoning, Galdós appears readily cognizant of the misogyny that subtends both heterosexual partnerships and doctor-patient relationships, both of which necessitate the importance of bodily autonomy and informed consent. The fleshly transformation of Tristana is, paradoxically, realized by her amputation as Don Lope attests to "la primera sangre" ("the first blood spilled"; *Tristana* [Cátedra] 243; *Tristana* [New York Review Books] 136), having borne witness to the entire operation. Upon returning to the social model of disability, the class comes to see medicine and patriarchy as twin disabling forces. Following the amputation, Tristana assumes the unlikely role of the angel of the hearth, abandoning her dreams of autonomy. The novel's ending becomes the topic of our final class debate.[8] Unsurprisingly, students are baffled by this conclusion, and some abandon their previous assertion that the text imparted a feminist perspective. Others argue that the representation of women's maltreatment is itself a feminist endeavor; in this way, I suppose Galdós does not disappoint. His fiction is always an invitation to dwell and debate.

I hope to have shown how disability as a central analytic can be productive for reading anew. Disability studies as a critical approach to narrative fiction does not only help us "see" new things. Instead, as a framework, it can reorient our reading such that we hear, feel, desire, and even recoil—apprehending literature in all its aesthetic horrors and delights and approaching medicine from the unique vantage point of narrative fiction. Galdós's works, for their part, provide a rich representational repository that allows us to apprehend the cultural history of disabled embodiment, the institutional power of medicine, and fiction's unique interventions into these timely matters.

NOTES

1. The term *bodymind* is frequently used in disability studies scholarship to emphasize the integration of mind and body and to challenge Western or Cartesian dualism, which treats the mind and body as discrete and hierarchical units.

2. A recent volume edited by Mara Mills and Rebecca Sanchez, *Crip Authorship: Disability as Method*, also explores this concept.

3. Clara Bell translates *sentir* in both instances as "heard," eradicating multivalent interpretations of the verb "to feel" or "to sense."

4. For advanced students, Foucault's essay "Open Up a Few Corpses" from *Birth of the Clinic* is helpful for illustrating this point (141–50).

5. Elsewhere I discuss the cultural significance of usefulness; see Chang.

6. My syllabus also notes that throughout the semester we will have frank conversations about bodies and sexual practices.

7. Dolors Aleu was the first woman in Spain to earn a medical degree, in 1882.

8. Luis Buñuel's filmic interpretation of *Tristana* provides a somewhat different ending. While film is not the focus of my class, instructors may find the comparison useful, especially in conjunction with Sara Muñoz-Mariana's article on the topic.

APPENDIX: SELECTED TEXTS AND TERMS

Further Reading for Students and Instructors

Chang, Julia Haeyoon. "Petrified: Debilitating Bodies in Benito Pérez Galdós's *Marianela* (1879)." *Journal of Literary and Cultural Disability Studies*, vol. 18, no. 1, 2024, pp. 35–51. *Liverpool University Press*, https://doi.org/10.3828/jlcds.2023.44.

Fraser, Benjamin. *Cognitive Disability Aesthetics: Visual Culture, Disability Representations, and the (In)Visibility of Cognitive Difference.* U of Toronto P, 2018.

———. *Disability Studies and Spanish Culture: Films, Novels, the Comic and the Public Exhibition*. Liverpool UP, 2013.

McRuer, Robert. *Teoría Crip: Signos culturales de lo queer y de la discapacidad*. Kaótica Libros, 2021.

Mitchell, David T., and Sharon L. Snyder. "Disability as Multitude: Reworking Non-productive Labor Power." *Journal of Literary and Cultural Disability Studies*, vol. 4, no. 2, 2010, pp. 179–93. *Project Muse*, muse.jhu.edu/article/390400.

Rodriguez, Erika. "The Essential Work of Crip Resistance: Demanding Dignity in Spain's Pandemic Austerity." *Disability Studies Quarterly*, vol. 41, no. 3, Sept. 2021, dsq-sds.org/index.php/dsq/article/view/8353/6192.

Willem, Linda. "Writing and Adapting Disability: Galdós' *Marianela* and Pablo Messiez's *Los Ojos*." *Bulletin of Spanish Studies*, vol. 95, nos. 9–10, 2018, pp. 109–20.

Key Terms for Disability Studies

Spanish	*English*
capacitismo	ableism
capacitista	ableist
cuerpomente	bodymind
discapacidad	disability
impedimento visual	visual impairment
neurodiversidad	neurodiversity
ocularcentrismo	ocularcentrism
ocularnormativismo	ocularnormativism
personas con discapacidad	people with disabilities

Teaching Contagion, Politics, and Epistemology through Galdós's Fiction and Journalism

Erika Rodriguez

Epidemics precipitate social crisis because the threat of contagion compels societies to reimagine intimacies and boundaries, from the scope of personal, everyday life to that of international policy. In the context of European and transatlantic readership, Benito Pérez Galdós's journalistic coverage of the 1885 cholera epidemic and later literary representations of contagion depict competing discourses on public health at a time when scientific theories of disease transmission were heavily politicized. Galdós's focus on legal policies, epistemic uncertainty, and an ethics of care offers fertile ground for students to examine the politics of contagion in ways that resonate with contemporary conversations on public health and are likely to remain relevant in coming years as climate change increases the risk of novel diseases. This essay delineates the materials and approaches I employed to discuss Galdós's works in Past and Future Plagues: Politics of Contagion, an undergraduate course cross-listed in English, Spanish, and international and global studies.

The purpose of Past and Future Plagues was partly to reframe controversial topics in present-day public health policy and rhetoric (such as vaccination, health care, and masking) through close reading and historical contextualization. Analyzing fictional and historical texts, helped my students approach high-stakes questions from new vantage points and move toward a deeper understanding of social constructions of the public and health. To this end, the scope of reading assignments included primary texts ranging from nineteenth-century journalism and anti-vaccine caricatures to *BPM* and Mario Bellatín's *Salón de belleza* (*Beauty Salon*), before turning to speculative fiction. By offering my own translations of selections from Galdós's publications on the 1885 cholera epidemic and assigning passages from *Nazarín* and *Misericordia*, which are available in English,[1] this essay takes into account the needs of Hispanist faculty members who may be required to teach outside of their discipline or faculty members from other national literatures or cultural studies disciplines invested in issues of health, care, and social control.

The journalism historian Juan José Fernandez Sanz describes Galdós's letters to the Argentine newspaper *La Prensa* as "sin lugar a duda, la visión más amplia y completa de una epidemia de cólera" ("undoubtedly the broadest and most complete vision of a cholera epidemic"; 437; my trans.). These journalistic publications are perhaps made most "complete" by the feeling of uncertainty they transmit, encapsulating public anxieties and political tensions as they unfold alongside new case reports and policy critique. Galdós explores similar issues in his novels, with the difference that care and contagion constitute vectors on which to explore the ethical values of his characters. *Nazarín* and *Misericordia* are part of the author's "spiritual turn," which combined realism's investment in scientific knowledge of social ills with the less material logic of spiritual redemption. For example, the protagonists of both novels take care of highly contagious subjects only to emerge from their caregiving unscathed. Instructors can invite discussion on ethical stances in fiction and journalism, particularly in thinking of literary realism as driven by claims to scientific empiricism and solutions to social problems. For students of Spanish literature, studying the historical development of public health can complement commonly taught topics (including the animosity between Carlists and liberals) or lead into burgeoning subfields in Iberian and global Hispanophone studies, such as critical disability studies. For students in other fields, public health history serves as a hook for this lesson: after all, debates about public safety, personal bodily autonomy, and the creation of empirical information continue to drive liberalism's complex relationship with contagion.

To introduce these topics, I ask the class what they would consider political influence on science and how such an influence could be beneficial or pernicious. After this discussion, I assign the introduction to Ann La Berge's *Mission and Method* (1–8) and Sylvia Tesh's "Political Ideology and Public Health in the Nineteenth Century." In the former, students learn how nineteenth-century hygienists' views on public health policies were inseparable from debates about statism (characterized by the belief that public health was the state's responsibility and could not be left up to individuals) and liberalism (which held that health reform was best handled at the individual level). Through Tesh's article, students learn that tensions between statism and liberalism shaped the arguments between contagionists and anticontagionists, which divided medical communities in France and England as well as in Spain. Contagionists, who believed diseases were transmitted through touch, were in favor of stronger borders, sanitary cordons, and quarantines; anticontagionists pointed out that contagion theory had failed to account for numerous instances in which people were exposed to disease but did not become ill (like the protagonists of *Nazarín* and *Misericordia*). Anticontagionists, therefore, argued that disease was primarily caused or facilitated by local factors and that quarantines and sanitary cordons were as ineffectual as they were draconian. At the time, the debate was scientifically irresolvable, but one thing was certain: contagion theory would cause the closure of important ports and other sites of commerce crucial to the merchant and industrialist class. For this reason, liberal physicians tended to argue against contagionism, associating it with the authoritarianism of the ancien régime, and defended their anticontagionist positions through economic arguments rather than empirical medical data. These texts emphasize that modern science has historically been political and encourage readers to examine contagion not only as a fact of disease transmission but as a cultural logic.

The class explores these issues through a series of asynchronous and in-person activities. In this lesson arc, I use two collaborative annotation activities and one shared document in which the whole class synthesizes their ideas toward the end of the lesson arc. The first annotation is of a document (see appendix) that contains translated excerpts from three of Galdós's letters to *La Prensa*: "Precauciones sanitarias" ("Sanitary Precautions), "La especulacion del miedo" ("Speculation of Fear"), and "El cólera y la política" ("Cholera and Politics"). The second includes translated excerpts from *Nazarín* and *Misericordia*. I assign the annotation of the journalistic texts as homework, but it can be done in class if the semester schedule permits. The instructor should create as many digital copies of the texts as needed to divide the class into groups of three to five (e.g., a class of thirty would have six identical digital copies to facilitate small group participation). Once grouped, students highlight and comment on instances in the journalistic texts that explain what is known with certainty and what is unknown about the contagion, identify social groups that align themselves with specific public health policies or politics, identify groups or regions most impacted by the contagion, or contain elements that students find confusing or surprising. In class, the instructor can share key annotations from each group before moving on to a jigsaw activity that will ask them to connect their observations to the political context of the nineteenth century introduced earlier in Tesh's reading.

To carry out this in-class jigsaw activity, the instructor separates the class into thirds and assigns each of those thirds one of the journalistic texts to summarize in relation to Tesh's work on liberalism and statism and their relation to contagionism and anticontagionism. If necessary, those thirds can be broken into smaller groups of three to five, depending on class size. Each group is tasked with writing one or two sentences synthesizing their analysis of either "Sanitary Precautions," "Speculation of Fear," or "Cholera and Politics" as a bullet point under the appropriate heading in a shared online document. In "Sanitary Precautions," students will notice the author's doubts about the effectiveness of the physician's administrative recommendations as well as his concern with social and economic disruption. The second selection, "The Speculation of Fear," showcases Galdós's mistrust of the government, which was reflective of popular sentiment. This text was published days after the announcement of cholera in Madrid, which was met with immediate protests by merchants and anarchist workers (Díaz Simón 467–71). Finally, "Cholera and Politics" paves the way for discussions about how people and governments should behave in moments of medical uncertainty about contagion. Galdós's questions about who appears to profit from claims of contagion are particularly fruitful, considering that Galdós himself is both skeptical of the medico-administrative policies and critical of popular myths about the origin of the outbreak. The urgency and stakes of a contagious outbreak such as cholera bring questions about knowledge and authority to the forefront: How do we know what we know? How should that influence behavior and policy? And what assumptions about authority can we find in the answers to these questions? This selection also provides an opportunity to discuss uneven health policy implementation across regions and classes. Depending on instructor interest, each selection from *Cronicón* offers possible parallels to COVID, monkeypox, or other recent outbreaks. To conclude the activity, the class assesses the summaries all together and the instructor offers corrections where needed before sharing the historical context of Galdos's politics. This lays the groundwork for a pre-reading conversation in which the instructor provides context on the two fictional texts and students discuss what aspects of the first annotation (knowledge and certainty about contagion, political divisions on contagion, and uneven social impact of contagion) they expect will be most important in the fictional texts.

After examining Galdós's journalistic depiction of contagion, we turn to chapter 38 through the conclusion of *Misericordia* ([Dedalus] 255–80) and sections 1 and 2 of part 4 of *Nazarín* ([Oxford] 113–25), focusing on connections and contradictions between Galdós's journalism and his fiction. I then introduce the novels by explaining that they were written at a time when Galdós was heavily influenced by Tolstoy's investment in spiritual crisis and moral regeneration. To help orient students in the reading, I provide a list of the main characters that appear in the novel's selections and a summary of the most relevant aspects of the plot for the scene to make sense. In the selection from *Nazarín*, the Christ-like, Don Quixote–inspired protagonist and two former prostitutes provide much-needed sanitation and medical care to a rural village when help from the national health ministry fails to arrive in time. This selection prompts discussion of anxieties surrounding contagion, community care, and inadequacies of official response to viral outbreaks. In *Misericordia*, the protagonist goes to her former employer, for whom she has been providing financially, to seek help caring for her sick friend, a Jewish beggar from Morocco. Instead of receiving help, the friend is accused of having leprosy and told to go back to Africa. This selection can be used to explore the relation between class control and fumigation or between the implementation of sanitary cordons at national borders, fear of infection, and xenophobia (Rodríguez 701–07). Teresa Fuentes Peris's arguments regarding Galdós's inconsistent stances on contagion are a helpful supplement to the discussion (163–69).

As with the collaborative annotation documents on Galdos's journalism, students are separated into small groups corresponding to a document in which they are asked to highlight and comment on instances in the text that can help them answer specific questions: First, what are the contagions depicted in each novel, and how do you know (e.g., what symptoms and diagnoses are depicted)? Second, how do different characters react to the threat of contagion? Students' answers lead into a class discussion on whether the characters' reaction to contagion can align with a contagionist or anticontagionist argument, how the texts invite us to agree or disagree with these characters' positions, and the most significant differences in Galdós's nonfictional and fictional works on contagion. This conversation allows for a deeper examination of state responsibility (as defended by statism and contagionists) and individual risks in caregiving (which may complicate anticontagionist and liberal perspectives on public health). The instructor can also lead the conversation in a new direction by considering that, though cholera was not known with certainty to be contagious, the two illnesses in *Nazarín* and *Misericordia* certainly were (smallpox and leprosy, respectively). This becomes an important distinction when asking what the logic of contagion does in these novels: What anxieties does it mobilize? What associations does it affirm or disrupt? Where does information become misused or become misinformation? For a graduate course, this line of questioning can find more depth alongside affect studies scholarship such as Brian Massumi's "The Political Ontology of Threat" and Sara Ahmed's *The Cultural Politics of Emotion*.

This progression through Galdós's texts develops students' awareness of medico-political and literary intersections while offering an opportunity to nuance their assumptions about public health. Just as nineteenth-century debates on contagion were influenced by economic factors and personal political leanings, present-day public health journals have noted that "predatory low-quality scientific journals, professional pressures to publish high quantities of manuscripts, and the exaggerated and uncontextualized dissemination of findings to the public are notable causes" of misinformation (Yudkin 1). Public health experts have called for a new epistemology of science that addresses uncertainty, improves science communication efforts with the public, and centers equity in scientific fields—particularly as it is expected that "science operating as crisis anticipation and management for the public good will become much more prevalent in the future" (Caniglia et al. 59). Although this is not the language surrounding epistemologies of science in the nineteenth century, the central questions resonate with Galdós's critiques of the medical profession, public confusion and mistrust, and violence through public health policy. Studying past examples of the creation and dissemination of scientific knowledge and the logic of contagion can help us all be more ethically and epistemologically prepared for future crises.

NOTE

1. There are two translations of *Nazarín*, one by Jo Labanyi, published in 1993 (Oxford), and a more recent translation, *The Forbidden*, by Robert Rudder and Gloria Arjona. *Misericordia* was translated by Charles de Salis (Dedalus).

APPENDIX: TRANSLATED SELECTIONS FROM GALDÓS'S LETTERS TO *LA PRENSA*

The following selections from Cronicón, *edited by Alberto Ghiraldo, are translated by the author.*

"Sanitary Precautions"

Madrid, 17 November 1884

Once again, the alarms of cholera have come to disturb the peace and happiness particular to this capital: once more, the terror of finding ourselves visited by the epidemic disrupts our peaceable spirits, upsets all our plans, paralyzes businesses, and establishes the anticipations of tragedy, which are not inferior to the tragedy itself. . . .

With the alarm has also come that medico-administrative calamity that goes by the name of *sanitary precautions*. These precautions seem like inventions of those physicians immortalized by Molière and toward whom the great poet had a dislike that he neither could nor wished to disguise. The lazarettos,* both on land and maritime, had been installed with their abuse and mistreatments.

The idea that *no one enters without speaking to the doorman*† is translated on our border into lockups, fumigations, and other annoyances whose real purpose does not seem to be public health but rather the unjust acquisition of money from poor travelers.

Meanwhile, here, the discussions between medical doctors renew the confusion of past days. There is a Council, which they say is Sanitary, in which contagionists and anticontagionists battle each day so fruitlessly that they would be better off going home. As the causes of the epidemic infection remain a mystery, everything that is said there only serves to make more noise and worsen the situation.

As for the rest, we have grown used to seeing the illness up close, and we have committed the impudence of laughing at it. For some time, the topic of microbes was a much-used gold mine for jokes and witty quips in Madrid. The topic has now passed on to popular theaters, precisely at the time of renewed danger. But this has not stopped the public from laughing (73–76).

"The Speculation of Fear"

19 June 1885‡

These days, our capital finds itself agitated by an important question that stirs up everyone's emotions: *Is there cholera here?* The government says there is cholera here and sustains this position in that official gospel known as the *Gazette*; and the neighborhood masses maintain that cholera is not here. The three, four, or five

* A room or building used to quarantine contagious diseases.

† A phrase indicating that anyone entering Spain had to go through the "doorman," the Carlist insurrectionists who would interrogate travelers.

‡ The presence of cholera in Madrid had been officially declared by the government three days earlier, on 16 June 1885.

cases that are recorded daily in sanitary statistics are considered by the popular masses to be cases of heatstroke, tuberculosis, or the afterpains of drunkenness.

Many of the cases of cholera these days have also been attributed to starvation, which is why some have recovered easily as soon as they were offered brunch. In those cases, a pork chop has been the most efficacious treatment.

The government's insistence that there must be cholera in Madrid and the tenacity of the neighborhoods to rebel against the governmental epidemic is one of the strangest things I have seen in my life. On comparable occasions, the Spanish government, like the governments in any country on earth, has insisted on minimizing illness, downplaying its gravity and reducing [reports of] the number of cases insofar as it is possible. But now the opposite occurs: the government stubbornly and unabashedly inspires fear, and undoubtedly obtains who knows what dark and mysterious advantages by keeping the people of Madrid living in anxiety . . . (197–202).

"Cholera and Politics"

14 August 1885

With a great portion of our peninsula invaded by cholera, we are witnessing the most senseless and outlandish things with regards to precautions. In some localities they take cordons and lazarettos so seriously that they commit true acts of cruelty against the unlucky travelers. In others, they fumigate to such an extent that those who are fumigated cannot help but be asphyxiated or develop a chronic case of bronchitis. . . .

In some towns, lazarettos refer to a barn's dilapidated hay loft, a mill that is no longer in use, a corral for livestock or some such thing, where there are no beds or food or comforts of any kind, nor even the bare necessities for existence.

All who arrive, regardless of where they come from, are put in there and locked away for seven or eight days, in accordance with the will of some little town's mayor. . . .

There are towns which, letting themselves be won over by terror, have seen the number of victims doubled because they have been abandoned. In such places, where egoism has decreed isolation, there have been cases of cadavers that remain unburied, infesting the atmosphere. Many who have fallen ill, and who would have been saved by regular assistance, have perished in such horrific loneliness. With familial ties broken, panic has separated father from child and brother from brother. . . .

This is why in all the invasions of this epidemic there are rumors of poisoned waters. In 1834, when our country was visited for the first time by travelers *from the Ganges*, the poisoning of wells was attributed to the friars. This stupid belief led to the atrocious assassinations perpetrated in Madrid and other capitals.

The invasions that followed have also had their myths, more or less ridiculous, and even now the popular mind, incapable of reaching the heights of doctors

Koch, Pasteur, and Ferrán in their appreciation of microbial organisms, explains the epidemic with the most laughable hypotheses.

At times the government is the author of this illness; other times it is the doctors. The first sends secret agents to empty bottles of pestilent liquids in our water sources, while the second administers terrible powders to the ill so they can die more quickly, increasing the statistics and profiting from the rising numbers.

Fortunately, these ideas are now less well-received and find a limited audience.

The general masses have enough sense not to circulate them.

But the grudge against doctors persists in some areas and in certain neighborhoods . . . (251–67).

Gothic Galdós: Unsettling Spanish Imperialism in "Tropiquillos"

Wan Sonya Tang

While Benito Pérez Galdós is much celebrated for what he called his "contemporary novels," the length and complexity of these works are often barriers to teaching them in their entirety, particularly in the undergraduate classroom. One solution is to teach the author's short stories, which are far less renowned but similarly engaged with political, economic, and social questions. In contrast to most of his novelistic writing, considered the gold standard of Spanish realism, Galdós's short fictions tend toward the fantastic, often featuring uncanny or outright supernatural elements.[1] This fantastic quality—and the potential for social commentary therein—provides a number of pedagogical advantages. References to the otherworldly tend to capture students' attention, and the obvious deviation from realist aesthetics facilitates contemplation of the text's symbolic dimension. Whereas students may be tempted to take more quotidian descriptions at face value, post-Enlightenment skepticism primes them to metaphorically read ghosts, monsters, and other unearthly beings. Thus, through thoughtful scaffolding with secondary readings and focused analysis of the primary text, instructors can direct students to identify specific cultural anxieties expressed in the text under supernatural guise. This essay provides a case study of how Galdós's fantastical short stories can be taught as surprisingly nuanced explorations of complex historical circumstances and social issues. Specifically, I describe my approach to teaching the story "Tropiquillos" (first published in 1884 as "Fantasía de otoño" ["Autumnal Fantasy"] and retitled in 1890) as a meditation on Spain's imperial decline that simultaneously reproduces and subverts the orientalizing rhetoric of the colonizer by means of gothic conventions and fantastic storytelling.

I teach this story as part of an upper-division undergraduate course titled Haunted Modernity: The Fantastic Short Story in Nineteenth-Century Spain. Enrolled students are mostly juniors and seniors majoring in Hispanic studies, and the course is designed to cultivate a general understanding of the sociohistorical landscape of late-nineteenth-century Spain through the period's fantastic literary production. I emphasize particularly the development of Spanish nationalism (in the face of imperial decline), changing gender roles, and the polemics surrounding urban poverty and the rise of the working class. Although this course has a specific thematic, temporal, and geographic focus, "Tropiquillos" could just as easily be included in wide-ranging survey courses of Spanish literature or topics-based seminars on the fantastic or the gothic in Spain and Latin America, the Hispanophone short story, or the history and legacy of Spanish imperialism, among other subjects. It likewise works well at the graduate level, where it can be paired with more extensive readings on Spain's imperial decline.[2] Unfortunately, "Tropiquillos" does not currently exist in English translation, which makes it impossible to assign to students who lack a fairly advanced reading knowledge of Spanish.

In Haunted Modernity, we begin the semester by establishing working definitions of the fantastic. What do we mean when we talk about fantastic literature? And, perhaps more important, what did it mean at the time when the authors under study were writing? Initial discussions are grounded in what are considered canonical critical texts by twentieth-century literary scholars. Students read chapter 2 of *The Fantastic: A Structural Approach to a Literary Genre*, in which Tzvetan Todorov defines the fantastic as a genre marked by unresolved doubt between a natural and a supernatural explanation of a story's events. David Sandner's *Fantastic Literature: A Critical Reader* provides an excellent abridged version of Todorov's theorization for instructors who favor brevity in secondary readings. Instructors who seek contemporary Spanish theory might include chapter 1 from David Roas's easy-to-read *Tras los límites de lo real: Una definición de lo fantástico* (available in translation as *Beyond the Frontiers of the Real: A Definition of the Fantastic*). In it, Roas defines the fantastic as an aesthetic that poses an epistemological quandary by representing a disquieting confrontation between the "real" (itself a social construction) and the impossible. After debates on what the fantastic is, we move on to what the fantastic does. To get students thinking about the subversive potential of fantastic literature, I assign the afterword to Rosemary Jackson's *Fantasy: The Literature of Subversion* (100–05), which views the fantastic in psychoanalytical terms as a form of storytelling that explores deep-seated anxieties at the individual or societal level.

Once students have a basic grasp of the fantastic aesthetic and its functionality, we turn to writings from nineteenth-century Spain to better understand what the fantastic meant for the society under study. For instance, José María Blanco White's 1824 essay "Sobre el placer de las imaginaciones inverosímiles" ("On the Pleasure of Implausible Imaginations") does not explicitly use the term "fantastic" but lauds literature that depicts the unreal with the utmost realism. More nationalistically, José Zorrilla's prologue to "La pasionaria" ("The Passion Flower"), from 1841, asserts that fantastic literary production from nineteenth-century Spain was distinct from other European variants by virtue of its Catholic grounding. Only religious fantasy, he argues, flourishes on Spanish soil. Throughout the semester, students judge for themselves to what degree the assigned short fiction adheres to the various theoretical models they have studied and how the interplay between the natural and supernatural within each tale may facilitate specifically Spanish social commentary. From Pedro Antonio de Alarcón we read the early novella "El amigo de la muerte" ("Death's Friend") and the author's most beloved tale, "La mujer alta" ("The Tall Woman"), which reveal interesting attitudes on social class, gender, and their intersection. Both are available in English. Any of Gustavo Adolfo Bécquer's *Leyendas* (*Legends*) provides a pleasurable atmospheric read, but I particularly enjoy teaching "El monte de las ánimas" ("The Spirits' Mountain"), "La corza blanca" ("The White Doe"), "El beso" ("The Kiss"), and "El miserere" ("The Miserere"). The first three lend themselves to discussions on Bécquer's portrayal of femininity and nineteenth-century gender expectations, whereas both "El beso" and "El miserere" reflect the author's thoughts on artistic greatness. All can be found in translation in *Project Gutenberg*'s online edition of *Romantic Legends of Spain*. Aside from "Tropiquillos," I teach Galdós's earliest published piece of fiction "Una industria que vive de la muerte" ("An Industry That Lives Off Death"), the popular "La novela en el tranvía" ("The Novel on the Tram"), and the little-known "La princesa y el granuja" ("The Princess and the Street Urchin"). These tales provide a panorama of life in nineteenth-century Madrid with their portrayals of a real-life cholera epidemic, contemporary public transportation, and urban poverty, and the latter two texts can be found in translation. Finally, I teach Emilia Pardo Bazán's "Maldición de gitana" ("The Gypsy's Curse"), "El antepasado" ("The Ancestor"), and "Vampiro" ("Vampire"), which trace the social impact of differences in race, gender, and class, often in combination. Of these, only "Vampiro" is available in an online English translation.

Students read "Tropiquillos" about halfway through the semester, when they are well versed in the fantastic aesthetic and have had ample practice dissecting the thorny questions of race, class, and gender behind the specters and monsters that lurk in the assigned readings. This previous exposure allows students to see through Galdós's disavowal of any political agenda in the text more quickly. In the prologue to the 1890 edition of *La sombra* (*The Shadow*), which also includes the short stories "Celín," "Tropiquillos," and "Theros," Galdós dismisses these tales as "obrillas" ("trifling works"), mere "divertimientos, juguetes, ensayos de aficionado" ("amusements, playthings, trials of an enthusiast [of the fantastic]") comparable to a giddy state of inebriation (7). Students can access this text online through the open-access *Biblioteca Virtual Miguel de Cervantes* (*Miguel de Cervantes Virtual Library*), and I ask how they interpret the author's dismissive stance considering that he first published "Tropiquillos" (then titled "Fantasía de otoño") in the Argentine paper *La Prensa* in place of his usual column on European news. Would nineteenth-century readers used to reading Galdós's insights on current events have viewed "Tropiquillos" as mindless entertainment? Or would they have been attuned to the story's sociopolitical commentary? Instructors may then assign "Tropiquillos" in digital form through the *Biblioteca Cervantes*, or as it appears in the collection *Cuentos fantásticos* (*Fantastic Stories*), edited by Alan E. Smith (Pérez Galdós, *Cuentos fantásticos*). Because the latter includes textual variants from the story's multiple editions, it is the version that I teach in class and cite throughout this essay.

For a fantastic text, "Tropiquillos" features no obviously supernatural antagonist, but it nevertheless disturbs readers' sense of reality with an unexpected and ambiguous final twist. The story follows Zacarías Tropiquillos, once a wealthy *indiano* (a Spaniard who sought his fortune abroad, often in the Americas, though here the protagonist seems to have amassed his riches in Asia), as he returns to Spain penniless and sick with tuberculosis. The moribund Tropiquillos heads home to the equally decrepit family vineyard, where *mestre* (Master) Cubas, a former family employee, rescues and nurses him back to health. By winemaking season, Tropiquillos has recovered both his health and his zest for life, happily marrying Cubas's daughter. However, the text shatters the illusion of a happy ending when the protagonist suddenly finds himself collapsed under a table in a seemingly drunken state of disarray. The story ends as an unnamed servant hands Tropiquillos a steaming mug of coffee, promising that "eso va pasando" ("this will pass"; Pérez Galdós, "Tropiquillos" 230).[3] Faced with this abrupt ending, readers infer that part, if not all, of what they had previously read has only transpired in the protagonist's imagination.

Although the title character's active participation in the colonial system precedes the story's action, it is nevertheless what sets the narrative in motion. Thus, imperialism is the specter that, although unseen, haunts the entire text of "Tropiquillos." Not only must the protagonist face the consequences of his exploitative adventures abroad, but his imperialist attitudes linger throughout his convalescence back home. In this regard, Galdós's short story exemplifies Alda Blanco's claim that an imperial consciousness is central to the Spanish identity and permeates the nation's cultural production of the late nineteenth and early twentieth centuries (Blanco, *Cultura* 17). To illustrate this point in class, we dissect the issues of Madrid's leading liberal newspaper, *El Imparcial*, and its literary supplement, *Los lunes de El Imparcial*, from 18 December 1893, the day "Tropiquillos" was printed there. Digital copies of both publications are readily available in the *Hemeroteca Digital* (*Digital Periodical Archive*) of Spain's Biblioteca Nacional, and I ask students to comb through them for traces of a Spanish imperial consciousness. Examples may include the day's lead story, a highly biased account of an armed scuffle between Moroccan pirates and Spanish troops in the Spanish-occupied city of Melilla, or color engravings of neatly uniformed Spanish soldiers in juxtaposition with turbaned and tunic-clad Moroccans.[4] These reports and images help students situate Galdós's fantastic fiction in a context of heightened imperialist sentiment at a moment when Spain was on the verge of losing the last of its colonial holdings and Britain was at the height of its imperial ascendance.

Contextualization helps students identify the imperialist prejudices informing Tropiquillos's descriptions of the foreign peoples he encountered overseas. Toward this end, we closely read the passage where the protagonist describes his swift and sudden downfall in section 2 of the story:

> Mi decadencia brusca pasó ante mis ojos envuelta en humo de incendios, en olas de naufragios, en aliento de traidores, en miradas esquivas de mujer culpable, en alaridos de salvajes sediciosos, en estruendo de calderas de vapor que estallaban, en fragancia mortífera de flores tropicales, en atmósfera espesa de epidemias asiáticas, en horribles garabatos de escritura chinesca, en una confusión espantosa de injurias dichas en inglés, en portugués, en español, en tagalo, en cipayo, en japonés, por bocas blancas, negras, rojas, amarillas, cobrizas y bozales. (Pérez Galdós, "Tropiquillos" 214–15)

> My abrupt decline took place before my eyes enveloped in the smoke of fires, in ship-wrecking waves, in the breath of traitors, in the evasive glances of a guilty woman, in the shrieks of seditious savages, in the racket of steam boilers that exploded, in the lethal fragrance of tropical flowers, in an atmosphere thick with Asian epidemics, in horrible scribblings of Chinese writing, in a horrific confusion of insults spoken in English, in Portuguese, in Spanish, in Tagalog, in the Sepoy language, in Japanese, by white, black, red, yellow, coppery, and black slave mouths.

In an analytical exercise, students highlight and examine descriptions of non-Europeans in the passage. The class may observe how the fires, shipwrecks, and equipment malfunctions that befall the protagonist are attributed to sabotage by native populations, though they could very plausibly be accidents. More obvious to students is the condescending attitude that Tropiquillos adopts toward colonized populations. In recalling the "alaridos de salvajes sediciosos" ("shrieks of seditious savages"), "horribles garabatos de escritura chinesca" ("horrible scribblings in Chinese writing"), and "confusión de injurias dichas por . . . bocas blancas, negras, rojas, amarillas, cobrizas y bozales" ("confusion of insults spoken . . . by white, black, red, yellow, coppery, and black slave mouths"), Tropiquillos shows an absolute disdain for the non-Spaniards around him. Not only is their use of language deemed nonsensical but they become a horde of disembodied, racialized mouths, represented with little sense of humanity, much less individuality. Here, Said's theorization of orientalism aids students' understanding of Tropiquillos's rhetoric as aggressively stereotyping based on the premise of Western superiority. Although I do not assign readings from Said's work in my class, the introduction to *Orientalism* is fairly accessible for advanced undergraduate students (1–28).

An examination of gothic undertones in the text further enriches the class discussion of the imperial consciousness pervading "Tropiquillos." Tasked with identifying gothic conventions in Galdós's story, aficionados of the genre will recognize such motifs as the extermination of the family line (Tropiquillos's parents and siblings have all died by the time he returns to Spain), the dilapidated ancestral home (and the symbolism therein), and the suggestion of supernatural intervention in Tropiquillos's rapid downfall, all of which can be read as karmic retribution for the protagonist's immoral activities overseas. I thus present "Tropiquillos" as an example of "imperial gothic," a category established by Patrick Brantlinger to describe a "literature of terror as it becomes obsessed with the perceived 'dusk' of an empire" whose decline is precipitated through contact with (and contamination by) more primitive native populations (qtd. in Höglund 8).[5] Common imperial gothic tropes include "going native," in which the colonizer adopts the supposed savagery of the colonized, and "reverse colonization," in which imperial powers are invaded and subjugated by their colonial subjects. I encourage students to view "Tropiquillos" as an original take on the narrative of reverse colonization. In Galdós's tale, Spain is not suddenly overrun with so-called seditious savages, but Tropiquillos's body has inarguably succumbed to the contagion of colonized lands. A broken man at the story's start, he laments, "Tengo el fuego del trópico en mis entrañas, el tifón en mi cerebro" ("I have the fire of the tropics in my bowels, the typhoon in my brain"; Pérez Galdós, "Tropiquillos" 218). The protagonist's debilitated body can easily be presented as an allegory for the ailing Spanish nation or, better yet, for what Lisa Surwillo describes as a "terminally ill imperialism" (90). This analogy is compelling given Tropiquillos's admission of his previous "fiebre de lucro" ("profit fever") and "sed insaciable de dinero" ("insatiable thirst for money") that could only be satisfied by extracting every last resource from colonized lands, violating nature and its inhabitants, animal and human, in the process (Pérez Galdós, "Tropiquillos" 214).

Students note, however, that Galdós's short fiction does not provide a straightforward cautionary tale against Spain's imperial project. Some may protest that although Tropiquillos suffers both mentally and physically as a result of exploiting foreign lands and peoples, the story does not track his definitive decline. Instead, the majority of the narrative follows the protagonist's recuperation and regeneration back at home in his motherland, where he is even allowed the luxury of falling in love. If Tropiquillos's predicament is allegorical, what does this contentment communicate about Spain's colonizing past or lingering imperial pretensions? The fact that we are reading a piece of fantastic fiction further complicates matters. The ending remains purposefully ambiguous, which becomes clear as students list multiple potential interpretations of Tropiquillos's final awakening in a heap on the floor. Perhaps he is actually a typical bourgeois gentleman who battles boredom by dreaming of an alternate existence marked by swashbuckling adventures abroad, a spectacular topple from grace, and an idyllic convalescence—or he is indeed a moribund colonizer whose fevered imagination has created a happy fantasy. Maybe all that has transpired—ascent, decline, and recuperation—has been true, but his life has been magically reset right at its happiest point as punishment for his past sins—or possibly nothing is amiss: he has simply had too much to drink during the wedding, and his new wife awaits him in their marital chamber. As students argue for one or another interpretive possibility, no definitive explanation of events emerges. This, I remind students, is the narrative ambiguity that defines the fantastic, according to Todorov, and it provides an excellent medium through which to convey ambiguous sentiments surrounding Spanish imperialism.

"Tropiquillos" offers no obvious answers, which is precisely why I teach it. Many students are left unsatisfied by the lack of certainty in the text at both the narrative and thematic levels. We have no more idea whether Tropiquillos has truly recovered—or whether he was ever ill in the first place—than we do if Galdós supported or critiqued Spain's clinging to the vestiges of its empire at the end of the nineteenth century.[6] We only know that Tropiquillos is unrepentant in his smug sense of European superiority. Even after his recovery and disavowal of the colonizing lifestyle, he lauds the Portuguese "[por] acercar la copa divina [de vino] a los labios amarillos del hijo de Confucio y despertar de su *nirvana* al bramín que tiene el mal gusto de emborracharse con agua y meditaciones" ("[for] bringing the divine glass [of wine] to the yellow lips of the son of Confucius and awakening from his *nirvana* the brahmin with the bad taste to get drunk off of water and meditations"; 226). To the protagonist's eye, the uncultured nature of the Chinese and Indians is displayed in their ignorance of European wine. At the same time, however, Tropiquillos's discombobulation in the story's final scene—potentially the only scene that occurs outside the protagonist's mind—seems to have resulted from said nectar of civilization. How cultured, then, is the Spaniard who finds himself prostrate beneath a table in a state he professes to approximate "la misma estupidez" ("stupidity itself"; 230)? The irony, though possibly unintentional, is unmistakable. Thus, the text of "Tropiquillos" presents unapologetically orientalizing attitudes but then undermines those who espouse them, just as Spanish society feared the end of Spain's imperial status even as public figures increasingly questioned the colonizing practices it entailed. When teaching complicated topics like Spanish imperialism at the turn of the twentieth century, assigning a fantastic short story like "Tropiquillos" may not seem like the obvious choice, but Galdós's play on the imperial gothic is ultimately effective in communicating to students the complexities of public opinion and pushing them to feel comfortable with the unknown.

NOTES

1. Galdós's early novella *La sombra* (*The Shadow*), the later novels *El caballero encantado* (*The Enchanted Gentleman*) and *La razón de la sinrazón* (*The Reason of Unreason*), and the fifth series of the *Episodios nacionales* (*National Episodes*) also include elements of fantasy to varying degrees.

2. Alda Blanco provides an excellent overview of Spain's awareness of and preoccupation with its changing imperial status throughout the 1800s (*Cultura*). With regard to Galdós specifically, Mary Coffey examines the author's attitudes toward Spanish imperialism as gleaned through his fictional writing. For an enlightening examination of how imperial decline translates into narratives of illness in nineteenth-century Spain, Susana Bardavío Estevan's "¡España es también aquí! Nación e imaginario colonial en los cuentos de Emilia Pardo Bazán" ("This Is Also Spain! Nation and Colonial Imaginary in Pardo Bazán's Short Stories") could easily be included in graduate syllabi.

3. All translations of "Tropiquillos" are my own.

4. An undergraduate-friendly analysis of these colonizing depictions can be found in chapter 3 of my book *Specters, Monsters, and the Damned* (113).

5. For more on the imperial gothic, instructors may assign Brantlinger's essay of that name or the introduction to his *Rule of Darkness* (3–16).

6. Galdós's own thoughts on Spanish imperialism are difficult to pin down, given his reticence to take a public stance and the mixed messages gleaned across his writing. As a counterpoint to "Tropiquillos," which quite clearly censures the greed involved in most colonizing endeavors, instructors may teach Galdós's journalistic piece "Furor colonial y otros furores" ("Colonial Furor and Other Furors"), published the following year, in which the author appears to laud Europeans' attempts to bring (their) culture to supposedly uncivilized Africans.

Galdós as Celebrity Playwright

Margot Versteeg

In this essay, I outline a pathway for guiding students in an exploration of Galdós's plays through the interpretive lens of literary celebrity studies. Celebrity culture has a pervasive presence in the everyday world of our students. It shapes the production and consumption of media content and the social values through which students experience the world. As a theoretical framework, the field of celebrity studies has generated a substantial body of scholarship. It strives to place literature into the bigger picture of society and considers the interplay between writer, audience, and the field of cultural production. The framework of celebrity studies can be used to emphasize the constructedness of the notion of the famous author or playwright.

"Galdós as celebrity playwright" could be taught as a section of an upper-division course on nineteenth-century literature but also as a component of a graduate class on Galdós. After discussing how we see (literary) celebrities in today's environment dominated by social media and how our perspective might illuminate the nineteenth century, when social changes and the rise of mass print technologies revolutionized the way people were informed about authors and works, instructors can guide their students through two short case studies—*Realidad* (*Reality*) and *Electra*, that will help them better understand how literary celebrity functioned in Galdós's time.[1] The goal is to encourage students to think beyond the strictly artistic value of the plays themselves and acknowledge that the success and significance of an author are also determined by extraliterary factors, both during his lifetime and posthumously.

A starting point would be a class discussion about how we see celebrity today. Students can read Sharon Marcus's excellent introduction to her book *The Drama of Celebrity* (1–20). Marcus defines celebrities as "people known *during their lifetimes* to more people than could possibly know one another" (9). She explains how celebrity culture involves three equally powerful groups: media producers, members of the public, and celebrities themselves (3–4). Once students are familiar with the basic notions of celebrity culture, they can explore the subcategory of *literary* celebrity. Instructors could ask why J. K. Rowling, Margaret Atwood, or any other writer of their students' choice would be considered literary celebrities. Is it only because of their writing, or are there other factors at stake?

Once students have formulated their own basic assumptions regarding the functioning of literary celebrity, they could be directed to a corpus of short theoretical texts to tease out how current scholarship defines this phenomenon. I recommend reading excerpts by P. David Marshall, Gaston Franssen and Rick Honings, and Rebecca Braun and Emily Spiers, supplemented by a short introduction to Pierre Bourdieu's ideas about the field of cultural production.[2]

Literary celebrity studies gained considerable popularity around the end of the twentieth century, when, as Marshall observes, researchers became interested in the ways in which public individuals and literary celebrities establish their audiences through their books and then strengthen that connection through public communications of aspects of their lives and the construction of public personas (xvi–xvii). The creation of the public persona of a literary celebrity, according to Franssen and Honings, involves three key players: the writer (textual self-image), the audience (reception of the work), and the field of cultural production (in Bourdieu's sense). The French sociologist Pierre Bourdieu situates artistic works within the social conditions of their production, circulation, and consumption. Bourdieu, who developed his ideas with the nineteenth century in mind, examines the role of writers and artists, but also publishers, critics, art dealers, galleries, and academies. He analyzes the structure of the cultural field itself and places this within broader social structures of power (Bourdieu, *Field*). Students need to be made aware of the importance of these broader structures. Instructors can discuss how books are not only written and produced but also marketed. Reviews in the press and interviews with the author (just like appearances in today's talk shows) drive up sales. A much-acclaimed work might also propagate values that can be given institutional approval, incorporated into other discourses, and recycled for new purposes (Braun and Spiers 453).

After asking the students how we see literary celebrity today and subsequently discussing the social changes and the rise of mass print technologies that in the nineteenth century revolutionized the way people read literature and considered literary celebrity, instructors could address Galdós's authorial self-representation and the role the media, his fans, and other writers and institutions played in portraying him. The media (newspapers, television, social media) available to authors to promote their artistic persona define the possibilities for self-fashioning in the service of celebrity status. We often see tensions, for instance, between the author's compliance with social norms and their desire to be unique and between economic success and authenticity (Farkas 2, 4).

Galdós was a popular author, but he was also recognized by official literary institutions, such as the Ateneo (Athenaeum) and the Real Academia (Royal Academy). He was very conscious of his literary project (see Pérez Galdós, "Observaciones") and keen on providing the Spanish nation-state with a literature, harking back to Cervantes, and a history, as he did with his *Episodios nacionales* (*National Episodes*). He sought to produce quality art, which meant novels as distinct from *folletines*, or serialized texts. Among other acclamations, he was nominated on three occasions for the Nobel Prize but never won it. He flirted with politics, and he was always eager to reconcile his status and artistic integrity with economic success (see Jagoe, "Disinheriting").

Galdós engaged in practices of self-representation to construct an authorial persona for public consumption in literary circles and the literary marketplace. His recent biographers have portrayed him as "callado y distante, pero de opiniones firmes, reflexivo y con especial sentido de la ironía" ("quiet and distant, but of strong opinions, thoughtful, and with a special sense of irony"; Arencibia 45), and "introvertido, metido en su propio mundo" ("introvert, inside his own world") with a "personalidad retraída" ("withdrawn personality") and a "carácter reflexivo" ("thoughtful nature"; Gullón, *Galdós* 169), a keen observer who preferred listening over speaking.[3] Students can delve deeper into Galdós's authorial self-representation by analyzing two famous interviews published in the Madrid journal *Por Esos Mundos* (*In This World*), excerpts of which are available online ("¿Cómo era Galdós?"). For the first of these, José María Carretero, who wrote under the pseudonym El Caballero Audaz (The Audacious Gentleman), visited Galdós at his home in Madrid in 1905 (Pérez Galdós, "Maestros"). The second interview, with Enrique González Fiol, who published as El Bachiller Corchuelo (The Bachelor Corchuelo), took place five years later, in 1910 ("Nuestros grandes prestigios"). Students may be asked what information these interviews provide regarding the author's personality, lifestyle, and work habits.[4] Other possible sources of information are Galdós's "Autocaricatura irónica" ("Ironic Self-Caricature"; Arencibia 125), the literary portrait that in 1889 Leopoldo Alas (Clarín) produced in the series *Celebridades españoles contemporáneas* (*Contemporary Spanish Celebrities*; Alas, *B. Pérez Galdós*), and Emilia Pardo Bazán's portrayal of the author's home office in 1891 (Arencibia 306, 345; Pardo Bazán, "Estudio"). Students may also read sections of the author's autobiography, *Memorias de un desmemorado* (*Memories of a Forgetful Person*).[5]

Galdós successfully cultivated his personal brand as shy and distant. However, *homenajes* ("tributes") and other unavoidable public events brought the author into contact with Madrid's bourgeois establishment and introduced him into literary and cultural circles (Gullón, *Galdós* 266). One of these circles was the theater world. In his *Memorias*, Galdós remembers his access to the Spanish stage as a casual event (76–79). In the author's version, Emilio Mario, director of the company performing in Madrid's Teatro de la Comedia, insisted that the famous writer adapt his dialogized novel *Realidad* into a play. These "memories," however, do not entirely conform to historical reality. The person who paved the terrain for Galdós's theatrical endeavors was none other than his friend and fellow novelist Emilia Pardo Bazán, who used her extensive social network to bring the author into contact with Mario. It is true that Galdós had a fascination with the theater and had long been experimenting with hybrid forms. For a public intellectual such as Galdós, playwriting was a way to influence public opinion. *Realidad* is, after all, a work with great societal resonance. It is a play about a husband who refrains from killing his adulterous wife in a country and time where an outdated honor code was still in place and domestic violence was rampant. Why, then, did Galdós wait until he was Spain's most popular novelist before finally premiering this, his first play, 1892?

Galdós's dream had always been to live by his pen, and although, from the 1880s on, he made a good living with the publication of his novels, his financial situation left much to be desired. Students can read a fragment from a recent biography that explains how the author's generosity with the numerous women in his life, the mortgage for his villa in Santander, his extensive travels through Europe, and the financial obligations he inherited from his family, all left Galdós plagued by debt till the end of his life (Gullón, *Galdós* 370–71). To alleviate his financial situation, the author needed a box office success; to obtain this, he had to change his position in the field of cultural production.

The field of cultural production, as the French sociologist Pierre Bourdieu envisions it, is a field of forces and struggles that represents an inversion of ordinary economic principles since disinterestedness in financial gains results in higher artistic value. The field is based on the relationship between two subfields: the subfield of small-scale, restricted production oriented towards the production of pure, artistic goods, and that of large-scale, mass production, oriented towards the production of commercially viable ones. The subfield of small-scale production has a high degree of autonomy and involves low levels of economic capital but high levels of symbolic capital. It brings prestige but rarely a lot of money. An example is poetry. On the other hand, the subfield of large-scale production has a much lesser degree of autonomy (numerous restrictions) and involves very high levels of economic capital but lower levels of symbolic capital. An example is bourgeois theater, which brings money but is not particularly prestigious. The novel, which in some cases can secure big profits, occupies a position in between poetry and theater. Other divisions in the field remain, such as the division between novice and consecrated writers.

Bourdieu's concept of "symbolic capital" is useful to give students insight into how Galdós seeks to improve his financial situation. As an acclaimed novelist, Galdós enjoyed a high level of symbolic capital. Bourdieu defines symbolic capital as residing in "the mastery of symbolic resources based on knowledge and recognition" (*Social Structures* 195); in other words, distinction and prestige are acquired through cultural recognition. While symbolic capital might seem far removed from economic capital, which is "immediately and directly convertible into money" (Bourdieu, "Forms"), Bourdieu considered symbolic capital as a crucial source of power in society that can be used to one's advantage, and even to obtain financial gains.

Galdós had accumulated prestige, celebrity, and honor and found ample recognition from his peers. He now aimed at obtaining higher financial profits without losing the symbolic capital (his artistic integrity and prestige) that he enjoyed as a consecrated author. Better still, he wanted to use his symbolic capital to enlarge his economic capital. Due to the immediate sanction of its bourgeois public, writing for the theater could provide both institutional consecration and considerable financial gains. Here, Galdós makes a move similar to one made by the French author Émile Zola, who tried to transfer into drama the symbolic capital he had previously won with his novels. Thanks to his literary fame, Galdós never suffered from being portrayed as a novice playwright. On the contrary, his celebrity gave him access to the best venues, actors, and directors, and as a former journalist, he could count on his buddies in the press to promote his plays.

Galdós's theatrical undertakings were eagerly anticipated, both in Spain and abroad. Students can carry out searches in the *Hemeroteca Digital* (*Digital Periodical Archive*) of the Biblioteca Nacional de España to explore how newspapers and magazines (such as *El Imparcial*, *Época*, and *Blanco y Negro*) accounted for the author's theatrical endeavors. Pardo Bazán announced the premiere of *Realidad* in the January issue of her *Nuevo Teatro Crítico* (*New Critical Theater*) and catered to the high expectations of the audience (Editor's column). The press dedicated ample attention to the premiere, which took place on 15 March 1892.[6]

Students can examine the reviews to see how they were designed to appeal to diverse audiences, although it is not always clear if the praise was intended for the recent dramatist or the consecrated novelist. Pardo Bazán, Alas, and Rafael Altamira wrote favorable reviews.[7] Pedro Bofill and Federico Urrechea, who wrote under the pen name Licenciado Amaniel, both produced negative critiques. *Realidad* turned Galdós into one of Spain's foremost playwrights without harming his reputation as a novelist. Playwriting brought him money, although not in the amounts he had hoped for.

As a second case study, we look at the promotional efforts (by the playwright and others) behind *Electra*, an admittedly provocative attack on the Spanish clergy that caused a monumental scandal at the time of its premiere in the Teatro Español by the company of Federico Balart on 30 January 1901, and earned the already famous playwright another big success. Galdós was acutely aware that he had created a risky and urgent work. In a letter to his friend Tolosa Latour, he described the work as "endemoniada" ("wicked"), "de mucho cuidado y compromiso" ("dangerous and risky"), and "de mucha miga. Más miga tal vez de la que conviene" ("very juicy. Juicier perhaps than appropriate"; qtd. in Menéndez Onrubia 325).

Always eager to enlighten his fellow Spaniards and with a solid feeling for the game—that is to say, well aware of the rules and expectations of the social context, or what Bourdieu calls *habitus*—Galdós had chosen yet another topic of tremendous societal interest, this time inspired by the real-life Ubao case, in which a clergyman influenced a young woman to enter a convent. The date of the premiere could not have been chosen any better, since it coincided with the trial of the case that inspired the play. Galdós's celebrity (both as novelist and playwright) made the Teatro Español decide to organize, on the eve of the first performance, a general rehearsal to which the members of Madrid's intellectual in-crowd received a personal and nontransferable invitation. As a result, "todo Madrid" ("Madrid's literary elite") talked about the play. The premiere, interrupted by applause and screams, brought a great triumph for the author, who was carried home on the shoulders of his admirers. Theater entrepreneurs approached Galdós for the exclusive rights to stage *Electra* in the provinces. The play attracted ample attention in Europe, from congratulations to anonymous threats. Ten thousand copies of the printed version of the play were sold, and the text was translated into numerous languages.

Electra resonated enormously with the Spanish public. Students can be encouraged to explore how the title of the play was used for all kinds of commercial products, such as sweets, lotions, digestives, and even a dessert in one of Madrid's most trendy restaurants. *Electra* also gave its name to a short-lived cultural journal that united numerous promising young authors. Instructors could explain how the reactions to *Electra* transformed a cultural product not only into a commercial item but also into a political manifesto with great impact on Galdós's public persona. Disturbances caused by the play brought about the fall of government and the formation of the liberal prime minister Práxedes Mateo Sagasta's so-called *Electra* cabinet in 1902, and all the upheaval around the play led Galdós himself to become more and more involved in republican politics.[8]

It is obvious that literary quality is just one of the aspects involved in a playwright's success. There are many extraliterary factors as well. Celebrities are constantly reinterpreted (Braudy), both during their lifetime and posthumously. During the Franco era, Galdós was ostracized for his anticlerical stance and republicanism. Now, he is a culturally appropriated commodity, a national icon with a larger-than-life public image. Students might explore how the Spanish government, the *Biblioteca Virtual Miguel de Cervantes* (*Miguel de Cervantes Virtual Library*), the Cabildo de Gran Canaria, the Casa-Museo Pérez Galdós, the Asociación Internacional de Galdosistas, journals, book clubs, and film adaptations currently promote his work. He is celebrated as "hijo de Gran Canaria" ("son of Gran Canaria") by local authorities in the Canary Islands, and in 2020 he was officially named "Hijo Adoptivo" ("Adoptive Son") of Madrid ("Galdós no es nuestro"; "Ayuntamiento"). He is lauded as "el segundo novelista patrio después de Miguel de Cervantes" ("the nation's second novelist after Miguel de Cervantes") on official sites such as *Instituto Cervantes* ("Centenario"), and a recent exposition dedicated to Galdós's life and work at the Biblioteca Nacional drew more than twenty thousand visitors (Briceño), which exceeds the more than twelve thousand visitors to the 2015 exhibition organized by Madrid's Instituto Cervantes and dedicated to Galdós's illustrious literary predecessor (Fernández Arribas). All these institutions work to preserve a legacy that goes far beyond the literary aspects of Galdós's work. Their efforts emphasize the constructedness of literary value and show students how literary celebrity is not exclusively the work of the writer alone. As Rebecca Braun and Emily Spiers state, "Celebrity authors . . . force reflection on the institution of literature: how it is constituted, why it matters and how it might be otherwise" (453).

Celebrity studies offers instructors the opportunity to show their students that the notion of Galdós as famous author and playwright is a construction. Students working within this framework are encouraged to think beyond the strictly artistic value of the works themselves and acknowledge that literary value is not the only factor that determines the success and significance of an author, both during their lifetime and posthumously.

As a final project for students, I suggest either a zine (a self-constructed, self-published, noncommercial magazine intended for a public space) or an author website. Both projects allow students to imagine themselves as press agents using a twenty-first-century medium and design strategies of their choice to reinforce Galdós's celebrity status. Instructors should provide an electronic template, samples, recommended resources, and suggested topics for discussion. A simple *Google* search on the phrase "how to build an author's website" yields numerous suggestions for both content and website builders; for a good starting point, see Jane Friedman's online guide. An excellent zine tutorial is "Creating a Digital Zine in Canva"; Santa Clara University's website also provides guidance and resources ("How to Make a Zine"). The Library of Congress has a research guide on zines and a database with an extensive collection of zines that can serve as examples ("Zines at the Library of Congress"). For a video demonstrating how to develop a zine in *PowerPoint*, see "Designing Magazine Using PowerPoint." Finally, the illustrator Greg Kletsel shows examples of the numerous creative possibilities of zines.

For both the author website and the zine assignment, students may write either one continuous piece or multiple short texts, each supporting the project's overall purpose as outlined in their abstract. Students are evaluated on their thematic framing, logical flow, creative elements, writing quality, and abstract effectiveness. These projects ask students to apply the takeaways of the cultural analysis of Galdós as a celebrity playwright to a product of their own creation. As they do so, they will not only be talking about culture but also producing a cultural artifact themselves.[9]

NOTES

1. *Electra* is available in an early-twentieth-century English translation by Charles Alfred Turrell (Pérez Galdós, *Electra* [Gorham]). *Reality* is a translation by Karen O. Austin of the novel *Realidad*. I am unaware of a translation of the play.

2. Students might read Randal Johnson's introduction to Bourdieu's *The Field of Cultural Production* (1–25) and Bourdieu's chapter of the same name (25–126). For an outstanding and fun introduction to Bourdieu, see Hage.

3. On Galdós's personality, see Arencibia 16–20.

4. For summaries of these interviews, see the virtual exposition *¿Cómo era Galdós?*.

5. I recommend the sections "Autor teatral" (76–79), "Estrenos de *Realidad* . . ." (80–83), "Ansó. *Los condenados*" (84–92), and "Galdós, editor" (103–12); these readings could be supplemented by the selection of paintings, photographs, and caricatures of the author curated on the Galdós portal on the *Biblioteca Virtual Miguel de Cervantes* website, see "Retratos del autor" and "Caricaturas."

6. For an account of the premiere, see Arencibia 361–65; for a detailed analysis, Menéndez Onrubia 101–05; see also Yxart 312–31.

7. See Pardo Bazán, Review of *Realidad*; Alas, Review [*Correspondencia*] and Review [*Imparcial*]; Altamira, Review [*Boletín*] and Review [*Justicia*].

8. For detailed studies of *Electra*, see Menéndez Onrubia 232–34; Catena. Additional, more recent sources include Fernández Cordero 33–39; Arencibia 508–20; Rueda. For press reviews, see Berenguer 203–38.

9. I want to thank my colleague at the University of Kansas, Megan Sheldon, for suggesting the creation of a zine as a final project.

The Author Is a Character: Fictional Embodiments of Galdós in the Twenty-First Century

Elena Cueto Asín

The centenary of Benito Pérez Galdós's death in 2020 inspired various artistic and academic evocations of the writer and his works that share a penchant for biographical detail. Alongside biographies, exhibits, and scholarly publications, there also appeared a significant number of novels, plays, films, and comics that explore the writer's personality and circumstances, and in which his persona is enlisted for a metaliterary and postmodern exercise in which he assumes the role of a historical character. The trend initiated in the years leading up to the centennial follows a broader biography boom registered in all areas of creative work, where artists and intellectuals are often portrayed against the backdrop of their lives and times. Such cultural products interweave facts about the author's life with fictional elements and encapsulate a didactic intent that can be tapped into for myriad classroom applications.

Noteworthy recent biographies of Galdós by Yolanda Arencibia, Germán Gullón (*Galdós*), and Francisco Cánovas certainly broaden academic knowledge and may even influence the training of future Galdós scholars and their teaching. Yet understandings of and interest in Galdós's literature are further enhanced by consideration of other recent works that fictionalize his private and public life while alluding to his significant novels and plays. Much may be gained by examining representations of the writer in other kinds of fictional texts—cataloged in an appendix to this essay—as a form of knowledge and a mode of vindication for his cultural and intellectual legacies. As I have suggested elsewhere, the extensive corpus of recent materials inspired by Galdós takes over the heritage-producing function of film and television adaptations of the late 1970s and 1980s that recovered his literature by underscoring its continued relevance for democratic Spain.[1] The writer's status as a heritage icon forged during Spain's transition to democracy goes largely unchallenged in these centennial treatments of the persona. Yet, as I outline below, these new cultural productions seek not merely to supplement the act of reading Galdós for present generations but also to offer alternative points of entry into the author's life and fictional world through which students can judge his cultural legacy for themselves.

Recent works in which Galdós appears as a character often conjure the same motifs and events, and together, they offer an almost complete recounting of his life and career. Novels, plays, short films, television programs, and comics depict his first love (Gil; Martínez; *Benito*), his work as a journalist (Gallardo; Faerna; *Prim*; Mayoral), his torrid affairs with writers and actresses (*Condesa rebelde*; Zurro), and the liberal political crusades of his final years (Molina; El Torres). Some representations center on specific moments, whereas others aim to portray his whole life chronologically or in snippets (Becerra and Hernández; Fernández Etreros and Menéndez Quirós). Additionally, theater and television appearances use reverie as vehicles to recreate Galdós's memories and retrospections, and present him near death, in the afterlife, or as a time traveler (Del Moral and Rodríguez; Ripoll and Llorente; Ripoll; Gallud).

Two of the most frequent ways in which Galdós is characterized in these works offer great possibilities for use in the classroom. The first are stories that explore the writer's love affairs with strong, independent women who recall some of his most memorable female characters. The second is through works that portray him as a journalist who bears witness to turbulent episodes of Spanish history. Both patterns reveal Galdós as a progressive writer who critically exposed social inequities and admired and loved women throughout his life. However, they also reveal a man who used his male privilege to avoid publicity and scandal while dodging long-term romantic commitments and marriage. In doing so, Galdós sidestepped the social alienation suffered by the women in his life who defied societal gender norms.

Using this body of work as a resource for teaching Galdós presents several challenges. Not all the plays are published, and some of the novels are long and require extra classroom time, which is hard to justify, especially in undergraduate courses where reading Galdós's texts already poses difficulties, given their length and complexity. Moreover, the author's works are often taught in topics-based seminars or panoramic surveys, where such digressions may be unfeasible. Even so, these materials can be valuable in the literature classroom since they offer a framework to introduce the author's biography. This approach has fallen out of fashion for critics despite its pedagogical potential. Nevertheless, examining portrayals of Galdós as a fictional or historical character can make students more aware of his role as a creator. Students in the typical language-literature classroom focus primarily on comprehending Spanish texts and their cultural context. In the case of so-called canonical or classic writers like Galdós, they often overlook the identity of the person behind the writing. This tendency stands in opposition to the importance recently given to questions of identity, where authors' backgrounds and life experiences are key considerations for inclusion or exclusion from curricula.

Introducing Galdós as a character in the classroom can be a strategy for approaching the actual writer who hides behind the persona of the omniscient narrator of his novels and who, like the fictionalized version of the writer in the works of others, is engaged with concerns that shaped nineteenth-century Spanish society and continues to have currency today. For twenty-first-century students, the metafictional commentaries made by the author's signature, intrusive third-person narrator become more accessible when personified and voiced by a liberal crusader who shares the author's penchant for social justice, animal welfare, and the feminist struggle. At the same time, invocations of Galdós as a human being with strengths and weaknesses place him in the position to be subject to judgment. Here is another opportunity for discussion by upper-level students interested and trained in the application of critical theory to analyzing behaviors such as patriarchal and hegemonic idealizations of romantic love, courage, and manly leadership.

Works featuring Galdós as a character often depict him in personal situations associated with the creation of specific novels and plays, which, curiously, are not among those regularly used in college courses. In this way, twenty-first-century books, films, and plays can encourage instructors to consider teaching works by Galdós that are taught less frequently, such as his plays or *Episodios nacionales* (*National Episodes*), which are neither more difficult nor less representative than the novels commonly read by undergraduate and graduate students. Among other things, incorporating these titles deepens the opportunities for literary analysis by inviting reflections on the author's varied form, style, and aesthetics. At the same time, the postmodern retooling of Galdós for present-day sensibilities through popular narrative forms, like graphic novels or crime fiction, sheds light on the lasting impact of the strategies of nineteenth-century realism forged in his works. Moreover, they connect his writing to the popular fiction and nonfiction genres of his day by unearthing the sources of the extraordinary situations and characters that inspired many of his stories.

In what follows, I suggest two approaches that examine Galdós's literary and historical legacy through the study of twenty-first-century texts that depict him as a man who loved and respectfully portrayed women and who applied a journalist's eye and historical perspective to the events of his lifetime. Both approaches involve texts readily available in print or online as class material, prompting instructors to consider teaching works by Galdós that are not usually included in course syllabi.

The Author Reflects on Women's Liberation

In the commemorative comic book *1892*, published in 2020, Antonio Becerra Bolaños and Alberto Hernández Rivero hit upon the original idea of focusing on one year in the life and work of Galdós as a way of resolving the challenge of summarizing both facets of his biography. *1892* focuses on two of the author's works written that year, the novel *Tristana* and the play *La loca de la casa* (*The Madwoman of the House*). These works expose both the limitations imposed by society on women with a desire to engage in activities outside the male-governed home and, as the graphic novel emphasizes, the abuse of power that men can exercise over women's bodies and wills in the domestic sphere. The connection between the two 1892 works in the comic is the author, who appears as a character seated at his desk engaged both in writing the play and in monitoring rehearsals. In these settings, he intermittently reflects upon his past experiences and his present situation. His youthful crush on a cousin in the Canary Islands in the 1860s and his affair with the actress Concha Morell in Madrid in the 1890s, shortly after having fathered a girl with another woman, Lorenza Cobián, are evoked to explore the unequal expectations placed on women and men during his lifetime.

A scholar and teacher, Becerra Bolaños set out to ensure his comic book would appeal to an audience that included Galdós specialists and lay readers, fans of graphic novels, and those unacquainted with the medium and its conventions (Willem, *Adapting Spanish Classics* 209). Linda M. Willem offers a detailed analysis of the techniques employed in *1892* to meet this challenge and to visually and thematically connect two Galdosian works that are not generally considered in parallel despite their coincidence in time of writing and subject matter. Willem's analysis serves as a guide to navigating the comic as the source for literary adaptation in vignettes and its ability to more graphically render, by visual means, the sexual abuse hinted at in Galdós's narration (*Adapting Spanish Classics* 210).

Depending on the course's scope and students' level, *1892* provides a variety of possible entry points for reading *Tristana* and *La loca de la casa* on the same syllabus. Putting the three works together, beginning with the comic book and then continuing with *Tristana* and *La loca de la casa*, engages students with two literary genres cultivated by Galdós and fosters discussions of the inequities women faced in late-nineteenth-century Spain. Reading the entire novel and the play alongside the comic is most plausible in graduate courses but may not be feasible for undergraduates. In this case, readings of Galdós's text could be abridged and supplemented by screening Luis Buñuel's film adaptation of *Tristana* and recordings of Burka Teatro's production of *La loca de la casa* ("Burka Teatro").

As a frame for studying the novel and the play, *1892* provides an opportunity for research and discussion about representations of Galdós and his birthplace in the Triana neighborhood of Las Palmas as an exercise in metafiction. Students discuss how the comic depicts Galdós's hometown and how his departure for Madrid to study affected his budding literary aspirations as an adolescent. The class also considers how the graphic novel represents Galdós's family situation and the conservative gender roles that surrounded his upbringing. These explorations can be supplemented with biographical research about the religiosity of the women in Galdós's family, a detail that becomes paramount as a potential influence on the development of Victoria's character in *La loca de la casa*. Finally, students are asked to comment on the change in visual style between the graphic rendering of 1870s Madrid and the re-creation of Galdós's recollections of Las Palmas as a way to think about the aesthetic and narrative choices writers make through the filter of memory.

The study of *Tristana* can be prefaced by a comparative analysis activity built around the repeated image in *1892* of Galdós engaged in the practice of reading and writing letters amid his creative endeavors. Here, students focus on Galdós's relationship with Concha Morell and how it might have influenced the writing of *Tristana*. In preparation for the class meeting, students should research and compile literary criticism that draws parallels between Morell and the protagonist of *Tristana*. In the classroom, using the compilation by Alan E. Smith, María Ángeles Rodríguez Sánchez, and Laurie Lomask (Pérez Galdós,

Correspondencia), the letters exchanged between Galdós and Morell are introduced by assigning pairs or small groups to examine selections from the correspondence and the accompanying critical analyses. Groups are asked to identify and discuss similarities between Morell's real-life situation and Tristana's fictional circumstances, particularly in terms of their respective relationships with older men and their struggles for independence. The groups then present their findings to the whole class to encourage a discussion about how Galdós's personal experiences might have influenced his characterization of *Tristana*. To conclude, students are prompted to reflect on the broader implications of using personal correspondence in biographical fiction and how this practice affects our interpretation of literary works. This activity explores the connection between Galdós's life and his writing and introduces students to the complexities of epistolary analysis and its role in understanding an author's creative process.

The analysis of *La loca de la casa* can be jump-started through a multimedia activity that further explores the intersection of Galdós's personal life and his literary works. In class, the panel from *1892* depicting a woman, possibly Lorenza Cobián, holding a baby and the text alluding to Morrell's potential pregnancy by Galdós is projected on-screen alongside a fragment from the scene from *La loca de la casa* in which Victoria's pregnancy is announced. In pairs or small groups, students are then asked to create a visual time line (or mind map) that connects these biographical elements to characters and plot points of the play they have just finished reading as well as to those of *Tristana*. In this context, they are encouraged to consider how Galdós's personal experiences might have inspired his fictional characters, paying particular attention to the portrayal of Horacio in *Tristana*. As a class, they then discuss the ethical implications of drawing from one's personal life to create works of fiction. To conclude, students can be assigned a reflective writing exercise to explore how Galdós's characterization of figures like Horacio might reflect his awareness of male privilege and societal constraints on women during his era. This activity promotes critical thinking about the relationship between an author's life and work while addressing broader societal issues reflected in literature.

As a culmination of the exploration of Galdós's life through the comic book, the novel, and the play, students engage in a reflective discussion of the cover image and the four panels on the final page of *1892*. In the first, Galdós hovers behind a startled-looking Tristana, and in the last, he appears beside her. While he is clearly figured as the author, the similarity between his likeness, rendered always in color, and those of *Tristana*'s Don Lope and Horacio and *La loca de la casa*'s Doctor Miquis, in black and white, injects a degree of ambiguity that provides a ripe context for discussion and debate. Using Willem's analysis as a guide, students are invited to debate the comic book creators' intentions regarding the author's identification with his characters and the underlying gender and power dynamics and creative control that inform the depictions. To facilitate a constructive and critical discussion about Galdós's stance vis-à-vis his female characters, students are asked to support their comments on previous analyses of *Tristana*, *La loca de la casa*, and the biographical details they have assembled and ultimately to consider the complexities of judging a nineteenth-century author by contemporary standards. To synthesize the discussion, students are tasked with creating a visual representation (e.g., a spectrum or a mind map) that illustrates Galdós's treatment of women in the two works they have read. This should incorporate elements from all the texts and biographical information they have studied, highlighting Galdós's depictions of women's socioeconomic status and chances for personal fulfillment. They might also be asked to write a brief reflection on how their understanding of Galdós as an author has evolved through this multifaceted examination of his life and works across the three texts. Ultimately, this approach allows for a summative discussion that ties together previous activities while encouraging critical thinking about the author's complex relationship with gender representation in his era.

The Author Investigates History

For the bicentennial of the birth of General Juan Prim in 2014, Nacho Faerna wrote the screenplay *Prim: El asesinato de la calle del Turco* (*Prim: The Assassination on Turco Street*) for a television movie recreating the prime minister's assassination in December 1870. The reconstruction of the event includes the investigations of a young gazetteer and emerging writer named Galdós seeking to discover the perpetrator of the crime, which remains a mystery to this day. Faerna subsequently wrote a tie-in novel with the same title as the telefilm that provides additional development of both historical and invented characters. Shortly afterward, the script was published in book form illuminating aspects of the creative processes involved in developing and writing both the script and the novel (Faerna and Yagüe).

The Faerna film and novel are both highly accessible and readily available and so could be studied in a graduate seminar alongside some of Galdós's historical novels. The telefilm and fragments of the novels by Galdós and Faerna might also be adapted for use in undergraduate courses; however, my suggestions here assume a higher level of reading and analytical skills. From Galdós's oeuvre, I recommend two particularly complementary works that, like the novel and play discussed above, also hinge upon a specific year in the author's life. In 1870, Galdós published his first historical novel, *La Fontana de Oro* (*The Golden Fountain Café*), set in the turbulent years of the Trienio Liberal (Liberal Triennium) in the 1820s, and witnessed the turmoil and controversy surrounding Prim's assassination. Almost forty years later, in 1909, he published *España trágica* (*Tragic Spain*), an *episodio nacional* that uses the 1870 murder as a historical backdrop. The period of Prim's short mandate featured in *Prim* introduces students to a young Galdós immersed in the moment of acute social and political tensions that moved him to set *La Fontana de Oro* against a background of comparable upheaval. At the same time, the depiction grounds the author's retrospective gaze on events of his youth in *España trágica*. By pointing out the overlap of the temporal settings of the two historical novels, the 1820s and 1870s, and the time frames of their writing, the 1870s and 1900s, the instructor could prompt a discussion of the functions of historical fiction as a reflection on the past mediated by present concerns.[2] The notions of presentism and universality can be applied to television series, movies, and other works of fiction set in the past. Students ponder how and why we can we draw parallels between past events or circumstances and present ones and consider how recognizing analogies in stories from other times helps us better reflect on or understand what is happening today.

Faerna's novel highlights correlations between the plot of *Prim* and that of *España trágica*, problematizing Galdós's version of events as based on his eyewitness account. Reading the two Galdós novels together raises multiple issues for discussion, including whether the reconstructions of the political climates of the 1820s and 1870s are relevant to understanding either period and whether the terror and surveillance characterizing both contexts can be equated. In class, students think about how these environments shape the protagonists of Galdós's novels, Lázaro and Vicente, and how those characters might be seen as Galdós's alter egos; it is key to remind them that Lázaro is roughly the same age as Galdós was at the time of writing, whereas Vicente reflects Galdós's mature reflections on his life. The class then creates profiles of both characters, identifying how they might represent Galdós at these different life stages. With this in mind, they debate the reliability of historical fiction, using Galdós's eyewitness account as a starting point, and examine the political climate of the 1820s and 1870s as portrayed in the novels, considering the works' relevance to each other and to contemporary issues. I conclude this unit with a brief writing exercise in which students reflect on how authors use historical settings to comment on their present day. This activity encourages critical thinking about the relationship between fiction, history, and authorial perspective while engaging directly with the assigned texts.

Students also explore the author's positionality by comparing the modes of observation adopted by Galdós in re-creating the past and chronicling his present. The postmodernity of Faerna's novel offers further possibilities for analyzing how the twenty-first-century representation of the historical episode replicates the structure of Galdós's works. To investigate these ideas in the classroom, the instructor can begin by introducing students to the concept of authorial positionality, using excerpts from Galdós's works that showcase his approach to chronicling past and present events. At this point, passages from Faerna's novel that feature Galdós as a character can be presented and students asked to analyze how Faerna's postmodern approach mirrors and reinterprets Galdós's narrative techniques. Next, the class can discuss the implications of featuring Galdós as a character in contemporary fiction by encouraging students to think about how this representation might influence their understanding of the original works and Galdós's status as a cultural icon. To make this more engaging, small groups or pairs of students can be asked to invent brief dramatic scenes that imagine

Galdós's reaction to his portrayal in modern literature. Finally, to draw parallels between Galdós's *episodio* format and contemporary storytelling techniques, students are asked to identify a current streaming series that deals with historical events and compare its narrative structure to Galdós's approach. This could lead to a creative exercise where students outline their own "episode" of a fictional streaming series based on a Galdós novel, emphasizing how they would balance entertainment and historical accuracy. This activity encourages students to engage critically with historical and contemporary narrative forms while exploring the enduring influence of Galdós's work.

The fictionalization of Galdós attaches his persona to a body with emotional and ideological traits, which the character displays in evocations of the historical figure's private and professional life. His incarnation by an actor on stage or screen, his reproduction in drawings, or his depiction on the pages of novels open different possibilities for honoring his legacy as an individual while also allowing him to be reconstructed as an icon who champions contemporary values. Providing Galdós with a recognizable human form and corresponding behaviors across different genres, formats, and media presents him as a human being with virtues and flaws rather than a national hero of mythic proportions. Portrayed as an eyewitness and interpreter of the sociohistorical context depicted in his novels and theater, the author himself becomes a text to be interpreted alongside or in conjunction with his literary production.

NOTES

1. See Cueto, "Pardo Bazán y Pérez Galdós" and "Galdós en el escenario."
2. Here, my article examining Faerna's work alongside the 1974 television adaptation of *La Fontana de Oro*, made on the eve of the democratic transition, could provide useful context (Cueto, "*Fontana de Oro*").

APPENDIX: WORKS FEATURING GALDÓS AS A CHARACTER

Fiction

Faerna, Nacho. *Prim: El asesinato de la calle del Turco*. Espasa, 2014.

Fernández, José Ramón. *Emilia, borriquita . . . : Cartas que no escribió Galdós*. Reino de Cordelia, 2020.

Gallardo, Carmen. *La reina de las lavanderas*. La Esfera de los Libros, 2012.

Gil, Santiago. *El gran amor de Galdós*. La Palma, 2019.

Mayoral, Carlos. *Un episodio nacional*. Espasa, 2019.

Molina, Mónica. *Los ojos de Galdós*. Edhasa, 2020.

Television

"Antes de que no haya tiempo." *El ministerio del Tiempo*, season 4 prequel, TVE, 2020.

Benito. Written and directed by Pedro Pérez, Lilium by APS, 2022.

La condesa rebelde. Directed by Zaza Ceballos, TVG, 2011.

Prim: El asesinato de la calle del Turco. Directed by Nacho Faerna, TVE, 2014.

Comics

Becerra Bolaños, Antonio, and Alberto Hernández. *1892*. Cabildo de Gran Canaria, 2020.

El Torres. *Galdós y la miseria*. Nuevo Nueve, 2020.

Fernández Etreros, Carmen, and Guillermo Menéndez Quirós. *Galdós, un escritor en Madrid*. Comunidad de Madrid, 2020.

Pulido Rodríguez, Rayco. *Nela*. Astiberri, 2013.

Drama

Del Moral, Ignacio, and Yolanda Rodríguez. *Galdós, sombra y realidad*. Directed and adapted by Pilar G. Almansa, 13 Nov. 2020, Teatro Español, Madrid.

Gallud Jardiel, Enrique. *Galdós en los infiernos*. VDB, 2022.

Martínez, Miguel Ángel. *El primer amor de Galdós*. Diputación de Granada, 2020.

Pérez Galdós, Benito. *Bien está que fuera tu tierra, Galdós*. Adapted by Alma García, Venecia Teatro, 15 Oct. 2020, Teatro Fernán Gómez, Madrid.

Ripoll, Laila. *Fortunata y Benito*. Directed by Ripoll, La Joven Compañía, 7 Feb. 2020, Teatros del Canal, Madrid.

Ripoll, Laila, and Mariano Llorente. *El último viaje de Galdós*. Directed by Mario Vega, Galdós Laboratory, 8 Oct. 2020, Teatro Pérez Galdós, Las Palmas de Gran Canaria.

Zurro, Alfonso. *Galdós enamorado*. Directed by Zurro, 25 Mar. 2020, Teatro Pérez Galdós, Las Palmas de Gran Canaria.

GALDÓS IN ADAPTATION

Teaching *Marianela*: From Galdós's Novel to Pulido's Graphic Novel

Linda M. Willem

The recent recognition of the graphic novel as a sophisticated genre worthy of academic study has opened avenues for its use in the classroom. The hybrid literary-graphic quality of these narratives enables students to experience story worlds through combined viewing and reading activities. Departing from the short, serialized plotlines and low production values of traditional mass-produced comics in newspapers and magazines, graphic novels are full-length bound books that develop their material with depth and subtlety, featuring intricate sequencing strategies and stylistically rich artwork, often by internationally known illustrators. Furthermore, today's graphic novel adaptations of world literature, such as Pablo Auladell's *El paraíso perdido*, based on John Milton's *Paradise Lost*, and Claudio Stassi's version of *Nada* (*Nothing*), by Carmen Laforet, are aesthetic works in their own right, offering original interpretations of previous works to a broad audience.

Below, I outline a plan to teach Galdós's *Marianela* in conjunction with its graphic novel adaptation, *Nela*. Available in both a hardcover print version and an internationally accessible downloadable format, *Nela* is adapted and illustrated by Rayco Pulido Rodríguez, winner of Spain's prestigious Premio Nacional del Cómic (National Graphic Novel Award). Pulido states in his preface that his two goals in creating *Nela* were to remain as faithful as possible to *Marianela* while making Galdós's nineteenth-century novel more attractive to the twenty-first-century audience. My approach is designed for an advanced undergraduate Spanish literature course in which both texts are read in Spanish and examined side by side, allowing students to analyze Pulido's use of the visuality of the page to communicate Galdós's novelistic content through the simultaneous presentation of images and words. Although two English translations of *Marianela* are available—a rather loose version by Clara Bell (William S. Gottsberger) and a more academic treatment by Gloria Bodtorf Clark (Juan de la Cuesta)—*Nela* exists only in Spanish, making a comparison of the two difficult without proficiency in the language. However, the inclusion of this adaptation in the advanced Spanish classroom not only helps undergraduate students engage with Galdós's original text and its sociocultural milieu but also raises their awareness of how the conventions of different genres shape the audience's reception of narratives.

Just as students will refer to elements of literary analysis—setting, characterization, plot structure, narrative voice, figurative language, themes, and tone—to discuss *Marianela*, so too will they need to use appropriate terminology to discuss *Nela* both as a graphic novel and as an adaptation. Instructors can provide a theoretical and stylistic framework for understanding the design elements of graphic novels by assigning chapters 2 ("The Vocabulary of Comics," 25–59), 3 ("Blood in the Gutter," 60–93), 4 ("Time Frames," 94–117), and 8 ("A Word about Color," 185–92) of Scott McCloud's *Understanding Comics: The Invisible Art* (available from Astiberri in Spanish translation as *Entender el cómic: El arte invisible*), as well as the following segments from *Drawing Words and Writing Pictures*, by Jessica Abel and Matt Madden: "Seven Types of Panel Transitions" (39–45), "Elements of Page Design" (71–75), and "Film Terminology and Comics" (154–55). For Spanish translations of terminology, instructors can also assign my "Elementos del cómic" ("Elements of the Comic") appendix at the end of this essay.

In addition, instructors can place Pulido's graphic novel in the context of adaptation studies by citing Linda Hutcheon's highly influential *A Theory of Adaptation*. Selections from Hutcheon's first chapter can provide a working definition of adaptation as a revisitation of a prior work, during which the adapter engages in a process of interpretation, creation, and reception (1–32). Moreover, Hutcheon's distinctions between various modes of engagement can help students understand the uniqueness of the graphic novel genre, which does not fit within either the telling mode of written narratives or the showing mode of audiovisual media. Also useful is Hutcheon's observation in chapter 4 that in order for an adaptation to be received as an adaptation, the audience must be familiar with the source text. The knowing audience mentally oscillates between the two versions while experiencing the adaptation. This contrasts with the adaptation not being received as such by an unknowing audience, who instead experiences it as a stand-alone work (120–28).

Provided with this information from McCloud, Abel, Madden, and Hutcheon, students can regard the various graphic choices made by Pulido as interpretive acts used to convey Galdós's written text through a combination of words and images. For an important additional insight into Pulido's creative process, instructors can cite from his blog, *Nunca trabajes solo* (*Never Work Alone*). In his 23 March 2013 posting, Pulido explains his practice of planning his graphic novels in double-page layouts, "tal y como las verá el futuro lector" ("as the future reader will see them"), with this double page serving as his "'unidad mínima,' abriendo fuerte y cerrando a través de un gancho que 'obliga' al lector a pasar a la siguiente unidad" ("'minimal unit,' opening strong and closing with a hook that 'obligates' the reader to continue to the next unit"; "Proceso"; my trans.). Based on this design principle, students can approach *Nela* as a series of double-page units contained within each chapter.

The text of *Nela* is unpaginated, but other than omitting Galdós's chapter 5 and placing chapter 10 before 9, it is structured to match the divisions of the original novel, thereby facilitating a comparative examination of the two texts. Before each class, instructors can assign the same chapters to be read in *Marianela* and *Nela*, allowing students to have a parallel reading experience of two different genres as they progress through the story. Ideally, students should vary the reading order between the two texts so they can alternate between both roles of reception—the "knowing" audience, who has read a particular portion of the novel before the adaptation, and the "unknowing" audience, who has not—which will aid them in appreciating the independent merits of each text. For an interesting topic of discussion, instructors may wish to restore chapter 5 by referring students to Pulido's 17 March 2013 blog post, which contains the discarded pages and the rationale for not including them in the published volume—namely, that the novelistic material yielded images that were graphically static and did not provide any significant new narrative information ("Trabajo").

Instructors can use the two most obvious visual aspects of Pulido's adaptation—its limited color palette and its abstract visual style—to orient the overall discussion of *Nela* as an adaptation of Galdós's novel. *Nela* is primarily presented in black and white, so the instructor can remind the students of McCloud's observation that "in black and white, the ideas *behind* the art are communicated more *directly*. Meaning transcends form. Art approaches *language*" (192). This is especially applicable to Pulido's treatment of settings. Rather than representing the novel's descriptions literally, Pulido captures the idea of place contained in Galdós's words.

For example, in chapter 2, Pulido expresses the awe-inspiring grandeur and fearful danger of the excavated mountain, mine, and chasm through his paneling, his sequencing, and his striking black-and-white drawings. Beginning with the chapter's initial double-page unit, instructors can ask students to give specific, detailed examples of the techniques Pulido uses to communicate the idea of this setting visually. For example, the artist draws Golfín and Pablo as tiny figures walking through the excavated mountain pass, presenting the scene from various angles and cinematic shots in different-sized panels, alternating black line drawings in moonlit white spaces with white line drawings in shadowed black spaces, and visually juxtaposing the words Pablo shouts against those that reverberate as echoes, showing both reaching into the vastness of space beyond the limits of the panels. The left page of the next minimal unit underscores the darkness and length of the mine's interior through white-outlined figures on a black background of identically sized small panels, a design that contrasts with the brightness of the right page when Pablo and Golfín move once again into the moonlight. The instructor can ask students to identify the *ganchos* ("hooks") that pique their interest and keep them turning pages and to note how the sudden appearance of an antique-gold streak in the last panel of the second two-page layout guides them to the third minimal unit of the chapter, where that color circulates around the figures as mysterious emanations from the Trascava chasm. Here, students begin to comprehend Pulido's sparing use of antique gold to indicate something that is not actually visible but nevertheless is sensed. Pulido's strategic inclusion of this single color within his overall black-and-white format allows him to attribute narrative meaning to its appearances. By noting each subsequent occurrence, students can examine how this color depicts the interplay between the seen and the unseen in different situations.

Turning next to the high level of abstraction in Pulido's drawings, it is useful to keep in mind McCloud's assertion that cartooning is "a form of *amplification through simplification*. When we abstract an image through cartooning, we're not so much *eliminating* details as we are *focusing* on *specific details*. By *stripping down* an image to its essential '*meaning*,' an artist can *amplify* that meaning in a way that realistic art *can't*" (30). Through this process of abstraction, Pulido presents the reader with the essence of Galdós's characters rather than just their surface appearance as described in the novel. Pulido's visual depictions of Pablo, Nela, and Florentina are blatantly unrealistic, serving not as indicators of their physicality but as vehicles for developing Galdós's themes of inner versus exterior beauty and blindness versus sight.

In chapter 1 of *Nela*, a frontal image of Pablo is withheld until the final panel, which is enlarged for emphasis, and his blindness is dramatically revealed through Pulido's depiction of his face without eyes. Here, abstraction and black-and-white presentation combine to communicate the ableist idea of blindness as an absence, which will serve as the central plot device of the story. Pablo is depicted with unseeing antique-gold eyes in chapter 7 while he imagines how Nela's outward appearance must match her inner goodness. Still, it is not until after his operation that his real eyes are drawn. Students can discuss how Pulido's images portray Pablo's ability to "see" Nela's inner beauty while blind but not while sighted. Nela's actual physical appearance is somewhat unclear in the novel. Although Galdós does describe her stunted body, he does not indicate the exact nature of the facial injuries Nela sustained in a fall as a baby, merely suggesting her disfigurement through her account that before the accident, she had been considered pretty, but now the townspeople call her a monster. This lack of specificity freed Pulido to portray Nela's facial features as changing depending on her own subjective feelings of how she sees herself and is seen by others. As students progress through the text, they can examine how Nela's facial representations—ranging from pretty to ugly—convey her fluctuating sense of self-worth as she reacts to those around her. Furthermore, the reader first sees Florentina not as she actually looks but instead through Nela's deification of her beauty. Pulido portrays this encounter as its own minimal unit, with a full "splash page" on the left side showing Nela's impression of Florentina as a dazzling antique-gold Virgin

Mary, followed on the right side by four rectangular panels in a grid pattern, each using less color than its predecessor as individual elements of Florentina's actual appearance are revealed in black and white. By comparing this visualization with the corresponding passages in the novel, students can appreciate how Pulido, rather than following Galdós's description, conveys the idea of Florentina as the personification of idealized beauty. As with Pablo and Nela, Florentina is presented through Pulido's interpretive lens. Since much of the scholarship on *Marianela* deals with the use of Pablo, Nela, and Florentina as metaphors for Galdós's exploration of philosophical concepts pertaining to the nature of beauty, reality, and knowledge, students can discuss how Pulido's nonrealistic imagery reinforces the characters' metaphorical function.

Instructors can also direct students' attention to the verbal component of *Nela*. By focusing on individual scenes, students can examine the selection and condensation involved in adapting Galdós's narration and dialogue to fit within speech or thought balloons or caption boxes and how Pulido's graphic elements work in consort with this pruned material to enhance what is being articulated. This interdependence of words and images is particularly effective in Pulido's presentations of concepts. An excellent example is in chapter 11, where Golfín describes Pablo's medical condition and the surgical process that could restore his sight. To make this lengthy and highly technical explanation more understandable to the average reader, Pulido culls its most essential elements, largely retaining Galdós's wording but also paraphrasing for brevity's sake. He then superimposes this information over the huge image of a cross-sectioned eye with the shadow of Golfín's profile in its center, thereby using a single panel to efficiently convey scientific information while establishing a visual link between Pablo's blindness and the surgeon who will cure it.

Similarly, Pulido presents Galdós's social criticism by visually supporting the concepts being verbally expressed. Students can examine how Pulido emphasizes Galdós's ideas about social inequality, education, and charity by giving prominence to the dialogues in the speech balloons. In chapter 4, Celipín's words stand out against the black background of his dark bedroom as he tells Nela of his desire to escape the miner's life and its animalizing effects by becoming literate. In chapter 10 (corresponding to chapter 9 in the novel), the conversation between Golfín and his family about personal versus institutional forms of charity dominates the space of a double page with a nearly blank background. In contrast, on the subsequent double page, the paneling and sequencing of Pulido's interlocking drawings emphasize the progression of Golfín's argument as the figures physically progress down the path they are following.

Instructors who wish to examine how disability is dealt with in both texts can assign David Mitchell and Sharon Snyder's *Narrative Prosthesis: Disability and Dependencies of Discourse*, in which the authors posit that nonnormative bodies function as metaphoric devices in mainstream narratives but must eventually become "normalized" through one of four "quick fix" prosthetic devices: a cure, a rescue from social censure, an extermination, or an alternative mode of being (53–54). Mitchell and Snyder state that literary narratives can subvert this pattern by exposing the artificiality of the prosthetic solution. Galdós does this by showing the negative consequences of Pablo's cure and by refusing to allow Marianela's disability to be erased by a rescue through adoption by Golfín or Florentina, an unquestioned death, or the alternative mode of being described in the newspaper account. By exposing the lie told by the English tourists, Galdós reinstates Marianela's nonnormative body, making it the narrative premise for his writing of the novel. In contrast, Pulido states in his prologue that he changed the ending to allow the newspaper account to remain unchallenged, thereby granting Nela "una pequeña victoria" ("a little victory"). Students can discuss how this change reinforces ableist assumptions concerning disability, and instructors can expand this conversation by asking for examples of the pattern of narrative prosthesis in today's mainstream media.

Pulido's nine-page microsequel, "Socartes-Madrid," also can be assigned to supplement both texts. Using the same graphic style and color system as in *Nela*, Pulido builds on elements from the novel to create a continuation of Golfín's story as he returns to Madrid by train and meets an impoverished widow and her son, who is a friend of Celipín. Students can discuss how Golfín's feelings of guilt for contributing to the death of Marianela are expressed through his dream of her pushing him into the Trascava chasm and how he puts into practice his views on humane personalized charity by offering the use of his home to the widow and her son while he travels to America. Students can also examine the parallels between the boy being helped by Golfín, and Golfín being helped as a boy by his benefactors as well as between the boy's future and that of Celipín.

For a creative final project, students might conceive their own microsequels to the novel, extending the stories of certain characters and developing thematic elements. They can write these as narratives or use online cartooning software to produce their own graphic novel pages. Alternatively, students can readapt a chapter or portion of the novel into a different medium of their choice, such as film, dance, theater, photography, song, or gaming. In keeping with the importance of both creation and reception in the revisitation of texts, students can present their projects to the entire class for discussion.

Hutcheon comments, "[W]e often come to see the prior adapted work very differently as we compare it to the result of the adapter's creative and interpretive act" (121). Instructors can open new perspectives for examining Galdós's novel by teaching *Marianela* and *Nela* in tandem. Through their final projects, students can contribute their own creative and interpretive endeavors to the afterlife of this nineteenth-century Spanish classic.

APPENDIX: ELEMENTOS DEL CÓMIC / ELEMENTS OF THE COMIC

Spanish	*English*
ángulo contrapicado	low-angle shot
ángulo picado	high-angle shot
bocadillo/globo	speech balloon
calle	gutter
cartela	caption box
cuadrícula	grid
dibujo	drawing
formato	page layout
gran plano general	extreme long shot
marco	frame
margen	margin
página	page
plano detalle	extreme close-up
plano general / plano entero	long shot
plano medio	medium shot
primer plano	close-up
rotulación	lettering
viñeta	panel

Transatlantic Adaptations: Teaching *Doña Perfecta* through Alejandro Galindo's Film

Luis Álvarez-Castro

Benito Pérez Galdós's fiction is fertile ground for adaptations. Galdós himself converted several of his novels—*Doña Perfecta* among them—into plays. Later, twelve film and six television versions of some of his classic titles cemented Galdós's status as a canonical figure in Spanish contemporary culture (Navarrete). Beyond Spain, Mexico's film industry became a significant hub for Galdós adaptations, producing eight films, including those by the Mexican director Alejandro Galindo, based on his novels (Sinnigen, *Benito*). In this essay, I propose Galindo's film *Doña Perfecta* as a case study of the pedagogical uses of film adaptations in the Spanish literature and culture classroom. Furthermore, the comparative analysis of Galdós's and Galindo's works provides an opportunity to reflect on the status of adaptation and transatlantic studies within present-day Hispanism.

The Novel and the Film

Whereas the *MLA International Bibliography* lists close to seventy essays on Galdós's *Doña Perfecta*, only a handful of studies—essentially, four articles (Gramley; Davies, "Space"; Sinnigen, "Benito"; Sinnigen and Medina Ramírez) and two book chapters (Dapena; Sinnigen, *Benito* 109–35)—examine Galindo's film version. It can therefore be surmised that the film remains relatively unknown to scholars and is therefore rarely used in classrooms. However, Galindo's adaptation allows for a fruitful comparative approach to teaching the novel. First, the combined study of these works facilitates a productive discussion on the theory and practice of adaptation (including the debated question of fidelity), the merits of the opposing views on adaptation as a discursive or affective process (Sánchez Noriega 47; Gimferrer 65), and the links between literary canon and film history. Second, Galindo's adaptation is representative of the transatlantic reception of Galdós's work and helps illuminate the cross-cultural exchange that resulted from the exile of Spanish Republicans in Mexico (including the case of Luis Buñuel and his film adaptations of Galdós's novels). Instructors may employ either approach in undergraduate and graduate courses on Spanish or Mexican culture as well as in undergraduate literature surveys. Galdós's novel is available in multiple Spanish editions (including annotated editions by Ignacio Javier López [Cátedra], Germán Gullón [Austral], and Linda Willem [Cervantes]) and in English translations, such as those by Mary J. Serrano (Harper) and, in a bilingual Spanish-English edition, by Graham Whittaker (Oxbow).[1] Galindo's film is available on DVD (*Doña Perfecta* [Vanguard]) and on *YouTube* ("*Doña Perfecta* México"); the online format features multilingual captions.

Doña Perfecta is a staple in Spanish high school literature courses. Despite that apparent popularity, though, it does not occupy a privileged position in Galdós's vast fictional production from a critical standpoint. Labeling it somewhat dismissively as a "novela de tesis" ("thesis novel"), scholars have noted the simplicity of its plot and the Manichaean nature of its characters (Sinnigen, "*Doña Perfecta*" 145), a negative characterization that recent studies dispute (López, Introduction 47–50; Pope). Nevertheless, *Doña Perfecta*'s purported narratological defects make it a highly productive text in the Spanish literature classroom, since undergraduate students usually feel confident expressing their views about what they regard as an easy-to-understand novel. In addition to being an accessible text on account of its structure and style, this novel resonates with students thanks to the generational and ideological conflicts that constitute its "tesis" ("thesis"), such as the city-country, science-religion, and liberalism-conservatism dichotomies.[2] Notwithstanding the novel's attachment to its historical context, these conflicts are anything but resolved in our present time, a fact that confers upon *Doña Perfecta* a universal and timeless appeal. Galindo's film exemplifies this enduring relevance.

The movie substitutes the imaginary city of Orbajosa and the political climate of the Spanish third Carlist War (1872–76) for the fictional Mexican town of Santa Fe at the time of the Reform Laws, during the early years of General Porfirio Díaz's authoritarian regime, known as the Porfiriato (1876–1911). Aside from these significant changes in the setting, announced at the beginning in a superimposed title—"Esta historia ha sido situada en el México del último tercio del siglo XIX" ("This story takes place in Mexico in the last third of the nineteenth century")—the film's plot is deceptively simple in that it appears to follow the source storyline quite closely. This initial impression quickly vanishes if an instructor or student attempts to divide the film's nearly two hours into narrative sections and then tries to match them with the novel's chapters. This exercise can be helpful to undergraduate students who prefer to work with the film in manageable fragments. Moreover, the challenging task of establishing correspondences between the film's and the novel's narrative structures illustrates the variety of interventions any adaptation requires. In the case of Galindo's version, the screenplay omits some chapters, combines others, and creates new scenes, such as Perfecta's burning of heretic books (00:22:30–24:00).

The following eight-part division of the film—each section is easily identifiable by fade-out transitions—includes time stamps and approximate correspondences with the novel's chapters. It serves as a guide for planning student-led presentations on the novel's plot and class discussions on the thematic, aesthetic, and ideological features of both the film and the book. Before or following the screening of each clip, instructors may assign the reading of the corresponding pages from the novel to the whole class or to a group of students, depending on the number of classes allotted to *Doña Perfecta* and students' reading proficiency. (The second option facilitates a faster pace, since groups can work on their respective readings simultaneously.)

Presentation of Perfecta and her circle. News of Pepe's impending visit to Santa Fe (ch. 3; 00:00:00–12:00).

Pepe's arrival in Santa Fe as a representative of the Ministry of Development. The first instance of conflict: Perfecta burns some heretic books that Pepe has brought to her brother, Don Cayetano (chs. 2–4; 00:12:00–24:00).

During a social gathering at Perfecta's home, there are ideological clashes between Pepe and Don Inocencio, followed by a dialogue between Perfecta and Don Inocencio regarding Pepe's qualities (chs. 6–7, 9–10; 00:24:00–39:00).

Pepe declares his love for Rosario. Perfecta admonishes her nephew for his irreverent actions during his visit to the town and clarifies that his advances on Rosario are not welcome. Pepe finds himself entangled in a lawsuit orchestrated by Jacinto (chs. 8, 11; 00:39:00–50:00).

Pepe encounters resistance among the town leaders to the government's development plans. Rosario admits her love for Pepe. Perfecta addresses the political leaders of Santa Fe regarding news of the governmental army's imminent arrival. Perfecta and Ramos discuss how many men he can enroll in an anti-government militia. Pepe receives notice of his sudden dismissal from his government position. Against Perfecta's plan, Pepe refuses to leave Santa Fe without Rosario (ch. 11; 00:50:00–01:07:00).

Perfecta secludes Rosario in her room to keep her away from Pepe under the pretense that she is sick. To cheer Pepe up, Juan Tafetán takes him to the house of "las Troyas," three orphan girls who live in poverty and are unjustly deemed indecent, prompting a scandal among Perfecta and her circle. Remedios demands that Inocencio take a more active stance in their plot to marry Jacinto to Rosario and proposes that Ramos threaten Pepe (chs. 12–13, 26–27; 01:07:00–21:00).

The conflict between Pepe and Perfecta intensifies. At night, Rosario takes Pepe to the chapel—she needs to confirm whether he is an atheist, as her mother claims. Under the image of a crucified Christ, they marry each other and kiss. Rosario faints before reaching her room, and Perfecta discovers them. Perfecta and Pepe argue, and she expels him from her house (chs. 16–17, 19; 01:21:00–37:00).

Remedios warns Perfecta that Pepe may take Rosario with him. After arresting most of the militiamen, the government troops enter Santa Fe. The commanding officer takes accommodation in Perfecta's house and gives Pepe a key. Remedios and Ramos follow Pepe to Perfecta's house. Perfecta discovers Rosario as she is getting ready to run away with Pepe, and she orders Ramos to shoot him in front of her daughter. Rosario abandons her mother (chs. 18, 20, 25, 30–31; 01:37:00–44:00).

Those familiar with Galdós's novel will notice a significant departure in the film's denouement. The ending of Galindo's film affords some level of agency to the character of Rosario, who repudiates her mother and leaves her house with the body of her murdered husband. In contrast, in the novel's definitive version—for Galdós experimented with different endings (Gullón, "Cinco")—the young woman loses her mind. To some extent, Galindo's ending exposes an underlying conflict that, according to Marilyn D. Rugg, provides the foundation for the novel's plot—namely, "the normative nature of patriarchy, and the insidious ways in which it still acts as a web to ensnare and subjugate women" (223). Indeed, we can regard Rosario's stance at the end of the film as a feminist gesture in an otherwise overwhelmingly patriarchal narrative universe.

In a typical approach to film adaptations, students read a literary text first. They then view the film inspired by it to detect changes in the narrative structure and the representation of characters, themes, and setting. Aside from implying a hierarchical relationship between literature and film, this methodology risks leading to the fidelity fallacy by means of mechanistic "spot the differences" tasks. Still, contrasting a novel with its film adaptation constitutes a valuable exercise to strengthen students' communicative and critical skills, especially at the undergraduate level. At the graduate level, students can engage in a metacritical analysis of the cultural role of film adaptations and, in the case of Galindo's *Doña Perfecta*, of the status of transatlantic studies in US academia. Regardless of the instructional setting, it is most productive when assessing similarities and divergences between novel and film to ask not "what" but "how" as well as "why."

Film Adaptation Studies and Transatlantic Studies

At the beginning of Galindo's *Doña Perfecta*, an intertitle acknowledges the film's artistic debt to Galdós's homonymous novel. This connection is further reinforced at the end of the movie by means of another intertitle that reproduces the novel's last sentence—"Es cuanto por ahora podemos decir de las personas que parecen buenas y no lo son" ("This is all we have to say for the present concerning persons who seem, but are not[,] good"; Pérez Galdós, *Doña Perfecta* [Cátedra] 404; *Doña Perfecta* [Harper] 319)—accompanied by the novelist's signature and name. By displaying this quotation and the writer's signature onscreen, Galindo invokes the intrinsic cultural authority literature confers on film adaptations—even if it creates the symbolic illusion that the novelist and not the director provides the film's ending. However, the last words spoken in the movie—Perfecta's cry of "¡Misericordia, Señor, misericordia!" ("Mercy, Lord, mercy!"; 01:54:00; my trans.)—are taken not from the novel but from Galdós's stage adaptation of *Doña Perfecta*, which premiered in 1896 (Pérez Galdós, *Doña Perfecta* [La Guirnalda] 87). Instructors may highlight this detail to students to illustrate that film adaptations do not result from univocal relations, wherein one literary text inspires one film version. Instead, they refer to multiple sources, just as novelists draw upon diverse experiences to create their works. Besides, film adaptations—and films in general—are shaped by myriad practical factors. Perhaps most significantly, film productions require substantial financial investments and large crews, whereas writers, as Luis Buñuel mentioned jokingly, only need pencil and paper to represent the most elaborate scenes (Colina and Pérez Turrent 232). Nevertheless, film adaptation studies, which are frequently produced by academics with a literary background, tend to overlook the pragmatics of filmmaking.

Scholars interested in formalist or narratological approaches to literature have embraced film adaptations to counter the academic dominance of post-structuralist theory and its subsequent developments in the last few decades.[3] This perspective entails the analysis of film adaptations as adaptations and not as independent creations, which at worst leads to the fidelity fallacy and at best may provide a more sophisticated understanding of films' literary sources. Judith D. Gramley's essay on Galindo's film *Doña Perfecta* exemplifies the critical ambiguity that often burdens adaptation studies. At the beginning of the article, Gramley states that "an adaptation's faithfulness to the novel on which it is based should not be the primary measure of its quality" (30). However, she cannot avoid the fidelity paradigm as, in the essay's last words, she concludes that "Galdós's novel has not been betrayed" by Galindo's version (36). Similarly, Rhian Davies analyzes features in Galindo's film that reveal the novel's artistic complexity, thus praising the film not for its own merits but rather for its ability to enhance audiences' appreciation of the book ("Space" 432).

Once we transcend the comparatist approach to focus on film adaptations as films, first and foremost, fidelity becomes a liability rather than a virtue. For instance, Navarrete justifies the hostile reception of César Fernández Ardavín's 1977 film version of *Doña Perfecta*—both at the box office and among critics—because it tried to follow the source text so closely that it failed to produce an original cinematic style (148). Galindo's version, in contrast, does feature a recognizable style that separates it from Galdós's novel: that of melodrama, which is particularly prominent in the film's soundtrack, the use of light, and close-ups of the characters' facial expressions. (Time permitting, instructors may show clips of the 1977 adaptation to clarify these points.) Moreover, the history of film adaptations provides valuable insights into sociopolitical and economic circumstances affecting the production of those films (including factors that can explain why those adaptations came to be and why their directors or producers chose their respective source texts). In this regard, Eduardo de la Vega Alfaro notes that Galindo's film was part of a Mexican trend in the 1940s and early 1950s: "All these films were super-productions intended to give the national industry a cosmopolitan flavor by way of adaptations for which, thanks to the war, no copyright fees had to be paid" (88). Economics aside, some of Galindo's artistic choices—such as changing Don Inocencio's occupation from priest to lawyer—may be attributed to the ideological climate surrounding the film's production, which compelled the director "to tone down the anticlerical tone expressed in Galdós's novel" (Davies, "Space" 427–28). Instructors can use this contextual information as a comprehension aid and as a basis for creative assignments in which students envision the main elements of a present-day film adaptation of *Doña Perfecta* produced in a Spanish-speaking country or in the United States.

The ideological landscapes that conditioned the creation and reception of both Galdós's novel and Galindo's film—not to mention the use of a Spanish novel as the source for a Mexican movie—underscore an additional comparatist dimension in the study of these works—namely, a transatlantic approach. Some scholars denounce this methodology as a neocolonial attempt by so-called Peninsularists—that is, scholars of the literatures and cultures of Spain—to remain relevant in the North American academy (Enjuto-Rangel et al. 6), thus perpetuating the Eurocentric and imperialistic tendencies that Herlihy-Mera observes in many Spanish departments in the United States. Indeed, if we liken the binaries literature/film and Spain / Latin America, the comparative nature of transatlantic studies could promote hierarchical biases analogous to those present in adaptation studies. However, in the case of Galindo's adaptation of *Doña Perfecta*, instructors can avoid both biases by presenting the film as a discrete cultural product, not merely as a derivative of a preexisting literary work. After all, the main pedagogical benefit of bringing a transatlantic adaptation to the classroom is to help students learn about the cultures represented by the film and the novel, with particular attention to the historical connections that link those cultures. By employing a genuinely comparative approach, Spanish instructors of either Spanish or Latin American specialization will meaningfully integrate works from either region into their syllabi. This conscious effort to decolonize the Spanish literature classroom is especially pertinent in relation to Galdós, a native of the Canary Islands who served as a parliamentary representative of Puerto Rico and depicted Spanish imperialism critically in many of his writings.

NOTES

1. Willem's edition, intended for the US academic market, includes an introduction and notes in English along with vocabulary glosses. Old translations, such as Serrano's, are freely accessible online (see, for example, www.gutenberg.org/ebooks/2462). In this essay, original quotations belong to López's edition, and translations are from Serrano's.

2. Varey's classic guide offers undergraduate students a good introduction to these themes.

3. For theoretical and critical instances of a structuralist approach to film adaptations in Spanish, see Sánchez Noriega; Faro Forteza.

Teaching Galdós through Film Adaptations and Filmmaking

Rhian Davies

Teaching Benito Pérez Galdós in the twenty-first century presents numerous challenges since students not only encounter linguistic barriers but are daunted by the length and breadth of Galdós's works. They may also feel alienated by the focus on what they perceive to be anachronistic values of little import. To give some examples, undergraduates studying *Doña Perfecta* often contend that the significance attached to religion is outdated since Catholicism plays a lesser role in contemporary Spain. (One student pointed out that only sixty-one percent of Spaniards are Catholic; see Espinosa.) Likewise, they find it difficult to relate to nineteenth-century concerns; some struggle, for instance, to comprehend Tristana's frustration with the restrictions imposed upon her as a woman since women in Spain have more rights and freedoms today. The challenge, then, is to find a way to break down barriers to students' comprehension and enjoyment of Galdos's works.

Film is a particularly useful medium because today's students respond more confidently and sensitively to dynamic visual representations than to static written materials such as novels. In this essay, I outline two ways of teaching Galdós through film: first by studying film and television adaptations of his works and, second, by involving students in filmmaking. These methods engage students in discussion, critical analysis, decision-making, and evaluation, thus mirroring approaches adopted by researchers and fostering autonomous learning.

Teaching Galdós's Tristana *alongside Buñuel's Film*

We begin by looking at Galdós's novel *Tristana*. Using *PowerPoint* presentations (including photographs of Galdós, his home, and scenes from the events of his day, such as Queen Isabel II's abdication), we examine the work's historical context as well as Galdós's life, career, and work alongside chapter summaries, discussing the main themes and key quotations from the novel before debating whether *Tristana* is feminist or anti-feminist. Catherine Jagoe's *Ambiguous Angels* provides a helpful overview of the situation of nineteenth-century Spanish women, and, for the benefit of intermediate students in the course, Colin Partridge's translations are given alongside Spanish quotations from *Tristana*. Our discussion of key quotations highlights the importance of close reading and the significance of particular terms, such as *muñeca* ("doll"), which can be reviewed alongside visual resources. For example, we consider how the title character corresponds to a photograph from a staging of Galdós's *Electra* of the actress Matilde Moreno holding a doll (published in *Blanco y Negro*, 23 Feb. 1901, p. 21), we reflect on the perception of nineteenth-century Spanish women as male-owned objects of beauty with few legal rights, and we link the work with Henrik Ibsen's *A Doll's House*.

Students complete worksheets in groups using *Google Slides*, which enables them to collaborate remotely if needed, and they report their responses to the class at the end of the session. Sample questions from week 2 include the following:

> What are the key themes of *Tristana*?
>
> Why is the ending left open?
>
> Why did Galdós write this novel?
>
> How do you think people responded to *Tristana* in the nineteenth century?
>
> How do you think people react to *Tristana* today? What is your response to it?

And the worksheet for week 3 asks:

> Was the amputation of Tristana's leg "cruel" (Miró)? What might it symbolize?
>
> Discuss the role of the men in *Tristana*. What ideas does the novel advance about masculinity?

Students are expected to consult Lisa Condé's critical guide and Gordon Minter's edition (Pérez Galdós, *Tristana* [Bristol]) to support their reading and should have a solid knowledge of *Tristana* before studying Luis Buñuel's film.

Next, students are asked to read Galdós's description of Tristana and draw a picture of her. If they are concerned about their artistic skills, they can suggest a picture or photograph that might evoke the character or name an actress to cast in the role. For example, one student proposed that Tristana resembled Berthe Morisot from Édouard Manet's painting *Le balcon*; another suggested Keira Knightley. Time permitting, other character descriptions can be included. Students share their worksheets with their peers, compare them, consider whether their picture matches the performer cast in the film (Catherine Deneuve, in the case of Buñuel's *Tristana*), and discuss the purpose of this exercise.

As noted in my article "New Ways of Teaching Literature," students frequently deviate from Galdós's description. They commonly draw Tristana with long, loose hair (even though the text tells us that she wore it in a bun), wearing a short, sleeveless dress that does not match the fashions of Galdós's time. They are initially startled by these "errors," but, as I explain, sometimes the human brain only retains certain details and, as the imagination takes over and processes the image, may subtract or even add elements. Some students, for example, draw a bucket or a brush alongside Tristana, portraying her as Don Lope's servant and subordinate.

The exercise is designed to actively engage students, to stimulate them to imagine some of the questions facing a film director, and introduce the idea that

Buñuel was, like them, a reader of Galdós. It also reveals that film can leave ineradicable impressions; we discuss whether anybody but Daniel Radcliffe could play Harry Potter and whether students will always associate Catherine Deneuve with Tristana henceforth.

Using a problem-based learning method, we then examine the changes Buñuel makes to setting (replacing nineteenth-century Madrid with Toledo in the 1930s) and style (such as the introduction of Surrealist elements). Students express their opinions on the director's decisions and debate the film's success. These exercises require them to know both the novel and the film well and to respond thoughtfully and sensitively to them. They come to appreciate that Buñuel's film was "inspired" by Galdós's *Tristana* and that, in line with Linda Hutcheon's *A Theory of Adaptation*, it not only differs on account of the generic differences between films and novels but is a work in its own right, matching Buñuel's interests. To encourage students to formulate their own opinions, we discuss whether they agree with the views of critics such as Condé, Gwynne Edwards, Joan Mellen, and Beth Miller, and whether the film reveals that Galdós's novel was ahead of its time.

As the students gain confidence and consider whether the film is superior (or inferior) to the novel, they realize that there are no wrong answers, that a great deal is open to interpretation, and they start to enjoy debating matters such as authorial intentions.

Students as Galdosian Filmmakers

Filmmaking is another effective means of engaging students, and I have used it in a final-year stand-alone course on Galdós. (Past students have selected sequences from the novel and play versions of Galdós's *Realidad* and *El abuelo* and turned them into films.) Galdós can also be taught alongside other authors; I have taught *Doña Perfecta* with Federico García Lorca's *La casa de Bernarda Alba* and Manuel Rivas's *¿Qué me quieres, amor?*, all of which have been adapted for the screen (the last of these as *La lengua de las mariposas*). Students are asked to reflect on generic differences and assess the works' modernity and universal relevance.

In the introductory session, students describe the generic characteristics of novels, plays, short stories, and films. They also discuss the nature and significance of dialogue in films and the importance of visual elements, considering quotations from Robert McKee's *Story*, including "Pity the poor screenwriter, for he cannot be a poet" (394), and "We watch a movie; we hear a play. The aesthetics of film are 80 percent visual, 20 percent auditory. We want to see, not hear as our energies go to our eyes, only half-listening to the soundtrack. Theatre is 80 percent auditory, 20 percent visual. Our concentration is directed through our ears, only half-looking at the stage" (389). Then, drawing on Hutcheon's *A Theory of Adaptation*, we deliberate whether fidelity theory is justified (or justifiable), if an adaptation is always doomed to be inferior to the original, and whether "'palimpsestuous' works [are] haunted at all times by their adapted texts," wherein the directors "transcod[e] into a different set of conventions" (Hutcheon 33). We also ponder whether Galdós, as the author of the original, always "got it right."

Finally, we consider Robert Stam's "Theory and Practice of Adaptation" and his question whether "[a] 'faithful' film [should be] seen as uncreative" whereas "an 'unfaithful' film [is] a shameful betrayal of the original" (8) before taking account of his view that "[e]very text, and every adaptation, 'points' in many directions, back, forward and sideways" (27). Another helpful resource to use alongside Hutcheon and Stam's works is Sally Faulkner's lecture "Galdós and Spanish Cinema."

We begin studying *Doña Perfecta* with an overview of the novel's historical context, including Galdós's life and work, and spend three weeks examining the key themes, comparing the novel with the film by Alejandro Galindo, and reviewing his decision to cast Dolores del Río as Perfecta. We use Rodolfo Cardona's edition, which comments on the manuscript and enables students to appreciate the creative transformation the work underwent, and we examine various secondary sources, including Gerard Dapena and John H. Sinnigen (*Benito*). We discuss the film's Mexican dimension, space and place (including the new setting), camera angles, and gender perspectives, particularly concerning Rosario. There are interesting links with the other works studied in the course, especially *La casa de Bernarda Alba*. For example, students can compare the protagonists and the situation of women as presented by Galdós and Lorca alongside the film adaptations. Linda Fox's article is useful for those wishing to explore the comparisons further. The first-semester assessment is a traditional essay weighted at forty percent of students' course grade for the year. Students compare and contrast an aspect of Galdós's novel (e.g., the role of Rosario or the chapel) with its treatment in the film adaptation and assess which version is more engaging.

In the second semester, students attend introductory practical sessions on filmmaking and then work independently in groups to make a five-minute film. They make creative decisions, such as which sequence they will film, where and when it will be set, and so on. They are also responsible for finding actors, costumes, and props and making technical decisions regarding roles, equipment, camera angles, and more. Rather than instructing them, we ask them questions about their choices and intentions, such as what effect a close-up shot of Rosario might convey, what they might lose or gain by setting a scene inside or outside, and so on. Although they are often unsure at the beginning, they gradually gain the confidence to make decisions autonomously and justify their choices.

In the past, students have engaged creatively with *Doña Perfecta*. One group turned Rosario into a man whose domineering, conservative mother struggled to accept his homosexuality. Another group focused on the novel's melodramatic and symbolic features, incorporating a thriller element, confining Doña Perfecta (rather than Rosario) to an asylum, and casting a student's two cats (one black, one white) as a symbolic nod to the novel's final words: "Es cuanto por ahora podemos decir de las personas que parecen buenas y no lo son" ("This is all we can say for now about people who seem to be good and are not"; Cardona 295; my trans.).

Filmmaking prompts students to make new connections; for example, those filming a news report sequence argued that this linked to Galdós's career as a journalist. Others, feeling that Pepe's move from Madrid to Spain's provinces in *Doña Perfecta* would not be sufficiently dramatic in the twenty-first century, decided to make immigration a key theme, turned Pepe into a Mexican refugee, and pondered whether his situation shared similarities with Galdós's move from Gran Canaria to Madrid.

Filmmaking also encourages students to reflect on the details in their films and make ambitious changes. One group argued that their use of cats not only complemented the tiger on the wall tapestry in (their) Rosario's bedroom, included to convey the character's newfound strength, but drew upon Galdós's *Miau*, where the female characters are compared to cats. Others also incorporated animal symbolism, using birds to highlight the theme of freedom, or including pictures of bullfighting to situate their sequence within "traditional" Spain and to portray the conflict between humanity and nature. Another group focused on the relationship between Rosario and Doña Perfecta, setting their film in a village called Esperanza ("Hope"), with a happy ending as the protagonist allowed her willful daughter to attend university, a deliberately dramatic contrast with the educational situation of Rosario and Tristana in Galdós's novels. At the end of the sequence, we see the now contented protagonist reading a copy of *Doña Perfecta* with a smile on her face, mocking her nineteenth-century counterpart.

In short, filmmaking is an effective means of encouraging students to gain an in-depth understanding of Galdós's works. Responses to the question "How do you think making a film contributed to your understanding of the work of Galdós?" repeatedly mentioned increased comprehension of the texts and highlighted the experience of engagement. Students find filmmaking accessible and enjoy the element of playfulness it releases into their learning, facilitating a relatively low-pressure environment conducive to creativity. They particularly enjoy working in groups, a process that helps them develop a sense of responsibility and work effectively both independently and in teams, learning from and helping each other. Another valuable gain is that students often become so engrossed in the filmmaking that their attention turns away from assessment; one wrote, "I enjoyed the break from focusing on exams and marks."

Students are not being trained to be professional filmmakers; filmmaking is an opportunity to test out their ideas. The key element of the assignment is "the process," not "the product," and therefore the films themselves are not assessed.[1] Instead, students submit portfolios, weighted at fifty percent of the course grade, evaluating the challenges of turning a literary text into a film, including diaries (containing a minimum of ten entries), storyboards, and scripts.

Diaries encourage students to "think forward," plan ahead, consider how the classes might help them, brainstorm, and weigh the pros and cons of specific ideas. They are beneficial as preparation for the pitch session when students present their ideas to their group members. They also enable students to "think backward," reflect, take stock, practice critical thinking (e.g., in response to an article they have read), and evaluate their progress or skills. They can additionally serve as a means of "crisis management," sometimes to let off steam, for instance, over frustrations that can arise in the course of a collaborative effort. Diaries place students "in the driver's seat," providing them with a record to which they can refer when writing up their portfolios. Students effectively begin writing earlier than when planning traditional essays and are gently prepared for the questions they will need to critically address when writing the portfolio, such as "Evaluate the success of your film" and "What would you do differently?" Diaries also require students to practice "deep learning" since they cannot forget about the activities they have undertaken in class. They encourage creative thinking and conversational writing, unlike the style expected in academic essays.

Finally, students complete peer evaluation forms (ten percent of their grade), wherein they assess the contribution and skills of other group members. This helps them appreciate the transferable skills they have gained, such as teamwork, leadership, negotiation, and organization—skills that will benefit them in their future working lives.

Presented with questions focusing on film adaptations of Galdós's works or practical filmmaking, students unleash their creative spirits as they decide what the works mean to them. They work hard but enjoy themselves. *Fun* is sometimes perceived to be a frivolous term, but literature is meant to be entertaining, and many nineteenth-century novels were arguably precursors of today's soap operas.

Filmmaking, in particular, enables students to interact creatively with Galdós's works and to advance fascinating insights. As students enthusiastically deliberate over what might initially appear to be minor details (such as the significance of flowers in the novel and film versions of *Doña Perfecta*, as well as in their own sequences), they undertake close readings of Galdós's work and gain a sense of ownership and pride.

Finally, a survey on undergraduates' attitudes to literature confirmed that "there was a social aspect of reading for [students] in that they like talking to friends about their reading" (Gallagher-Brett 26). In my experience, teaching Galdós with film and filmmaking helps remove students' fear of reading as a solitary activity and mirrors nineteenth-century group reading sessions. Students often invite friends and relatives to watch their film; others put their films on *YouTube*. I'm not sure they treat their undergraduate essays with the same enthusiasm.

NOTE

1. I later devised marking criteria for assessing the film, but students declined the option.

Reading Pretty Privilege in *Marianela*

Lennie Amores

"What is a privilege?" I ask students from my nonchronological, theme-based survey of Spanish literature. A first-year heritage learner who has not yet completed any of the prerequisite language courses responds, "A gift." A graduating senior gasps at the response, itching to jump in. The other students squirm when the first-year student adds, "It's like a minority scholarship gifted to someone because of their identity." I look at the senior about to explode. She corrects her classmate by explaining how privilege is an advantage some people have that ends up disadvantaging others. We then begin a preliminary brainstorming of privileges and how they complicate the notion of merit-based opportunities, such as scholarships. I ask if romantic love is merit-based or whether some privileges make certain people more desirable as a prelude to my two-and-a-half-week course module, "Pretty Privilege."

Because I teach at a small, urban liberal arts college where most of our student body is first-generation college students and about half belong to a minority population, primarily identifying as Black and Latinx, discussions of privilege resonate deeply with students' lived experiences of colorism, European beauty standards, and financial accessibility to cosmetic enhancements, making these conversations especially lively. Spanish minors of all language levels make up the majority of students in my classes, and heritage and second-language learners take the same courses together. My greatest challenge, therefore, is fostering dialogue and paragraph-level discourse among students of varying proficiency levels. Because I am sensitive to my students' social, economic, racial, and popular cultural contexts and their varying language skills, I develop course themes that reflect current conversations in and outside the classroom. For instance, in approaching the topic of pretty privilege, students bring up a myriad of films during the discussion, such as the musical *Dreamgirls*, in which Beyoncé's character's beauty capital grants her more opportunities for success and romance in contrast to Jennifer Hudson's character. Similarly, they comment on the comedic film *The DUFF,* whose title features an acronym for "designated ugly fat friend." Drawing on their experiences of having, witnessing, or desiring pretty privilege, I emotionally engage them with the topic as I discover their beliefs about privilege and beauty.

In this "Pretty Privilege" course module, we read the abridged Santillana edition of *Marianela,* which is accessible for undergraduates at the "intermediate high" level (*ACTFL* 7) while preserving the novel's essential elements, and Rosa Montero's Generation X short story "La gloria de los feos" ("The Glory of Ugly People"). Both literary texts address how beauty currency operates in distinct social milieus, as evidenced in the authors' attitudes toward the unattractive protagonists they describe. Through comparison, we generate shared knowledge in the classroom, where student readers notice a detail in one text by virtue of its absence from another text. Hands-on activities compare aspects of assigned texts students have already read and absorbed, thus allowing for more thoughtful analysis than when students encounter new literature, films, or cultural theories for the first time during class.

Focusing on pretty privilege instead of a generalized examination of *Marianela,* my students think more deeply about how conventional, alternative, and evolving beauty standards intersect with race, gender, socioeconomic status, disability, and neurodiversity in society. Students' understanding of the destructive implications of pretty privilege on individuals and groups is at stake in my approach to teaching *Marianela.* My goal is for students to recognize their biases and reflect on ways to describe beauty diversity. By expanding their vocabulary to include more inclusive and nuanced descriptive words, such as *convencionalmente atractivo/a/e* ("conventionally attractive") or *tener una vibra radiante* ("to have a radiant vibe"), students can focus on a person's unique qualities rather than simply rating their looks using basic adjectives like *fea* ("ugly") and *bonita* (pretty"). Furthermore, by promoting an ethos of *la belleza inclusiva, accesible, y más allá de la talla* ("inclusive, accessible, and size-inclusive beauty"), students are encouraged to imagine new possibilities for seeing others. Imagining an inclusive beauty paradigm is a lofty course goal, so I list the more measurable learning outcomes in the syllabus but discuss with students the overall goal of reimagining what beauty means.

Compare beauty standards of nineteenth-century Spanish bourgeois women with present-day American beauty ideals, exploring differences and universal themes that persist.

Explain how a person's beauty capital affects their opportunities in society.

Interpret both literary texts in the module using close reading strategies and support from academic articles.

Advocate for the importance of inclusive representations of beauty that embrace intersections of race, gender, socioeconomic status, disability, and neurodiversity.

Day 1: Capturing Students' Attention

Most of my classes incorporate prediction activities to increase learning retention. In *Small Teaching*, James Lang notes that "making predictions about material that you wish to learn increases your ability to understand that material and retrieve it later" (43). To grab my students' attention and set up a common first experience with the text, I start with the moment when Dr. Golfín first meets Marianela. Students first encounter the scene in the audiobook format. I play the audiobook excerpt twice. During the first listen, students focus solely on comprehension. For the second listen, I ask them to jot down key descriptive words or phrases. This dual-listening approach helps students with varying proficiency levels engage with the text more deeply.

> Era muy delgada, demasiado delgada quizá. Tenía el cuerpo pequeño y débil de una niña de doce años, pero su mirada era grave. En sus grandes ojos negros había siempre una luz triste que le hacía parecer mucho mayor. Tenía la cara delgada, una nariz graciosa y un pelo rubio oscuro casi sin color por culpa del sol y del polvo. Sus labios eran pequeños, tan pequeños que casi no se veían, y siempre estaban sonriendo. Pero su sonrisa se parecía a la de los muertos que han dejado de vivir pensando en el cielo.
> (Pérez Galdós, *Marianela* [Santillana] 10)

> She looked a child, for she was but a tiny creature, extremely thin and undeveloped; but she seemed like a little woman, for her eyes had not a childlike expression. . . . Her forehead was narrow, her nose sharp but not ill-shaped, her eyes black and brilliant, but their light shone but sadly. Her hair, naturally of a golden brown, was dull for want of care, and from exposure to the sun, wind and dust. Her lips were so thin as to be hardly visible, and always wore a smile, but it was like the faint smile of the dead who have died dreaming of Heaven. (*Marianela* [William S. Gottsberger] 25, 27)

Students decipher the text and paraphrase the passage in pairs. We clear up misunderstandings and define new vocabulary words. Students imagine who Marianela is, what she desires but lacks, why the narrator treats her this way, and what kind of fate Marianela's family background seems to portend for her. My questions lay the groundwork for a close reading: What words or phrases stood out? Did you notice any literary figures? What effect do they produce? Students always comment on Marianela's smile.

Indeed, Nela's deceased alcoholic mother and presumably abusive father make it easy for my students to imagine what kinds of circumstances await their now orphaned daughter—sex work, drug addiction, and unintended pregnancy. Nobody expects Nela to live a good life. My students call Galdós a "mean girl" author supported by bourgeois readers who want to read about the sad, brutal lives of the people they would ignore in real life. At this point, during a fifteen-minute class discussion, I invite them to investigate Galdós's intellectual motivation for subjecting poverty-stricken characters to trauma. What, I inquire, did Galdós believe about social mobility and education?

To accommodate varying levels of reading ability and cultural knowledge, I ask a few more questions: Why call her "La Nela" instead of Marianela? What does her thinness signify culturally in her context? At this point, I show images of 1870s fashion to compare the busty hourglass models to the description of Marianela's frame. Because students read more carefully when they are already curious, I remind them to answer the questions they posed during our initial reading.

Next, we move to reading comprehension. Assigned as homework, the vocabulary worksheets include three types of exercises: matching definitions, providing synonyms, and fill-in-the-blank paragraphs. Each worksheet focuses on ten to fifteen key words from the assigned reading. For the fill-in-the-blank exercise, I create short paragraphs that summarize plot points, ensuring students understand the vocabulary in context. All students, including heritage learners, benefit from expanding their vocabulary, so the vocabulary activities encourage them to use new words in the ensuing discussions and assignments. Additionally, I assign a discussion forum where they submit their video responses to the question "What is pretty privilege?" Considering examples from real life, literature, or television and film, students provide their examples and respond to their classmates' posts in writing. For the video response, I ask students to record a two-to-three-minute video in Spanish discussing their understanding of pretty privilege. They must include at least one example from real life and one from media (literature, television, or film). Students then comment on at least two classmates' videos, fostering further discussion and allowing quieter students to engage more comfortably. Letting students expand on the previous class discussion gives quiet students another opportunity to contribute.

Day 2: Reading in Class Together

Before we read aloud together, I introduce a dynamic brainstorming activity to explore the nineteenth century. I begin by dividing the class into small groups and providing clear instructions: "In your groups, brainstorm everything you know about the nineteenth century, including history, literature, and art from the United States, the United Kingdom, France, and Spain. Your goal is to generate as many unique points as possible." After a few minutes of initial brainstorming, I introduce a twist to encourage active participation and knowledge sharing. I announce, "Now, one person from each pair will move to the next group. Share your ideas with your new partners and learn from them." This process repeats several times, allowing students to circulate and exchange information.

As students engage in these continuous conversations, I move around the room, listening and intervening when necessary. I correct misinformation, offer clues to prompt further thinking, and encourage students to dig deeper. About halfway through the activity, I introduce an additional resource: "If you're struggling to recall certain details, you may use your smartphones to quickly search for information. Remember, our goal is to compile the most comprehensive list of unique points about the nineteenth century."

This approach not only expands students' knowledge of the nineteenth-century cultural, historical, and literary contexts that define Galdós's novels but also enhances learning retention and language fluency through active engagement and peer-to-peer teaching. The activity typically lasts about twenty minutes, culminating in a brief whole-class sharing session where groups highlight their most interesting or surprising findings. Then we start to read *Marianela* together. I begin, then pass off paragraphs to students to read aloud as I stop and ask comprehension questions, point out the vocabulary words, and ask the class to make predictions. Starting a novel is often the most challenging part for my students, so I ask them to describe what they are picturing in their minds. I believe vivid descriptions, especially in nineteenth-century Spanish realism, cultivate strong reading comprehension skills for language learners. Although reading together during class means less time for discussion, reducing the frustration of approaching a new text in Spanish means greater buy-in from students. When I pause to connect with the background information we have already discussed, ask them to recall a new word, or briefly summarize what is going on, I set up a model for my students to go on to engage with the texts independently.

Guided reading prompts pose basic *who, what, when, where,* and *how* questions, and I summarize important contextual information missing from the abridged edition. In the past, I would assign analytical questions for homework, but the students' answers were vague and without sufficient textual support. I now ensure students have spent enough time working through the text by giving basic yet detailed reading comprehension assignments. That way, students can quickly locate the textual evidence they need as we analyze passages in class.

Day 3: Close Reading with Scholarly Texts

We begin with a one-minute reading quiz that assesses students' comprehension of the assigned reading thus far, emphasizing details that an attentive reader who thoroughly engaged with the material would recall—for example, features of the region's landscape or the names of the characters who accompany Pablo and La Nela on their walks. The quiz also reminds students that careful reading will make it easier for them to find textual evidence. Using their guided reading comprehension questions as notes, we summarize the assigned reading before going deeper.

When introducing scholarly articles, I first model how to skim for main ideas by reading the introduction and conclusion together as a class. Then, in small groups, students focus on assigned sections, identifying key arguments and evidence. We reconvene to share findings, creating a collaborative understanding of the text. Dividing students into small groups, I assign different short passages from secondary texts about *Marianela* or related topics (e.g., bourgeois women, nineteenth-century beauty standards, and Galdós and his works) to each group.

Examples include articles such as Linda Willem's "Writing and Adapting Disability: Galdós' *Marianela* and Pablo Messiez's *Los ojos*" and visual digital texts from Fashion Institute of Technology's Fashion History Timeline website (Franklin). Students discover the claims and observations put forth by authors, searching for passages that support or connect with those ideas. They take literary and cultural studies criticism examples as models for their own interpretations and will notice more details in their next reading. Once they have located some evocative passages, we return to our discussion, in which students explain how pretty privilege intersects with other privileges such as socioeconomic status, race, culture, gender, disability, and neurodiversity. I ask about the intersectional identities that inform Marianela's physical attractiveness and require them to find evidence for their answers in the novel. We end the class with a lively discussion in which students defend these popular sayings using our readings of *Marianela* and our conversations on privilege to build their arguments:

"No eres feo, solo te falta dinero." ("You're not ugly; you're just broke.")

"Cada cosa tiene su belleza, pero no todos pueden verla." ("Everything has beauty, but not everyone sees it.")

"La belleza es riqueza, o por ella empieza." ("Beauty is wealth, or it starts with it.")

"La aceptación del cuerpo es una herramienta de salud mental." ("Body acceptance is a mental health tool.")

Days 4–6: Thinking about Beauty in New Ways

Our final discussion, following the assignment of reading questions for the second half of the abridged novel, focuses on a clip from the 1972 film *Marianela*, which features Rocío Dúrcal, a famous Spanish musical actress and singer. I use an *Edpuzzle* interactive video that pauses as students answer comprehension questions. I then show images of Dúrcal from the 1960s and '70s and ask why the actress might have been cast as Nela. Further questions include: How is Dúrcal made to appear less conventionally attractive in the film, and are those methods effective? What examples do we find of conventionally attractive people playing an "ugly" person in films and television? What do these castings say about beauty standards? In addition to offering a bit of amusement for students when Nela scurries away from her own reflection in the pond (1:48–2:20), the clip makes visible the character's lack of body confidence as described by Galdós.

Although it is cliché, I ask my students to consider how beauty is more than just skin-deep. Because they are missing parts of the original full text, I add a few parts that tell Marianela's story from different characters' points of view. Finally, I ask them to list the positive traits Marianela possesses, irrespective of her physical appearance. Students observe that Marianela has not had the opportunities, support, or nutrition that would have strengthened her beauty currency, but her sense of direction in the region of the mines, creative thinking, pleasant voice, helpful nature, and ability to survive trauma are all factors that make her an admirable young woman.

To further explore the theme of beauty beyond conventional physical standards, we move into Rosa Montero's short story "La gloria de los feos." This contemporary text serves as a counterpoint to Galdós's nineteenth-century perspective, allowing students to compare and contrast societal attitudes toward beauty across different time periods. Students read the story in class and then take part in a guided discussion. Key questions include the following: How does Montero's portrayal of Lalo and Lupe challenge conventional beauty standards? Comparing the narrator's initial description of the characters with the moment they fall in love, how does the language shift? What parallels and differences do you see between Marianela and the characters in "La gloria de los feos"?

We pay particular attention to the pivotal moment when Lalo and Lupe meet: "Fue un 11 de mayo y, aunque ustedes quizá no lo recuerden, cuando los ojos de Lalo y Lupe se encontraron tembló el mundo, los mares se agitaron, los cielos se llenaron de ardientes meteoros. Los feos y los tristes tienen también sus instantes gloriosos" ("It was May 11 and, although you may not remember, when Lalo and Lupe's eyes met, the world shook, the seas were agitated, the skies filled with burning meteors. The ugly and the sad also have their glorious moments"; Montero 114; my trans.). Students analyze this passage, discussing how Montero uses hyperbolic language to elevate what society might consider an unremarkable moment between two "ugly" people into something cosmically significant.

These comparative discussions often lead to insightful observations from students. For instance, one student drew an interesting parallel between the two works and contemporary pop culture. They observed that Marianela's situation was reminiscent of teen movies where the weird girl is a secret best friend to a misunderstood popular athletic guy, but Marianela doesn't end up getting the guy. In contrast, they noted that Lupe and Lalo in Montero's story find community and acceptance in each other. In this comparison and others, students connect these literary works to familiar cultural narratives, deepening their understanding of how societal attitudes toward beauty and acceptance are portrayed across different time periods and media.

To deepen engagement, I assign a creative writing exercise. Students write a short scene from Marianela's perspective, imagining her reaction to witnessing Lalo and Lupe's meeting. This activity encourages students to synthesize their understanding of both texts while practicing their Spanish writing skills. Finally, we have a class debate on the proposition "Conventional beauty standards are more fluid and inclusive in contemporary society than in Galdós's time." Students must use evidence from both texts to support their arguments.

Through these activities, students enhance their Spanish language skills and critically engage with evolving societal attitudes about beauty, love, and self-worth. This comparative approach helps students understand how literature reflects and challenges cultural norms across different historical periods. The first higher-stakes assignment in the "Pretty Privilege" module is a three-to-four-page rough draft of a paper including background information about the two authors studied and their sociocultural and literary contexts; evidence of the ways pretty privilege works in each text, gathered using close reading strategies; and at least one of the snippets of literary criticism we used during our discussions. Outside research is not required since the purpose is to practice communicating complex ideas in Spanish while meeting the module's learning outcomes. Having noted what students contribute during the discussions, I am looking for a deeper level of engagement when students articulate their ideas in writing.

To prepare students for this assignment, I dedicate a class session to developing strong thesis statements. Students come to class with a proposed thesis, and we workshop these as a group. We focus on ensuring each thesis is clear, arguable, and directly addresses the module's themes of pretty privilege and beauty standards. I also provide a structured outline template that guides students in organizing their ideas, ensuring they include all required elements. This preparatory work helps students approach the writing task more easily.

Once we have explored how our uniqueness makes us beautiful in unconventional ways, I ask students to rewrite Marianela's fate. In Marianela's voice, they often explain how she healed from heartbreak and learned to accept her physical appearance. Students can bring Marianela into the present or change her racial or cultural identity while preserving her essential characteristics as poor and conventionally unattractive. They write a Marianela without a Prince Charming, cosmetic surgery, or a lottery payout. The new, empowered Marianela accepts her unique physical appearance and values her creative thinking as an attractive quality. In Marianela's new voice, students write a story where she defines an alternative beauty paradigm that includes her. My students have enjoyed turning a tragic ending into a satisfying one that resonates with their own experiences and observations.

Students become curious when reading literature is an act of self-discovery. The tragic story of Marianela "la fea" makes sense for students in their own contexts. Despite changing beauty standards, gender norms, and social mobility, a nineteenth-century Spanish realist novel about a disenfranchised young woman means something to my predominantly first-generation college students. Moreover, comparing the novel to Montero's "La gloria de los feos" prompts them to imagine the possibility of a world where conventional beauty—often built on racist, ableist, and classist attitudes—ceases to define a person's worthiness of romantic love.

By juxtaposing Marianela and "La gloria de los feos" within the framework of pretty privilege, my pedagogical approach provides students with a unique opportunity to grapple with diverse notions of beauty, societal norms, and self-worth. Through the comparative analysis of texts spanning distinct time periods and participation in interactive activities, students not only enhance their Spanish language proficiency but also develop critical thinking skills regarding privilege and representation. This methodology empowers students to challenge ingrained biases, expand their descriptive vocabulary, and imagine more inclusive paradigms of beauty. Ultimately, by reimagining Marianela's destiny and engaging with contemporary perspectives, students acquire the ability to discern beauty in unconventional forms and comprehend the capacity of literature to both mirror and contest cultural norms. This approach moreover exemplifies how canonical texts retain their relevance and potency as instruments for examining contemporary social issues in the language classroom.

Orienting Bodies in *Electra*: Teaching Galdós through History and Embodiment

Laurie Lomask

Debuting in January 1901, Benito Pérez Galdós's play *Electra* caused an international stir that not even the author had expected. Indeed, Galdós confessed in a letter to José María de Pereda on 1 March, "Nunca sospeché que esta obra levantara tan gran polvareda, y el día anterior al ensayo general creía firmemente, me lo puede creer, que el drama produciría poco o ningún efecto. En fin, me equivoqué en aquella apreciación, y todavía no *he vuelto de mi apoteosis*" ("I never suspected that this work would cause such a commotion, and the day before the general rehearsal I firmly believed, you can believe me, that the drama would produce little or no effect. In brief, I was wrong in that assessment, and I still haven't *returned from my apotheosis*"; Pérez Galdós, *Correspondencia* 514).[1] Within a year, the play had run over one hundred times at the Teatro Español in Madrid, toured Spain's outer provinces and various cities in Argentina, sold some twenty thousand copies, and been translated into German, Dutch, Portuguese, and English; three years later, it was translated into French (Ortiz-Armengol 577). The play enthused and elated liberals, including younger artists who were in the audience on opening night, such as José Martínez Ruiz (also known as Azorín) and Pío Baroja. It also aroused reactions from conservative factions, who were already concerned about the nation's splintering commitment to religious traditionalism.

Although Galdós's liberal politics were no secret, it is too simplistic to characterize the play's overarching theme as a one-sided critique of the Catholic Church. Galdós was uncomfortable with the intertwining of religion and politics—even complaining of "una plaga intolerable de frailes, clérigos y jesuitas" ("an intolerable plague of friars, clergymen and Jesuits"; Pérez Galdós, *Correspondencia* 510)—and recognized his own struggles to embrace faith, yet he longed for a recovery of sincere religious sentiment in his life and in Spanish society (Valis, *Sacred Realism* 124). He described the chaos of public celebration and denunciation of *Electra* in a letter to the Peruvian writer Ricardo Palma more than eight months after the play's debut: "pero no hay ninguna sobre la cual se haya escrito tanto en tan corto tiempo. . . . Lo reunido hasta la fecha es un fárrago que asusta" ("but there is no [play] about which so much has been written in so little time. . . . What has been collected to date is a frightening jumble"; Pérez Galdós, *Correspondencia* 529). In addition to matters in the author's personal life that detracted from his typically prolific output, the uproar around *Electra* seems to have slowed his creative turbine: it would be fourteen months before his next literary publication and two years before his return to the theater (Ortiz-Armengol 579).

When teaching *Electra*, it is both vital and challenging to convey to students, at both the undergraduate and graduate level, the scandal that this play aroused in turn-of-the-century Spain. Participants in my classes easily identified the plot twists of Pantoja's attempt to end the romance between Electra and Máximo by alleging their fraternity, and they also felt great empathy for the young Electra and her deceased mother. What I found difficult to impress upon students, however, was the bold and groundbreaking quality of the work in the context of Spain at the turn of the century. The country was still coming to terms with the end of its status as an empire, torn between efforts to modernize and the desire to preserve its traditional religious and social foundations, simultaneously trying to keep pace with the rest of Europe and to respect the mores of its smaller villages and pueblos. Artists speaking to this social moment, like Galdós, took complex positions that cannot be adequately represented by labels like *liberal*, *conservative*, *Republican*, or *Carlist*. For these reasons, the most effective way to study *Electra*, I have found, has been through heavy use of primary resources in the forms of newspaper articles and the author's personal letters and through employing theater games and exercises with students in the classroom.

I teach *Electra* in an advanced seminar on nineteenth-century Spanish literature at a community college in a large urban center. The majority of the students in these classes are native Spanish speakers of Caribbean descent. Given the economic realities of many of our students, I have taken to using the free online text offered through *Project Gutenberg* (Pérez Galdós, *Electra* [American Book]). Although this version does not offer much textual commentary, it includes a Spanish-English glossary. Other print versions I have used are the 1981 edition by Editorial Hernando and the 1998 edition by Biblioteca Nueva, depending on availability through the university's library.

For classes teaching the text in translation, the play and a great deal of historical information are available in English; there is even a recorded reading published by Librivox and available through *Internet Archive*. For general historical background on the period, I have used Adrian Shubert's *A Social History of Modern Spain*, and my approaches to teaching theater are informed by Augusto Boal's *Theater of the Oppressed*. I do use several primary resources, however, for which there are no English translations. In this case, the instructor may choose to translate passages from the primary documents discussed below. The newspaper articles are all available for download through the *Hemeroteca Digital* (*Digital Periodical Archive*) of the Biblioteca Nacional de España, and even if not assigned as reading, are very much worth showing in class so students may observe the format and structure of the press at the turn of the twentieth century. The theatrical games and activities I have used to deepen students' understanding of the visceral impacts of the play work in any language and, in fact, highlight one of the benefits of using physical play and games in the classroom: they become a low-stakes equalizer of participation. There is no right or wrong, and the experience is as much personal as it is communal.

The discussion of *Electra* spans two weeks of class time. The first week supplements a more traditional close reading of the text with sociohistorical background information for context. I give them an excerpt from chapter 4, "Identities," of Schubert's *Social History*, "The Church, Religion and Belief" (145–68), that traces the relationship between Catholicism, the state, and the public from a variety of perspectives throughout the long nineteenth century. On the one hand, the church was unable to integrate with the modernization and social restructuring of the country, even ignoring the growth of the middle class (popular sermons tended to address only the rich and the poor [156]). On the other, it played a vital role in welfare and charity initiatives when Spain's economy took a downturn as the century ended (158). In applying historical knowledge to dramatic work, students also highlight social justice and the role of gender in the work. It is no accident that the play's victim is a young woman subjected to the supposed guidance of older men. Pantoja's actions are not merely the manipulations of a jealous, power-hungry entrepreneur but also symbolize the pressures that Spanish society imposed upon women, including limitations on their physical freedom. Electra manifests her free-spirited personality through movement and uncontrollable sensation and thus attracts and fascinates everyone in her coterie, including the malevolent Pantoja. She even resists the latter's moralizing by insisting on her right to be a woman in flesh and blood, full of both joys and defects: "Salimos otra vez con la tecla de que yo he de ser ángel . . . ? Soy muy terrestre, Don Salvador. Dios me hizo mujer, pues no me puso en el cielo, sino en la tierra" ("Are you playing again on the same key about my being an angel? . . . I am very worldly, Don Salvador. God made me a woman, since he put me on earth and not in Heaven"; Pérez Galdós, *Electra* [American Book] 112; *Electra* [Gorham] 105; act 4, scene 8). With great physicality of character, Electra is not just a reference to the ancient Greek plays by Sophocles, Euripides, or Aeschylus[2] but is also *electric* in her dynamism and fervent spirit.[3] Why her character would stir such emotions among all levels of Spanish society is difficult to explain outright. To this end, the primary resources and theater games become most useful in that they highlight both the aesthetic merits of the play and the social impact of its debut.

In the second week of working with the play, we transition to looking more closely at primary resources. I give students PDF copies of four Madrid newspaper articles that document the fervent enthusiasm and criticism with which the work was received. In the first, from page three of *El Día* on 30 January 1901, the date of the premiere, we read that Galdós's play was already expected to cause a sensation for evidencing the tension between "lo *hipócrita* y lo *moderno*," ("the *hypocritical* and the *modern*"; Círculos políticos)—a projection most likely based on what had been seen and commented upon in rehearsals during the preceding weeks. The next day, on the front page of *El Imparcial*, the famed Spanish theater critic José de Laserna notes that by the third act of the play, the audience could barely stay in their seats, applauding and screaming "mueras" ("death") to the power of the church and comparing the theater to a "club revolucionario" ("revolutionary party"). On the second page, there are descriptions of rowdy groups that took to the streets to cheer on the playwright and chant similar anticlerical slogans late into the night. Two later articles show the contrary opinions the play generated as it exhilarated audiences in the Teatro Español: the conservative publication *La Lectura Dominical*, which calls itself the "órgano del apostolado de la prensa" ("voice of the ministry of the press"), on 10 February 1901 claims the drama has little literary merit and is most impressive to an irreligious and irreverent public that will jump at any chance to criticize the church (Christián); meanwhile, the magazine *Nuestro Tiempo* connects the play to the highly contested Caso Ubao (Ubao case)[4] and the newly reinstated liberal government of Práxedes Mateo Sagasta (Canals). These articles represent a small sample of the press coverage of *Electra*, which, as noted above, received more discussion than any of Galdós's other works; an excellent assignment is to ask students to find their own articles on the *Hemeroteca Digital* and bring them to class for discussion.

Following this exercise, I ask students to go deeper by embodying aspects of the play through several physical games adapted from Rosa Luisa Márquez's pedagogical theater manual *A-Saltos*. For example, students play a kind of charades, where they act out a character from the play—including at least Electra, Eleuteria, Máximo, Pantoja, Don Urbano, Evarista, and the Marqués de Ronda—either in front of the whole class or, if the class is large, in groups. Another option is to do the same activity with key lines of dialogue that invite physical action, such as the following from early in the play:

> Electra: "Soy una gran artista para todo lo que no se parece a mí" ("I am a great artist for all that I have not experienced"; Pérez Galdós, *Electra* [American Book] 24; *Electra* [Gorham] 38; act 1, scene 7).
>
> Pantoja: "Este libertino incorregible . . . este veterano del vicio se atreve a poner su mirada venenosa en esta flor" ("That incorrigible libertine . . . that veteran of vices dares to cast his poisonous glance upon this flower; *Electra* [American Book] 33; *Electra* [Gorham] 46; act 1, scene 10).
>
> Máximo: "Electra, defiéndete" ("Electra, defend yourself"; *Electra* [American Book] 38; *Electra* [Gorham] 49; act 1, scene 13).
>
> Evarista: "Gozar, gozar, gozar: esto queréis y por esto vivís en continuo ajetreo . . ." ("Pleasure, pleasure, pleasure: that is what you want and for which you live in continual movement . . ."; *Electra* [American Book] 42; *Electra* [Gorham] 53; act 2, scene 1).

In another activity, students are split into groups of five wherein each member is assigned a character from the play. They must choose a few words (or a short phrase) plus a movement to associate with that character and then work in their groups to combine the individual pieces into one sequence. The groups then take turns performing their montage on repeat for a few minutes to the class, and we discuss the effects of each of their representations. Key questions to reflect upon are: Which representation was the most rhythmic? Which one was faster or slower? Which one was funnier or more somber, and why? The purpose of both these activities is to encapsulate an entire character from a play in a minuscule fragment and then portray the distilled idea of the character to the class. Students can also defend their characterization with examples from the text. This works to develop their sensitivity to the texture of dramatic literature.

These activities have several benefits for student engagement with and comprehension of the play. First, they help students remember that theater is not merely the script and notes we are reading; it is, first and foremost, a performance. Furthermore, to create an effective performance, the actors and director must make many decisions about body language, placement, and interaction among the characters, because even slight differences in movement and posture can drastically affect the meanings of every scene. Second, using theatrical exercises in class asks students to embody characters or significant moments from the play, using their own states of animus and emotion as a resource through which to engage and interpret. Thus students practice what Boal describes as a productive kind of empathy—dianoia, or "character's thought–spectator's thought" (102)[5]—which results in critical comprehension: "A good empathy does not prevent understanding and, on the contrary, needs understanding precisely in order to avoid the spectacle's turning into an emotional orgy and the spectator's purging of his social sin" (103). This practice helps many students deepen their analytical capabilities by utilizing the fervent emotions of the play in conjunction with critical reasoning. As Márquez explains, "El teatro traducía a lenguaje expresivo, las lecciones de historia, de ciencia y hasta de matemáticas" ("Theater translated history, science, and even math lessons into expressive language"; 10). When at the end of the unit on *Electra* I ask students to work in small groups to perform a scene of their choosing,[6] and to explain the rationale for their selection, I find that these preparatory exercises greatly improve the quality and depth of the execution. Students are able to bring to life not only their understanding of Galdós's dramatic work but also of the craft of theater in general.

An additional benefit of using embodiment exercises in the classroom, especially in the case of Galdós, is that it highlights the links between the literary realism traditionally associated with the author and his incorporation of more symbolic themes bordering on the supernatural.[7] There is also a connection to be made between realism in the novel and its application to theater in the early twentieth century. As Serge Salaün has shown, Spanish theater took on many of the artistic trappings of European symbolism and Spanish modernism (which Salaün equates as two vertices of the same aesthetic doctrine) at the turn of the century. However, Salaün posits symbolist theater as paradigmatically opposed to the tenets of realist theater and so dismisses Galdós as one of the stalwarts of the traditional style based on "rescoldos patéticos" ("pathetic embers") of "el lenguaje de la Razón, . . . la deducción analítica . . . la convención" ("the language of Reason, . . . analytic deduction . . . convention"; 296–97). However, Salaün is strict in his classification of dramatic styles, and while it would be a far cry to call Galdós a symbolist, there is a line of continuity. The common ground for both the late realist schools and the symbolist experiments with pure representation onstage is the emphasis on the body, sensations, and presence, which becomes the "medicación necesaria para todo tipo de mensaje" ("necessary medication for any kind of message"; Salaün 302). The immediacy of unfiltered expression became the foundation for new twentieth-century artistic movements, and direct physical sensation took priority. At the same time, the theater represented for writers like Galdós a concise embodiment of the meticulous detail and description of manners that fill the pages of their best-known fictional works. Studying Galdós's theater in this way shows that symbolist and modernist movements are not starkly opposed to the ideals of realism but rather can represent an extension of and homage to their realist predecessors who gave audiences such close, even microscopic, access to their subjects. To make this point to students is another reason one might opt to teach *Electra* instead of Galdós's better-known works, or at least in conjunction with one of his novels, to show the evolution of and exchange among artists of different aesthetic styles.

Artistically, *Electra* demonstrates both Galdós's practice of literary realism and his application of that aesthetic to theater. Lilian Furst's description of framing in realist literature—that is, an embedding of the fictional narrative in a coherent, self-contained world *(All Is True* 49)—creates a parallel between the narrator of a novel and the stage manager of a play, who is present and in control of the show and yet disappears in favor of the characters and principal action. A critical aspect of narratology is thus the "acceptance of pretense and performance" (Furst, *All Is True* 59) and an awareness of the reading audience that must agree to and complete the fictional illusion of the work (65). The narrator in Galdós is always performative and often playful with the reader, and his theatrical pieces show his mastery at creating a world that is both separate from and intimately connected to the lived reality of the audience.

Galdós's fiction exemplifies a "humanitarian predisposition" and a "sacred vision of the social" (Valis 138). However, the same can be said about his dramatic work. Political and religious allegiances, ultimately seen as small-scale power plays, give way to human connection and compassion. Although these themes resound in Galdós's novels, theatrical works lend themselves to elucidating empathy, an almost symbiotic identification with the characters on the stage, because of their direct contact with an audience. In the classroom, teaching *Electra* has greater potential to bring to life the themes of individual autonomy, familial responsibility, social expectation, and respect for personal liberty, bringing human bodies to the forefront amid different backdrops of historical circumstances.

NOTES

1. Translations are my own unless otherwise attributed.

2. When teaching this play, I make only brief comments about the ancient Greek origins of the protagonist's name and the later Freudian psychoanalytical complex. I have

found that students discover these references on their own, while the sociohistorical context and the public response to the drama are a source of investigation and discovery for them.

3. For an interesting comparison of the play to scientific innovation in electric currents, see Rueda.

4. See "Joven fugada" for the breaking news of the "young runaway." Galdós drafted *Electra* in the summer of 1900 (*Correspondencia* 505; Ortiz-Armengol 571).

5. I would extend, here, to "character's feeling–spectator's feeling," and perhaps even to "character's being–spectator's being."

6. Students are drawn to the scene of the apparition of the ghost of Eleuteria, probably for its thrilling dramatic effect, so it is a good idea to assign scenes to avoid repetition: I use 1.2, 2.1, 2.9, 3.1, 4.8, 4.10, and 5.8.

7. An interesting discussion could be had comparing *Electra* to Galdós's 1888 novel *Miau*, though I have never been able to teach both in one semester.

Meeting Galdós through Open Pedagogy

Juan Jesús Payán and Robin R. Miller

The year 2020 marked the centenary of Benito Pérez Galdós's death. This commemoration set in motion a wide array of celebratory events. In Madrid, the center stage of many of the writer's novels, the government declared it the "Year of Galdós." Unfortunately, the celebrations faced an unexpected setback with the outbreak of COVID-19. Seemingly overnight, many educational institutions around the world transitioned from in-person instruction to full remote learning. In the fall of 2020, at the City University of New York (CUNY), located in New York City, one of the epicenters of the global pandemic at the time, the need for creative solutions regarding course offerings became immediately pressing.

During this challenging period, we took the opportunity to explore open pedagogy and new multimodal paths for teaching Galdós by creating an open educational resource course on the digital publishing platform *Manifold*.[1] We called this project *Conociendo a Galdós* (*Meeting Galdós*). The title expressed our desire to make the author's work and legacy an immediate experience for our students, circumventing the distance of time by creating as personal an encounter as possible. In this essay, we discuss how using open pedagogy and social annotation enhanced student learning and reflect upon the experience of teaching Galdós on *Manifold* and the lessons we learned along the way.

Our course was originally designed as a seminar for our master's students in Spanish literature and education. Its pedagogy and technology can also be used with more advanced texts in a course for PhD students or with translations of the novels for courses taught in English. Additionally, its model could be offered to undergraduate students with native or near-native fluency in Spanish (including advanced heritage learners).[2] It is particularly suitable for modern Spanish literature courses, within the scope of realism or nineteenth-century literature in general. Our students were Spanish speakers with varying levels of competence in reading and writing (heritage and native speakers). None of them had prior exposure to Spanish geographical and historical references, so we made use of *Manifold*'s capacity to add multimedia resources to our project and used class presentations to provide the necessary background.

We chose three novels for the course: *Marianela*, *Tristana*, and *Misericordia*. Since our course design was part of CUNY's open educational resource and Zero Textbook Cost initiatives ("Open Educational Resources"), we made use of openly licensed versions of the texts from the *Textos.info* digital library.[3] We privileged novels of moderate length (roughly three hundred pages), led by strong female protagonists. In doing so, we aimed to represent different epochs of Galdós's production and interconnected themes, such as intersectional dimensions of discrimination (mainly based on gender and class), reflections on imagination and realism, the limitations of science's power to achieve social justice, and the author's ultimate belief in philanthropic altruism. Our students incorporated additional themes concerning ableism, aporophobia (i.e., "fear, or an attitude of rejection, towards impoverished people"; Cortina 21), the role of religion in modern societies, and the short- and long-term effects of orphanhood, especially for women.

The use of social annotation was central for student engagement throughout the course and replaced other common activities, such as pop quizzes and reaction papers. Although social annotation can also be done using tools such as *Hypothesis* and *Perusall*, we chose to create our course in *Manifold* because it offers the ability to use EPUBs, multimedia resources, and built-in social annotation features in a single course site. We created a private reading group on *Manifold* that enabled the students to annotate as a cohort in a safe and controlled environment, where their annotations were visible only to other members of the group. Students were asked to provide five meaningful annotations per session across different sections of their assigned readings. They could choose between two options: adding critical notes to the text or producing questions for the group to answer. We accepted short contributions (fifty to one hundred words) as long as these guidelines were followed. Critical notes could comment on possible allegorical meanings (colors, names, situations, etc.); elucidate implicit messages within the text; provide literary, artistic, or historical clues or establish meaningful intertextual associations; or reflect on passages students deemed strongly impactful or problematic. Questions could not be merely plot-oriented or descriptive but needed to be interpretative in character and not answerable with a simple *yes* or *no*. During the first two weeks of class, we modeled the type of questions that lead to analytical discussions.

As Remi Kalir insightfully reminds us, annotating is often entwined with the act of active reading: "when you read, you probably make your thinking visible . . . you're probably marking up a book, or you're probably taking notes in some kind of way." Kalir and Antero Garcia provide one of the most comprehensive definitions of the purposes of annotation: "Annotation is a form of self-expression, a way to document and curate new knowledge, and is a powerful means of civic engagement and political agency" (ch. 1). The authors' theoretical framework has been key in informing our project and this article.

Despite its importance, annotation is not often taught outside remedial education. Jennifer Gonzalez's overview analyzes the traditional framing of instruction in note-taking as a remedial practice at the college level, limited to helping "under-achieving students" (Robin et al. 81–85) or students with disabilities (Haydon et al. 226–31). Note-taking thus has not been conceived as a broader skill for all students in higher education, regardless of their background. Also, discussions in the field are noticeably characterized by binary views opposing low-tech education, with which note-taking is typically associated, to high-tech education (Gonzalez). Yet, as is widely acknowledged by scholars and expert readers alike, annotating skills are central to the task of abstracting or selecting relevant information, summarizing and retrieving data from a text, creating associative trails between different texts, and scaffolding ideas for later scholarly writing and research. Without annotation, abstract thinking can hardly take root (Bell and Cohn 12).

Through the practice of social annotation, reading and annotating a text as a group, students engage with each other and with their respective thinking processes, not just with the text itself. Social annotation is beneficial not only for individual knowledge building but also as a conduit for interpersonal exchange. It can mitigate the risk of isolation that threatens many remote teaching practices. Students also develop a stronger sense of community, a factor that is hard to cultivate through more traditional approaches of remote teaching. Social annotation bolsters continuous learning while also developing analytic and peer engagement skills. Students experience how scholarship is informed by the act of "entering [into] a conversation with other's views" (Graff et al. 4). Finally, as Jojo Karlin and colleagues point out, it is worth considering how the praxis of social annotation provides formal training in the type of interactions that dominate the digital public sphere (269).

Student annotations were due the night before each class meeting. When we reviewed them, we could see a heat map emerge as annotations clustered around certain areas or topics in the text. A heat map is a way to visualize data using colors: for example, red represents more data, and black, no data. Having access to this heat map provided us with insight into where students could be struggling before we met as a group. For instance, we received immediate feedback regarding passages whose difficulty we had not anticipated (such as the first chapters of *Misericordia*). Thus, social annotation allowed us to review our lesson plan prior to the session and make adjustments where needed. Conversely, social annotation also provided insight into passages whose importance our students were at risk of overlooking (such as Galdós's abundant homages to Cervantes through quixotic characters). Unannotated areas were as pedagogically insightful as the most annotated passages. Using student ideas as a starting point for discussions was extremely useful in helping us move away from an instructor-centered classroom to a more deliberately student-centered pedagogy. For example, early on, several students expressed a profound interest in disability studies theory (especially after discussing in class the plight of characters such as Tristana in the eponymous novel and the unhoused people attended by Benina in *Misericordia*). Knowing this allowed us to build our discussions around these interests. Thanks to social annotation, our course became a more inclusive space, where students knew their voices were heard and their role as knowledge creators was valued, because their ideas steered the direction of our class themes and discussions.

Social annotation also provided additional benefits. From a linguistic standpoint, the annotations provided a way to identify grammar and spelling challenges early in the course. Thus, we had time to address these aspects before our students were asked to write a longer research essay. Social annotation had a positive impact on class participation as well in that it provided a platform for those students who were uncomfortable speaking in class or needed more time to process discussions and articulate answers. By offering an alternative way to participate in discussions, we were able to balance student participation and counter the possibility that one or two students would dominate conversations. By following student engagement and replying to annotations during the week, we boosted students' confidence in their own analyses, encouraged further reflections, and energized their exchanges. These public interactions created a sense of cohesion, and students felt that they were part of a lively intellectual debate.

In addition to the novels, we included a wide array of multimedia resources that painted a more complete picture of the author and his works. They included biographical data; original drawings and manuscripts; epistolary exchanges with Concepción Ruth Morell and Emilia Pardo Bazán; historical references; audiobooks; theater and film adaptations of *Marianela*, *Tristana*, and *Misericordia*; online materials from the "Year of Galdós" in Madrid; virtual visits to the family house and museum in Las Palmas; graphic novel tributes (Pulido, *Nela*; El Torres); Galdós-focused open academic journals, and repositories of the writer's complete works for further reading. By adding multimedia resources, we were able to expand the course beyond the act of reading, annotating, and discussing literary texts; we introduced the students to the complex individual that Galdós was and shed light on his immense cultural interdisciplinary impact. We used and referenced these resources in class, which made it possible for our students to participate in the commemorations of the Year of Galdós.

Participation included the optional open publication of students' final essays on *Manifold* (i.e., making their work available outside the class group). Giving students the opportunity to be creators of knowledge and to share their work with others on a professional platform was another exciting way our course embraced open pedagogy. Our students were invited to immerse themselves in the intense process of writing and revision that defines scholarship. This project not only provided them with an intrinsic motivation for their work but also made them accountable. If they wanted to publish their essays for general consumption, they had to work hard. The students submitted individual academic essays on topics they had chosen with guidance. The last weeks of the class included peer review on their abstracts, selected sources, and citations and the creation of outlines and first drafts. After receiving individual feedback, students were invited to submit a final version for the online publication. Their work is publicly available under the title *Vigencias de don Benito* (*The Current Relevance of Don Benito*; cuny.manifoldapp.org/read/vigencias-de-don-benito).

While our course model was very successful in terms of social engagement and was extremely well received by the students, there are some aspects that prospective instructors need to consider before applying it to their own courses. First, consider the ratio between class size and the length of primary texts. The praxis of social annotation works best, in our opinion, when the class is relatively small (between ten and fifteen students) and the readings covered per session are thirty to sixty pages long. When those two conditions are met, it is possible to assign portions of the text to individual students for commentary. In our seminar of fifteen students, keeping up with annotations was never overwhelming for the instructor or for the students, since annotations were evenly distributed among diverse assigned passages. Multiple reading groups may work better for a larger class. In undergraduate courses, instructors may wish to use reading prompts or questions to which their students should reply; for our graduate seminar, however, we were not very prescriptive with respect to the content of annotations. Social annotation is an easy and flexible way for instructors to create engagement with a text, better understand the interests and needs of their students, and create an accessible space where students feel their voices are heard and their knowledge is valued.

Embracing open pedagogy provided a new and innovative way for students to engage not only with the texts that Galdós wrote but also with the world in which he wrote them. Using multimedia resources, such as an interactive map or 3-D virtual visits, gave students the opportunity to explore the places Galdós wrote about and called home. For this course, the instructor chose these secondary resources, but inviting students to find and add resources to the project is also a great option, especially for those students who wish to become educators themselves.

In reflecting upon the final open student publication, we realize that even though the prospect of openly publishing their work generated initial excitement, as the semester progressed and their workloads increased, students' excitement waned. Many students submitted their final essays, but after grades were released and final feedback given, others did not make final edits, and therefore their essays were not included in the collection. While this type of open student project is rewarding, the time frames for a project like this need to be recalibrated so that more students can provide a final version before the semester ends.

Finally, although *Conociendo a Galdós* was born in the context of remote learning, an open pedagogy project such as this is not limited to online instruction and is equally useful for in-person instruction. We were thrilled with the reception of this project and to have the opportunity to bring Galdós and his work to our students on *Manifold*. Thanks to social annotation and multimedia resources, our students were able to engage with the texts, the author, and one another in exciting new ways. As instructors, it is common practice to silo our courses on learning management systems, such as *Canvas*, *Brightspace*, or *Blackboard*, restricting texts and resources to just the students enrolled in the course. By embracing open educational resources and open pedagogy we can open our courses to students and instructors everywhere.

NOTES

1. Open pedagogy is working collaboratively with students as creators of knowledge, not just consumers. Open educational resources are teaching, learning, and research resources that are free of cost and access barriers and carry legal permission for open

use. Generally, this permission is granted by an open license that allows anyone to freely consult, adapt and share the resource ("Open Education"). *Manifold* is a digital publishing platform developed by the University of Minnesota Press; the Graduate Center, City University of New York; and Cast-Iron Coding. Originally designed for academic publishers, it is increasingly being used by colleges and universities as a platform for publishing open educational resources.

2. The proficiency of our students ranged from "advanced mid" to "superior." None of them were within the parameters of the "distinguished" level (see *ACTFL* 4–5). Therefore, this model can be applied not only at the master's level but also for undergraduate groups with a high level of proficiency.

3. We would like to thank Edu Robsy for the EPUBs.

Tweeting *Tristana*: Bringing the Literature Classroom Online through Microblogging

Stacy L. Davis

If Benito Pérez Galdós were alive today, he would marvel at the advances of our digital society. As an author keenly aware of the technological and societal innovations of his day and the ways these modernizations enhanced communication, Galdós would be amazed at the ease and speed of global connections in the digital era. This essay proposes using social media in the form of microblogging to enrich students' appreciation of the content and form of Galdós's novels. At the same time, the use of social media can constitute a meta-exercise through which students reflect on how advances in the technologies of Galdós's time compare to those of their own. Since today's students are highly skilled at navigating social media, using *Facebook*, *Instagram*, and *Twitter* (rebranded in 2023 as *X*) on a daily basis, this essay provides examples of activities that incorporate *X* before, during, and after reading *Tristana* to encourage learners to connect with the novel. Interaction on this platform results in deeper meaning-making, increased engagement and motivation, and richer communication, both in and out of the classroom.

Statistics on the overwhelming use of social media support implementing microblogging in the design or redesign of course activities. Reporting on his own age group in 2023, Eliot Zedd writes, "College-aged students, generally between the ages of 18–22, are the first generation to be raised in a social-media dominated world." An estimated seventy-three percent of prospective and first-year students spend two or more hours daily on social media, and twenty-six percent spend over five hours ("Social Brand University"). Cambridge International Education reports that over half the world's population averages two hours and twenty minutes a day on social media, suggesting that incorporating these widely used platforms into educational settings may enhance learning and knowledge sharing, improve collaboration and communication, boost creativity and self-expression, and develop digital and media literacy skills ("Ten Unbelievable Benefits"). Learners have attested to preferring brief online informational formats over print and longer-form digital media; for example, in 2016, less than twenty percent of high school seniors reported reading a book or magazine as a daily activity, whereas more than eighty percent used social media daily. The authors declare, "There's no lack of intelligence among young people, but they do have less experience focusing for longer periods of time and reading long-form text" (Twenge et al.). Further, according to a recent survey, seventy-five percent of the public prefers to read online content that does not exceed a thousand words (Teicher). Given statistics supporting a media-rich learning environment, microblogging can provide an innovative approach to teaching literature.

Microblogging refers to the act of creating concise posts for quick online interactions. Applications like *X* allow users to deliver multimedia content that incorporates a limited amount of text. With 353.9 million active users tweeting 500 million times a day (5,787 tweets per second), the platform opens virtual lines of communication (Lin). The benefits of "participatory learning through social media" support *X* as the "networking platform most amenable to ongoing, public dialogue" on account of its brevity—posts must be under 280 characters—and ease of use as learners take part in the "participatory culture" of social media (Carpenter and Krutka 415). Engaging students through familiar media platforms enhances their ability to interpret texts by connecting the material to their daily lives, making reading more personalized and reducing reluctance to read. Integrating posts students make outside class that contain memes and links to materials related to the works they study can spur livelier in-class discussions and strengthen insights into novels like *Tristana*. Such peer-to-peer interactions allow students to see that nineteenth-century literature is not outdated or irrelevant to their lives but rather offers meaningful insights and connections to their experiences today. Much like Galdós and his readers in the nineteenth century, today's learners are navigating an increasingly interconnected world. From the invention of trains and streetcars that joined members of different social classes in the author's time, today's digital applications have likewise created an interconnected community in which individuals cross borders of time and space. Students regularly share their lives online; thus, uploading reactions to character descriptions and plot events allows them to collaboratively construct meaning while envisioning historical and cultural differences and forge connections between the nineteenth century and today.

Using *X* in the classroom can enhance student engagement with *Tristana* by enabling students to break the novel into manageable sections, fostering discussion around its critical themes and diverse narrative styles. *Tristana* is a short, easy-to-read work. Given that the novel is under two hundred pages, it lends itself well to undergraduate courses like Introduction to Literary Analysis or Survey of Spanish Literature as well as advanced topics-based senior or graduate seminars organized around critical issues in Hispanism. The text employs the preterit and the imperfect alongside detailed character descriptions in the present tense that are easily understandable by intermediate and advanced language learners. The compelling plot explores the power structures that underlie the relationships of its three main characters; its focus on Tristana's desires to transcend the constraints imposed on women in nineteenth-century Spain posit topics like idealistic passion, innocence, resistance, and rebellion, with which students can identify. The novel's mix of omniscient narration, dialogue, and letters offers a variety of written formats with which students can interact as they learn to appreciate the complexity of nineteenth-century literature. Don Lope's sexual exploits can be linked to prior readings about Don Juan to support discussion of models of masculinity as well as masculinities in transition (Zaviezo).[1] Students can similarly be prompted to consider the era's prominent models of femininity, such as the *ángel de hogar* ("angel of the house"; Aldaraca, "*Ángel*" and Ángel), issues of love and matrimony (Moreno), and the heroine's struggle for autonomy (Tsuchiya, "Struggle"), as they consider the novel alongside scholarly articles. The novel invites comparisons with Luis Buñuel's movie adaptation and pairs nicely with criticism that addresses fetishism and sexual difference (Labanyi, "Fetishism"), subjugation and rebellion (Kirtland Grech), and notions of agency (Otero Luque) in both works.

Guidelines for Using X in the Classroom

Short-form media communications are more compelling than traditional written assignments or LMS discussion boards because the social media format is familiar to learners, making it easy for them to participate more frequently. In response to teacher-directed comprehension and analysis questions, students can post answers on *X*, quickly reacting to readings in short bursts of conversation. Instructors must first create a unit hashtag, such as #TristanaFans, so that students can comment in a closed forum. Next, clear expectations must be set regarding the types of posts instructors want, delineating the rules of proper netiquette with examples and stressing how an academic usage of social media differs from a private one. Afterward, instructors will need to indicate how often students should post, perhaps providing a list of nineteenth-century scholars and journals with which they can engage. Reminding students always to use the class hashtag, instructors should discuss the mechanics of creating an academic account with an emphasis on protecting privacy settings.

Pre-Reading Activities

After addressing these initial guidelines, educators can employ various pre-reading activities to activate prior knowledge and aid learners in understanding new material. One effective tool is a three-column graphic organizer that students complete during class time and before beginning to post. Taking nineteenth-century Spain as their subject, students label the columns *K* ("what I *know*"), *W* ("what I *want* to know more about"), and *L* ("what I have *learned* so far"). The *L* column is particularly useful when *Tristana* concludes a unit where students have already encountered other period texts, and revisiting this column after completing the novel can serve as a summative assessment. To complement the organizer, instructors can facilitate an in-class exploration of nineteenth-century artwork from the Museo Nacional del Prado's website: students can peruse the interactive video of the Sala del siglo XIX and subsequently search the XIX collection to explore portraits and landscapes by artists like Joaquín Sorolla and Eduardo Rosales Gallinas. As students report on their findings, instructors should project the visuals under discussion on the screen, soliciting opinions and sharing what students glean about the era from such paintings. (As an extension activity outside of class, learners can upload similar images on

X and, assuming the role of art critics, describe what their chosen images convey about the time period.) This use of visuals promotes oral communication as students infer historical concerns and are exposed to different aesthetic movements. Collectively, such activities reinforce vocabulary, build cultural background knowledge, and address potential gaps in knowledge before students delve into the novel. Given that *Tristana* meditates on the relationship between love and art through Horacio's and Tristana's characters, students can later revisit this assignment to reflect on the characters' abandonment of their creative endeavors, speculating on the importance of this plot development.

In addition to illustrating the mechanics of searching for tweets and using online tools to create posts that express the novel's material visually, instructors should also model how to perform keyword searches on *X*, using #Galdos175 to demonstrate how to find groups discussing Galdós's fiction on the platform. For example, searching "@literlandweb1" and "Tristana" yields an engaging post to project on the classroom screen; the handle @literlandweb1 often quotes Galdosian novels, and this search yields a direct quotation from chapter 17 about Tristana's desires to be independent: "Quiero ser algo en el mundo, cultivar un arte, vivir de mí misma. ¿Será verdad, Dios mío, que pretendo un imposible?" ("I want to be something in the world, cultivate an art, make a living off of myself. Is it true, my God, that I am trying to achieve the impossible?"; Galdós, *Tristana* [Cátedra] 206; *Tristana* [New York Review Books] 95; see also Literland). This post piques students' interest in the novel's theme of autonomy, enticing learners to read further because they may identify with a desire to rebel against social conventions. Likewise, learners can return to the letter to Horacio in which Tristana declares, "Aspiro a no depender de nadie, ni del hombre que adoro. No quiero ser su manceba" ("I aspire not to depend on anyone, not even the man I adore. I want to be married to myself"; *Tristana* [Cátedra] 206; *Tristana* [New York Review Books] 95) and discuss why the statement was revolutionary when the novel was written. Considering these and other passages from the text, students can expound, either in class discussion or in writing, on why the protagonist can be considered an early feminist.

As students read, instructors should skim the class *X* stream as a part of their lesson preparations, grading students' posts if desired. Online discussions allow learners to participate in more original ways, resulting in much livelier exchanges in and out of the classroom. Instructors should choose key passages for students to comment on, prompting learners to respond to specific passages before tweeting other, related excerpts. These assignments can replace reading quizzes and short reaction papers, allowing instructors to provide quick formative feedback on reading comprehension. For instance, *Tristana* opens with a lengthy description of Madrid that students can immediately engage with:

> En el populoso barrio de Chamberí, más cerca del Depósito de Aguas que de Cuatro Caminos, vivía, no ha muchos años, un hidalgo de buena estampa y nombre peregrino, no aposentado en casa solariega . . . sino en

> plebeyo cuarto de alquiler de los baratitos, con ruidoso vecindario de taberna, merendero, cabrería y estrecho patio interior de habitaciones numeradas. (*Tristana* [Cátedra] 119)
>
> In the populous quarter of Chamberí, toward the water tower end rather than Cuatro Caminos, there lived, not so many years ago, an agreeable-looking gentleman with a most unusual name, and he lived not in an ancestral mansion . . . but in a cheap, plebeian rented room, with, as noisy neighbors, a tavern, a café, a shop selling milk fresh from the goat, and a narrow inner courtyard with numbered rooms.
> (*Tristana* [New York Review Books] 1)

This quotation orients students to the novel's setting; using *Google Maps* or *Google Earth*, they can search images of Madrid for houses or neighborhoods similar to Galdós's description to enrich their visualizations of late-nineteenth-century Madrid—especially helpful for students who have never visited Spain.

Tweeting for Active Reading

While reading, students can create and tweet summaries of character descriptions in the form of memes, as if they were the narrator gossiping about protagonists. This creative exercise compels learners to pay careful attention to the text, encouraging them to capture the nuances of character portrayal in a succinct and witty manner. By blending humor with analysis, students engage with the text on a deeper level, reflecting on the intersection of characters' personal and public lives, both in the context of the novel and in modern social media. In memes, students can pair lines from the text with images found online. For example, tweeting images related to Don Lope's slippers or Tristana's amputated leg, along with short passages, elicits responses that students can further develop in extension assignments. Making memes forces students to create a tangible product demonstrating reading comprehension; students make personal connections as they develop empathy for a particular character. Memes can capture important themes; for example, possession is crucial to the novel, whose narrator compares Tristana several times to inanimate objects: "linda muñequita de papel" ("that pretty little paper doll"; *Tristana* [Cátedra] 124; *Tristana* [New York Review Books] 8). These types of posts allow students to combine pictures and passages from the novel to respond to specific issues of their choosing, make predictions of what is to come in the plot, and practice succinct writing in the target language given *X*'s character limit.

Tweeting images forces learners to synthesize their reading in an easily demonstrable format. Students can likewise post definitions of key terms, link to biographical information about Galdós, share facts about nineteenth-century Spain, and include a wide array of related multimedia resources. They can add critical interpretations about particular episodes, point out overlooked passages from class discussions, and interpret the meanings of symbols used in the novel.

Learners can submit questions for their peers to answer and, in their reflections about noteworthy or hard-to-understand excerpts, answer one another before the instructor does. As students ask questions about plot and character, these conversations will clarify problematic concepts. If instructors review tweets before class, they can adjust lesson plans accordingly to tailor discussions to learners' interests and identify important grammar and vocabulary issues that must be addressed.

As students read, they can post inspirational quotations from the novel to spark in-class discussions, such as the powerful passage describing Tristana's feelings as she endures Don Lope's advances—"se despertó en ella un anhelo de independencia" ("there awoke in her a desire for independence"; *Tristana* [Cátedra] 124; *Tristana* [New York Review Books] 8). This line can serve as a catalyst for conversation, inviting students to examine themes of autonomy and resistance. Learners may identify with the twenty-one-year-old heroine, who desires to be her own person and break free of societal restraints. Instructors can measure reading comprehension rapidly by asking students to match affirmations and utterances with the characters who make them. In addition, students can upload a short chapter summary each week, mimicking publishing *por entregas* ("in installments"), allowing the instructor to discuss publishing practices in Galdós's time. As learners imitate the idea, rather than passively learning about it, they can also rewrite chapter endings and tweet diary entries from Tristana's or Don Lope's perspectives. This ongoing format mirrors the novel's original form as students produce short posts that focus on key vocabulary and plot elements, practicing narrative analysis while also demonstrating a cultural understanding of nineteenth-century publishing practices. Students may also post an imaginary interview with a character or tweet as if they were this persona in order to practice grammatical and lexical structures in a meaningful context, creatively and personally engaging with the novel's material.

Post-Reading Activities

Post-reading activities consolidate students' learning, confirm their understanding, and move learners from content to analysis, synthesis, and creation. For example, students can read the blog post "Galdós y la a pierna de Tristana" ("Galdós and Tristana's Leg") and tweet questions to the author, David Torres, in Spain. Writing comments to a Spaniard knowledgeable about the topic consolidates students' understanding of the material and allows them to express their opinions in the target language. To forge interdisciplinary connections, students can write a cinquain (a stanza of five lines that conveys a strong emotion or image) or create a comic strip inspired by themes they find relevant. Instructors can post a final open-ended question to be developed in a longer written essay or an in-class presentation. For example, Tristana laments the "lazo de matrimonio" ("ties of matrimony"; Galdós, *Tristana* [Cátedra] 231; *Tristana* [New York Review Books] 122) despite agreeing to marry Don Lope; students can post brief reflections or questions about this tension, which they can later expand into opinion-based essays. Final tweets can completely rewrite the novel's ending—a creative extension activity in which learners assume an authorial role to reenvision Tristana's journey as one of positive self-fulfillment if they choose. Posting an online teaser, students can turn their submissions into a more extensive essay that addresses whether Don Lope and Tristana, finally joined in matrimony, are happy, taking into account the narrator's final "tal vez" ("perhaps"; *Tristana* [Cátedra] 272; *Tristana* [New York Review Books] 169). Such wrap-up activities enable learners to express their opinions, using evidence from the text to support their claims, thus practicing an important skill in literary criticism.

In conclusion, *X* leverages students' love of microblogging to examine the themes, styles, and tone of *Tristana*. Virtual dialogue makes assignments more personalized; in turn, students gain greater insight into the reading, boosting confidence in their ability for textual analysis. *X* can create a space for shy learners uncomfortable speaking in class or needing more time to articulate answers. These benefits promote a more profound engagement with the text, as the social-media-style interaction makes Galdós's novel germane and accessible to learners' daily lives. As instructors take advantage of the enhanced engagement, students take an active, hands-on approach to their reading. If our goal as instructors is to contextualize literature and encourage learners to see the relevance of nineteenth-century literary works, then microblogging is one way to enrich their enjoyment of wonderful works like *Tristana*.

NOTE

1. For more on teaching Don Lope as a donjuanesque character, see Cope in this volume.

NOTES ON CONTRIBUTORS

Luis Álvarez-Castro is professor of Spanish and chair of the Department of Spanish and Portuguese Studies at the University of Florida. He is the author of *Los espejos del yo: Existencialismo y metaficción en la narrativa de Unamuno* (2015), *La palabra y el ser en la teoría literaria de Unamuno* (2005), and *El universo femenino de Ángel Ganivet* (1996) and the editor of *Approaches to Teaching the Works of Miguel de Unamuno* (2020). He has published annotated editions of Ángel Ganivet's *Teatro y poesía*, Luis Bonafoux's *El avispero*, Eugenio Antonio Flores's *Trata de blancas*, and Eduardo López Bago's *Carne importada* and is coeditor of the journal *Decimonónica* and associate editor of the journals *Siglo Diecinueve* and *Hispania*.

Lennie Amores directs the Center of Excellence in Teaching and Learning and serves as an adjunct faculty member in languages and literature at Lincoln University, a historically Black institution. Focusing on undergraduate education, she curates and creates language learning experiences that foster students' critical engagement with Spanish and global Hispanophone cultural products and practices.

Julia Haeyoon Chang is associate professor in the Department of Romance Studies at Cornell University, where she is also affiliated with the Feminist, Gender, and Sexuality Studies Program and the Southeast Asia Program. Her areas of research and teaching include modern and contemporary Iberian literature and culture, race and empire, feminist and queer theory, disability studies, and game studies. Chang is the author of *Blood Novels: Gender, Caste, and Race in Spanish Realism* (2022).

Brian Cope is associate professor and Raymond and Carolyn Dix Chair of Spanish at the College of Wooster. His research areas include philosophy and literature, the modern Spanish novel, and contemporary Spanish film. He is currently completing a book on the role of philosophical skepticism in Miguel de Unamuno's critical and philosophical outlook and the sophisticated constructs of skepticism that appear in Unamuno's major novels. His articles have appeared in *Hispanic Review*, *Revista de Estudios Hispánicos*, and *Anales de la Literatura Española Contemporánea*.

Elena Cueto Asín is professor of Hispanic studies at Bowdoin College. Her research and teaching focus on contemporary literature, especially theater, film, and television, with an emphasis on the representation of history and cultural heritage in genres that combine text and visual media. She is the author of forty articles and of the books *Autos para siluetas de Valle-Inclán* (2005), *Reconciliaciones en escena: El teatro de la Guerra Civil* (2008), and *Guernica, en la escena, la página y la pantalla* (2017). She is also coeditor of the volumes *Historias de la pequeña pantalla: Representaciones históricas en la televisión de la España democrática* (2009) and *The Graphic Past: Comic and History in Twenty First Century Spain* (2023).

Rhian Davies is senior lecturer (associate professor) in Hispanic studies at the University of Sheffield. Her research interests include nineteenth-century Spanish literature and culture, the role of the press during the *fin de siglo* and contemporary Canarian literature and culture. Her publications include a monograph and articles on the cultural review *La España Moderna* (1889–1914), an electronic edition of Benito Pérez Galdós's *Torquemada en la hoguera*, and articles and chapters on the *Torquemada* novels, *Doña Perfecta*, and Galdós's work as a journalist.

Stacy L. Davis teaches all levels of Spanish language and literature at Truman State University. She also serves as the director of second language instruction for Truman's master's program in education, teaching the graduate-level methods course for preservice teachers. Her research focuses on late-nineteenth- and early-twentieth-century literature and, in particular, the figure of the *indiano* as an intersection of gender and empire in the works of Benito Pérez Galdós and Emilia Pardo Bazán. She has published in *Decimonónica* and *Anales Galdosianos* and is currently working on an anthology of Pardo Bazán's *indiano* short stories.

Liana Ewald is senior lecturer in global languages at the Massachusetts Institute of Technology and was formerly associate professor in the Department of Spanish and Portuguese at San Diego State University. She has dedicated much of her career to the study of modern Spanish literature and culture. More recently, her pedagogical interests have centered on second language studies, with a particular interest in the integration of content and language at all levels of the curriculum. She has published her research in journals such as *Second Language Research and Practice*, *Hispanic Review*, *Revista de Estudios Hispánicos*, *Bulletin of Spanish Studies*, *Revista Canadiense de Estudios Hispánicos*, and *Bulletin of Hispanic Studies*.

David R. George, Jr., is senior lecturer in the Department of Hispanic Studies, and affiliated faculty in the European studies and Asian studies programs, at Bates College. He has published more than thirty articles and book chapters on a variety of aspects of nineteenth-, twentieth-, and twenty-first-century Iberian literature, film, and television. He is coeditor of the volumes *Historias de la pequeña pantalla: Representaciones históricas en la televisión de la España democrática* (2009) and *Televising Restoration Spain: History and Fiction in Twenty-First Century Costume Dramas* (2018). He is also the author of annotated editions of Leopoldo Alas's *Doña Berta* (2008) and Benito Pérez Galdós's *Tormento* (2012).

Laurie Lomask is associate professor of Spanish and Portuguese at Borough of Manhattan Community College, City University of New York. She coedited *Correspondencia* (2016), a collection of the personal letters of Benito Pérez Galdós, and has published on walking and landscape in Galdós and other Spanish authors. She has also studied theater and movement arts and investigates the expression of the body in Latin American literature.

Collin McKinney is professor of Spanish at Bucknell University. He is the author of *Mapping the Social Body: Urbanisation, the Gaze, and the Novels of Galdós* (2010) and coeditor of *Spanish Graphic Narratives: Recent Developments in Sequential Art* (2020) and has published articles and chapters on various topics related to gender and Spanish culture.

Gabrielle Miller is associate professor of Spanish at Baylor University, where she has taught a variety of courses, from introductory language classes to graduate seminars. With expertise in Iberian literature and culture from the eighteenth century to the present, she specializes in nineteenth-century Spanish realism, age studies, feminist and gender studies, and disability studies. She has published numerous articles in journals such as *Revista de Estudios Hispánicos, Revista Canadiense de Estudios Hispánicos*, and *Hispanic Review*. She is also associate editor for *Anales Galdosianos*. At present, she is finishing her first monograph, entitled "Aging into Agency: Spinsterhood in Nineteenth-Century Spain."

Robin R. Miller is an open educational technology specialist at the Graduate Center, City University of New York (CUNY). She is currently a member of the Graduate Center's digital initiatives team, where she provides workshops, training, and project support for the digital publishing platform *Manifold* to the twenty-five-campus CUNY community. She holds degrees in Arabic and Islamic studies from the University of California, Los Angeles, and in library and information science, with a specialization in digital humanities, from the Pratt Institute. She is a former open educational resources librarian.

Sara Muñoz-Muriana is associate professor of Spanish at Dartmouth College, where she teaches and specializes in eighteenth- and nineteenth-century Spanish literature and cultures. Her research interests include urban and gender studies, the role of affects in cultural works, modernity and its connections with peripheral identities, and the relationship between illness, society, and literature. She is the author of *Andando se hace el camino: Calle y subjetividades marginales en la España del XIX* (2017) and coeditor of *Freakish Encounters* (2018). She is associate editor of the journal *Anales Galdosianos*, and her current book research is about the role of disease, pain, and healing in Spanish cultural modernity.

Juan Jesús Payán is associate professor in the Department of Language and Literatures at Lehman College, City University of New York. He has specialized in twentieth-century Latin American poetry and, more recently, in nineteenth-century literature and Spanish fantastic aesthetics. He is the author of more than twenty articles in academic journals and four books: *Entre las dos orillas: Lírica Hispánica en RevistAtlántica de Poesía* (2005), *Vida y obra del músico gaditano Antonio Escobar Perera* (2006), *Cadencia rota* (2022), and *Los conjuros del asombro: Expresión fantástica e identidad nacional en la España del XIX* (2022).

Erika Rodriguez is assistant professor of Spanish at San Diego State University. Their current book project, "Disabling Progress: Degeneration, Eugenics, and Futurity in Modern Spain," scrutinizes the connective tissue between visions of progress in degeneration theories and early eugenics and examines how Spanish authors challenged the social values that cast abject bodies as threats to the national future. Another book in progress examines representations of labor movements in Catalan, Cuban, and Filipino literature. Rodriguez's work on critical disability studies and Iberian culture studies has appeared in *Disability Studies Quarterly*, the *Revista Canadiense de Estudios Hispánicos*, and the *Hispanic Research Journal*.

Erika M. Sutherland is professor of Spanish and director of the Spanish program at Muhlenberg College. Coedited with Elizabeth Smith Rousselle, her *(Con)textos femeninos: Una antología de escritoras españolas* (2019) is a critical anthology of Spain's women writers, both well-known and unjustly forgotten. Her research in contemporary Spanish narrative focuses primarily on the representation of disease, health, and the female body in both literary and medical texts. Her essay in *Approaches to Teaching the Writings of Emilia Pardo Bazán* (2017) outlines this pedagogy, and other articles explore different aspects of medical knowledge in nineteenth-century literature. Sutherland's current research explores narratives of women's medical examinations and women's representation of hunger before and after the Spanish Civil War.

Wan Sonya Tang is associate professor of Hispanic studies and director of Asian American Studies at Boston College, where she teaches on a variety of topics relating to modern and contemporary Spanish literature and culture. She is currently the treasurer of the Asociación Internacional de Galdosistas, having previously served as an executive board member. She is coeditor of *Televising Restoration Spain: History and Fiction in Twenty-First-Century Costume Dramas* (2018) and the author of *Specters, Monsters, and the Damned: Fantastic Threats to the Social Order in Nineteenth-Century Spanish Fiction* (2024).

Margot Versteeg is professor of Spanish at the University of Kansas. A native of the Netherlands, she has published numerous articles and book chapters on nineteenth- and early-twentieth-century literature and culture. She is the author of *De fusiladores y morcilleros: El discurso cómico del género chico* (2000), *Jornaleros de la pluma* (2011), and *Propuestas para (re)construir una nación: El teatro de Emilia Pardo Bazán* (2019). Versteeg coedited, with Susan Walter, *Approaches to Teaching the Writings of Emilia Pardo Bazán* (2017) and, with Mary Coffey, *Imagined Truths: Realism in Modern Spanish Literature and Culture* (2019). She is currently working on a book on female performers in turn-of-the-century Spain.

Linda M. Willem is the Betty Blades Lofton Distinguished Professor of Spanish at Butler University and past president of the Asociación Internacional de Galdosistas. She is on the advisory board of *Anales Galdosianos* and has been named a "Galdosiana de Honor" by the Casa-Museo Pérez Galdós. Among her book-length publications are *Adapting Spanish Classics for the New Millennium: The Nineteenth-Century Novel Remediated* (2022) and *Galdós's Segunda Manera* (1998) as well as edited volumes on Galdós, Emilia Pardo Bazán, and the filmmaker Carlos Saura. She has published over forty articles on Spanish literature, film, and television, and has presented papers both nationally and internationally.

SURVEY RESPONDENTS

Luis Álvarez-Castro, *University of Florida*
Lennie Amores, *Lincoln University*
Frieda Blackwell, *Baylor University*
Joanne Britland, *University of Florida*
Julia Haeyoon Chang, *Cornell University*
Brian Cope, *College of Wooster*
Elena Cueto Asín, *Bowdoin College*
Rhian Davies, *University of Sheffield*
Stacy L. Davis, *Truman State University*
Megan Echevarria, *University of Rhode Island*
Hazel Gold, *Emory University*
Ignacio Javier López, *University of Pennsylvania*
Mark Mascia, *Sacred Heart University*
Ana Mateos, *Ludwig-Maximilians-Universität München*
Gabrielle Miller, *Baylor University*
Francesc Morales, *The Citadel*
Mario Ortiz-Robles, *University of Wisconsin, Madison*
Juan Jesús Payán, *Lehman College*
Susan Polansky, *Carnegie Mellon University*
Anton Pujol, *University of North Carolina, Charlotte*
Erika Rodriguez, *San Diego State University*
Sarah Sierra, *Virginia Tech University*
Erika M. Sutherland, *Muhlenberg College*
Margot Versteeg, *University of Kansas*
Linda M. Willem, *Butler University*

WORKS CITED

Abel, Jessica, and Matt Madden. *Drawing Words and Writing Pictures: Making Comics: Manga, Graphic Novels, and Beyond.* Roaring Brook Press, 2008.

El abuelo. Directed by José Luis Garci, Nickel Odeon, 2001.

ACTFL Proficiency Guidelines 2012. American Council on the Teaching of Foreign Languages, 2012, www.actfl.org/uploads/files/general/ACTFLProficiencyGuidelines2012.pdf.

Adams, Michelle, and Scott Coltrane. "Boys and Men in Families: The Domestic Production of Gender, Power, and Privilege." *Handbook of Studies on Men and Masculinities,* edited by Michael Kimmel et al., Sage, 2005, pp. 230–48.

Ahmed, Sara. *Cultural Politics of Emotion.* Edinburgh UP, 2014.

Alarcón, Pedro Antonio de. "El Amigo de la Muerte." Alarcón, *Narraciones inverosímiles,* pp. 13–89.

———. "Death's Friend." *Stories of Enchantment from Nineteenth-Century Spain,* translated by Robert M. Fedorchek, Bucknell UP, 2002, pp. 134–88.

———. "La mujer alta." Alarcón, *Narraciones inverosímiles,* pp. 91–109.

———. *Narraciones inverosímiles.* Edited by Francisco J. Arellano, Clan, 2000.

———. "The Tall Woman." *"The Nun" and Other Stories,* by Alarcón, translated by Robert M. Fedorchek, Bucknell UP, 1999, pp. 153–69.

Alas, Leopoldo. "Benito Pérez Galdós." *Galdós, novelista,* edited by Adolfo Sotelo Vázquez, Editorial Promociones y Publicaciones Universitarias, 1991, pp. 7–26.

———. *B. Pérez Galdós: Estudio crítico biográfico.* Madrid, 1889. Celebridades españolas contemporáneas.

———. Review of *Realidad,* by Benito Pérez Galdós. *La Correspondencia de España,* 18 Mar. 1892, pp. 1–2. *Biblioteca Nacional de España,* hemerotecadigital.bne.es.

———. Review of *Realidad,* by Benito Pérez Galdós. *El Imparcial,* 18 Apr. 1892, p. 1. *Biblioteca Nacional de España,* hemerotecadigital.bne.es.

Aldaraca, Bridget A. El Ángel del Hogar: *Galdós and the Ideology of Domesticity in Spain.* U of North Carolina P, 1991.

———. *"El Ángel del Hogar*: The Cult of Domesticity in Nineteenth-Century Spain." *Theory and Practice of Feminist Literary Criticism,* edited by Gabriela Mora et al., Bilingual Press / Editorial Bilingüe, 1982, pp. 62–87.

Alonso y Rubio, Francisco. "La mujer." 1863. Jagoe et al., pp. 65–71.

Altamira, Rafael. Review of *Realidad,* by Benito Pérez Galdós. *El Boletín de la Institución Libre de Enseñanza,* 15 Apr. 1892.

———. Review of *Realidad,* by Benito Pérez Galdós. *La Justicia,* 16 Mar. 1892, p. 1. *Biblioteca Nacional de España,* hemerotecadigital.bne.es.

Álvarez Junco, José. *Mater dolorosa: La idea de España en el siglo XIX.* Penguin Random House Grupo Editorial España, 2010.

Arenal, Concepción. "La mujer de su casa." 1883. Jagoe et al., pp. 493–500.

Arencibia, Yolanda. *Galdós: Una biografía.* Tusquets Editores, 2020.

Arkinstall, Christine. "Forging a Nation for the Female Sex: Equality, Natural Law, and Citizenship in Spanish Feminist Essays, 1881–1920." Bermúdez and Johnson, pp. 147–57.

Átame. Directed by Pedro Almodóvar, El Deseo, 1989.

Auladell, Pablo. *El paraíso perdido.* Editorial Sexto Piso, 2015.

"El Ayuntamiento de Madrid concederá el título de Hijo Adoptivo a Benito Pérez Galdós." *Madrid Destino,* 4 Mar. 2020, www.madrid-destino.com/prensa/el-ayuntamiento-de-madrid-concedera-el-titulo-de-hijo-adoptivo-benito-perez-galdos.

Bacon, Francis. "Of Studies." 1597. *The Essays; or, Counsels Civil and Moral,* London, 1891, pp. 11–12.

Bakhtin, Mikhail. *The Dialogic Imagination: Four Essays.* Translated by Caryl Emerson and Michael Holquist, U of Texas P, 1981.

Barbado Hernández, F. J. "Medicina y literatura en la formación del médico residente de medicina interna." *Anales de Medicina Interna,* vol. 24, no. 4, 2007, pp. 195–200.

Bardavío Estevan, Susana. "'¡España es también aquí!': Nación e imaginario colonial en los cuentos de Emilia Pardo Bazán." *Castilla: Estudios de Literatura,* vol. 9, 2018, pp. 176–203.

Barthes, Roland. *The Rustle of Language.* U of California P, 1989.

———. "Toward a Psychosociology of Contemporary Food Consumption." *Food and Culture: A Reader,* edited by Carole Counihan and Penny Van Esterik, 3rd ed., Routledge, 2013, pp. 23–30.

Bebe. "Bebe—Malo (Videoclip Oficial)." *YouTube,* uploaded by Bebe, 15 July 2015, www.youtube.com/watch?v=90GqAf3zJ8s.

Becerra Bolaños, Antonio, and Alberto Hernández Rivero. *1892.* Cabildo de Gran Canaria, 2020.

Beck, Ulrich. *Risk Society: Towards a New Modernity.* Sage Publications, 1992.

Bécquer, Gustavo Adolfo. "El beso." Bécquer, *Obras,* pp. 253–70. *Biblioteca Virtual Miguel de Cervantes,* www.cervantesvirtual.com/obra-visor/obras-de-gustavo-a-becquer-tomo-primero--0/html/00cbc210-82b2-11df-acc7-002185ce6064_291.html.

———. "La corza blanca." Bécquer, *Obras,* pp. 185–208. *Biblioteca Virtual Miguel de Cervantes,* www.cervantesvirtual.com/obra-visor/obras-de-gustavo-a-becquer-tomo-primero--0/html/00cbc210-82b2-11df-acc7-002185ce6064_223.html.

———. "El Miserere." Bécquer, *Obras,* pp. 311–23. *Biblioteca Virtual Miguel de Cervantes,* www.cervantesvirtual.com/obra-visor/obras-de-gustavo-a-becquer-tomo-primero--0/html/00cbc210-82b2-11df-acc7-002185ce6064_349.html.

———. "El Monte de las Ánimas." Bécquer, *Obras,* pp. 271–81. *Biblioteca Virtual Miguel de Cervantes,* www.cervantesvirtual.com/obra-visor/obras-de-gustavo-a-becquer-tomo-primero--0/html/00cbc210-82b2-11df-acc7-002185ce6064_309.html.

———. *Obras de Gustavo A. Bécquer.* Vol. 1, Fortanet, 1871.

———. *Romantic Legends of Spain.* Translated by Cornelia Frances Bates and Katharine Lee Bates, Thomas Y. Crowell, 1909. *Project Gutenberg*, www.gutenberg.org/files/50044/50044-h/50044-h.htm.

Bell, Margaret, and Sharon Cohn. "The Use of Abstract Modeling to Teach Note-Taking Skills." *Middle School Journal*, vol, 16, no. 3, 1985, pp. 12–14.

Bellatín, Mario. *Salón de belleza.* Tusquets, 1994.

Benito. Written and directed by Pedro Pérez, Lilium by APS, 2022.

Benjamin, Walter. "The Collector." *The Arcades Project*, translated by Howard Eiland and Kevin McLaughlin, Harvard UP / Belknap Press, 1999, pp. 203–11.

Berenguer, Ángel, editor. *Los estrenos teatrales de Galdós y la crítica de su tiempo.* Consejería de la Cultura de la Comunidad de Madrid, 1988.

Berkowitz, Hyman Chonon. *Pérez Galdós, Spanish Liberal Crusader.* U of Wisconsin P, 1948.

Bermúdez, Silvia, and Roberta Johnson, editors. *A New History of Iberian Feminisms.* U of Toronto P, 2018.

Bernard, Claude. *An Introduction to the Study of Experimental Medicine.* Translated by Henry C. Greene, Dover, 2018.

Biasin, Gian-Paolo. *The Flavors of Modernity: Food and the Novel.* Princeton UP, 1993.

Bieder, Maryellen. "First Wave Feminisms, 1880–1919." Bermúdez and Johnson, pp. 158–81.

———. "Women Authors in the Romantic Tradition (1841–1884) and Early Feminist Thought (1861–1893)." Bermúdez and Johnson, pp. 126–46.

Blanco, Alda. *Cultura y conciencia imperial en la España del siglo XIX.* U of Valencia, 2012.

———. "Domesticity, Education and the Woman Writer." *Cultural and Historical Grounding for Hispanic and Luso-Brazilian Feminist Literary Criticism*, edited by Hernán Vidal, Institute for the Study of Ideologies and Literature, 1989, pp. 371–94.

———. "Teóricas de la conciencia feminista." Jagoe et al., pp. 445–67.

Blanco White, José María. "Sobre el placer de las imaginaciones inverosímiles." *Antología de obras en español de José María Blanco White*, edited by Vicente Llorens, Editorial Labor, 1971, pp. 212–19.

Blumenberg, Hans. *La legibilidad del mundo.* Paidós, 2000.

Boal, Augusto. *Theater of the Oppressed.* 1974. Translated by Charles A. McBride and Maria-Odilia Leal McBride, Theatre Communications Group, 1995.

Bofill, Pedro. Review of *Realidad*, by Benito Pérez Galdós. *La Época*, 16 Mar. 1982, p. 1. *Biblioteca Nacional de España*, hemerotecadigital.bne.es.

Bolt, David. *The Metanarrative of Blindness: A Re-reading of Twentieth-Century Anglophone Writing.* U of Michigan P, 2014.

Bourdieu, Pierre. *Distinction: A Social Critique of the Judgement of Taste.* Cambridge UP, 1984.

———. *The Field of Cultural Production.* Columbia UP, 1993.

———. "The Forms of Capital." *Handbook of Theory and Research for the Sociology of Education*, edited by J. Richardson, Greenwood, 1986, pp. 241–58.

———. *The Social Structures of the Economy*. Polity Press, 2005.

BPM. Directed by Robin Campillo, Memento Films, 2017.

Brantlinger, Patrick. "Imperial Gothic." *Teaching the Gothic*, edited by Anna Powell and Andrew Smith, Palgrave Macmillan, 2006, pp. 84–106.

———. *Rule of Darkness: British Literature and Imperialism, 1830–1914*. Cornell UP, 1988.

Braudy, Leo. "Knowing the Performer from the Performance: Fame, Celebrity, and Literary Studies." *PMLA*, vol. 126, no. 4, Oct. 2011, pp. 1070–75.

Braun, Rebecca, and Emily Spiers. "Introduction: Re-viewing Literary Celebrity." *Celebrity Studies*, vol. 7, no. 4, 2016, pp. 449–56. *Taylor and Francis Online*, https://doi.org/10.1080/19392397.2016.1233709.

Bretón, Tomás. *La verbena de la Paloma: El boticario y las chulapas y celos mal reprimidos*. Libretto by Ricardo de la Vega, Madrid, 1894.

Briceño, José. "Exposición de Galdós en la BNE recibe más de 20.000 visitantes." *RevistaDeArte.com*, 4 Dec. 2019, revistadearte.com/libros/exposicion-de-galdos-en-la-bne-recibe-mas-de-20-000-visitas.

Brillat-Savarin, Anthelme. *The Physiology of Taste; or, Meditations on Transcendental Gastronomy*. Heritage Press, 1949.

Brittan, Arthur. "Masculinities and Masculinism." *The Masculinities Reader*, edited by Stephen Whitehead and Frank Barret, Polity, 2001, pp. 51–55.

Brooks, Peter. *Reading for the Plot: Design and Intention in Narrative*. Alfred A. Knopf, 1984.

Brown, Bill. *The Material Unconscious: American Amusement, Stephen Crane, and the Economies of Play*. Harvard UP, 1996.

Brumberger, Eva. "Visual Literacy and the Digital Native: An Examination of the Millennial Learner." *Journal of Visual Literacy*, vol. 30, no. 1, 2011, pp. 19–46.

Burgos, Carmen de. *La entrometida*. Prensa Popular, 1921. *Biblioteca Virtual Miguel de Cervantes*, www.cervantesvirtual.com/nd/ark:/59851/bmc1053266.

"Burka Teatro *La Loca de la Casa* resumen." *YouTube*, uploaded by BurkaTeatroX, 24 Mar. 2017, youtu.be/cEZvTICkFpQ?si=JE91qxxvvfxsBh8b.

Butler, Judith. *Gender Trouble: Feminism and the Subversion of Identity*. Routledge, 2007.

Calle Mayor. Directed by Juan Antonio Bardem, Suevia Films, 1956.

Canals, Salvador. "De 'Electra' á Sagasta." *Nuestro Tiempo*, Mar. 1901, pp. 3–8. *Biblioteca Nacional de España*, hemerotecadigital.bne.es.

Caniglia, Guido, et al. "COVID-19 Heralds a New Epistemology of Science for the Public Good." *History and Philosophy of the Life Sciences*, vol. 43, no. 2, 2021, pp. 1–6.

Cánovas, Francisco. *Galdós: Vida, obra y compromiso*. Alianza, 2019.

"Caricaturas." *Biblioteca Virtual Miguel de Cervantes*, www.cervantesvirtual.com/portales/benito_perez_galdos/imagenes_caricaturas/. Accessed 24 Oct. 2024.

Carpenter, Jeffrey P., and Daniel G. Krutka. "How and Why Educators Use *Twitter*: A Survey of the Field." *Journal of Research on Technology in Education*, vol. 46, no. 4, 2014, pp. 414–34.

Carr, Raymond. *Spain, 1808–1939*. Clarendon Press, 1966.

La casa de Bernarda Alba. Directed by Mario Camus, Cinemateca, 1987.

Casalduero, Joaquín. *Vida y obra de Galdós*. Editorial Gredos, 1951.

Casanova, Sofía. *Princesa del amor hermoso*. Ena Bordonada, pp. 151–94.

"Centenario de Benito Pérez Galdós, 1843–1920." *Instituto Cervantes*, 16 Sept. 2020, cultura.cervantes.es/manchester/es/Centenario-de-Benito-Pérez-Galdós,-1843-1920/135618.

Cervantes Saavedra, Miguel de. *Don Quixote*. Translated by John Ormsby, Lerner Publishing Group, 2014. *ProQuest Ebook Central*, ebookcentral.proquest.com.

———. *El ingenioso hidalgo Don Quijote de la Mancha*. Edited by Francisco Rico, Instituto Cervantes, 2025, cvc.cervantes.es/literatura/clasicos/quijote/edicion/default.htm.

Chang, Julia. "Becoming Useless: Masculinity, Able-Bodiedness, and Empire in Nineteenth-Century Spain." *Unsettling Colonialism: Gender and Race in the Nineteenth-Century Global Hispanic World*, edited by N. Michelle Murray and Akiko Tsuchiya, State U of New York P, 2019, pp. 173–202.

Charnon-Deutsch, Lou. "Death Becomes Her." *Fictions of the Feminine in the Nineteenth-Century Spanish Press*, Pennsylvania State UP, 2000, pp. 223–56.

———. *The Spanish Gypsy: The History of a European Obsession*. Pennsylvania State UP, 2004.

Christián. Review of *Electra*, by Benito Pérez Galdós. *La Lectura Dominical*, vol. 8, no. 371, pp. 83–86. *Biblioteca Nacional de España*, hemerotecadigital.bne.es.

Círculos políticos. *El Día* [Madrid], 30 Jan. 1901, p. 3. *Biblioteca Nacional de España*, hemerotecadigital.bne.es.

Coffey, Mary L. *Ghosts of Colonies Past and Present: Spanish Imperialism in the Fiction of Benito Pérez Galdós*. Liverpool UP, 2020.

Colina, José de la, and Tomás Pérez Turrent. *Objects of Desire: Conversations with Luis Buñuel*. Marsilio, 1992.

"¿Cómo era Galdós?" *Gobierno de Canarias*, 19 Dec. 2019, www3.gobiernodecanarias.org/medusa/ecoescuela/galdos2020/tag/como-era-galdos/.

Condé, Lisa. *Critical Guide to* Tristana. Grant and Cutler, 2000.

La condesa rebelde. Directed by Zaza Ceballos, TVG, 2011.

Connell, R. W. *Masculinities*. U of California P, 2005.

Cortina, Adela. *Aporofobia, el rechazo del pobre: Un desafío para la democracia*. Paidós, 2017.

"Creating a Digital Zine in Canva." *YouTube*, uploaded by Fountaindale Public Library, 8 May 2023, www.youtube.com/watch?v=ss-c5H6-s_M.

Cruz, Jesús. *The Rise of Middle-Class Culture in Nineteenth-Century Spain*. Louisiana State UP, 2011.

Cueto Asín, Elena. "*La Fontana de Oro* en la proyección televisiva de Galdós: Del espacio Los libros al telefilme Prim, el asesinato de la calle del Turco." *Moenia: Revista Lucense de Lingüística y Literatura*, vol. 26, 2020, pp. 27–41.

———. "Galdós en el escenario conmemorativo: El recuerdo delirante como construcción de memoria pública." *Talía: Revista de estudios teatrales*, vol. 4, 2022, pp. 31–39.

———. "Pardo Bazán y Pérez Galdós: Una intimidad imaginada en público." *Anales Galdosianos*, vol. 57, 2022, pp. 213–31.

Dapena, Gerard. "Galdós on Film: *Doña Perfecta*, a Mexican Melodrama." *The Hispanic Connection: Spanish and Spanish-American Literature in the Arts of the World*, edited by Zenia Sacks DaSilva, Praeger, 2004, pp. 313–22.

Davies, Rhian. "New Ways of Teaching Literature." *Centre for Languages, Linguistics and Area Studies*, 2006, web-archive.southampton.ac.uk/www.llas.ac.uk/resources/gpg/2593.html.

———. "Space and Place in Alejandro Galindo's 1950 Film Adaptation of Benito Pérez Galdós's *Doña Perfecta* (1876)." *Bulletin of Hispanic Studies*, vol. 95, no. 4, 2018, pp. 417–34.

Del Moral, Ignacio, and Yolanda Rodríguez. *Galdós, sombra y realidad.* Directed and adapted by Pilar G. Almansa, 13 Nov. 2020, Teatro Español, Madrid.

Del Valle-Inclán, Ramón. *Sonata de invierno: Memorias del Marqués de Bradomín.* Renacimiento, 1927. Vol. 8 of *Opera Omnia.*

Dendle, Brian J. *Galdós: The Early Historical Novels.* U of Missouri P, 1986.

———. "Shipwreck and Discovery: A Study of Imagery in 'Marianela.'" *Neuphilologische Mitteilungen*, vol. 74, no. 2, 1973, pp. 326–32.

"Designing Magazine Using PowerPoint." *YouTube*, uploaded by Chuah Kee Man, 15 May 2013, youtu.be/mLNDxTAzfyM?si=cMTaFjEZAy90rajH.

Díaz Simón, Luis. "El cólera de 1885 en Madrid: Catástrofe sanitaria y conflicto social en la ciudad epidemiada." *Veinticinco años después: Avances en la Historia Social y Económica de Madrid*, Ediciones Universidad Autónoma de Madrid, 2014.

Doña Perfecta. Directed by César Fernández Ardavín, Azor Films, 1977.

Doña Perfecta. Directed by Alejandro Galindo, Cabrera Films, 1951.

Doña Perfecta. Directed by Alejandro Galindo, Vanguard Cinema, 2005.

"*Doña Perfecta* México, 1951 Dirección Alejandro Galindo." *YouTube*, uploaded by María Navarro, 24 July 2024, www.youtube.com/watch?v=bisUcopo160.

Eagleton, Terry. "Edible Ecriture." *Times Higher Education*, vol. 24, 1997, pp. 25–27.

Edwards, Gwynne. *The Discreet Art of Luis Buñuel: A Reading of His Films.* Marion Boyars, 1982.

El Torres. *Galdós y la miseria.* Illustrated by Alberto Belmonte, Nuevo Nueve, 2020.

Ena Bordonada, Ángela, editor. *Novelas breves de escritoras españolas, 1900–1936.* Castalia, 1989.

Enjuto-Rangel, Cecilia, et al., editors. *Transatlantic Studies: Latin America, Iberia, and Africa.* Liverpool UP, 2019.

Espina, Concha. *La esfinge Maragata.* Edited by Carmen Díaz Castañón, Castalia, 1989.

———. *La niña Luzmela.* Espasa-Calpe, 1985.

Espinosa, Catalina. "Proportion of Catholics in Spain 2011–2024." *Statista*, 22 Jan. 2025, www.statista.com/statistics/992681/share-of-catholics-in-spain/.

Ewald, Liana. "Playing the Part: Performance and Identity in *Tristana.*" *Revista de Estudios Hispánicos*, vol. 44, no. 1, Mar. 2010, pp. 57–79.

Faerna, Nacho. *Prim: El asesinato de la calle del Turco.* Espasa, 2014.

Faerna, Nacho, and Virginia Yagüe. *Prim: El asesinato en la calle del Turco (Guión).* Ocho y Medio, 2016.

Farkas, Zita. Review of *Idolizing Authorship*, edited by Gaston Franssen and Rick Honings. *Authorship*, vol. 6, no. 2, 2017, dx.doi.org/10.21825/aj.v6i2.7010.

Farmacopea oficial española. 6th ed., Gregorio Estrada, 1884.

Faro Forteza, Agustín. *Películas de libros.* Prensas Universitarias de Zaragoza, 2006.

Faulkner, Sally. "Galdós and Spanish Cinema." 11th Pérez Galdós Lecture, *University of Sheffield*, 2011, sites.google.com/sheffield.ac.uk/gep/events/lectures/lecture-11-2011-gald%C3%B3s-and-spanish-cinema.

Fernández Arribas, Javier. "La exposición 'Quijotes por el mundo' supera los 12.000 visitantes." *Atalayar*, 16 June 2016, www.atalayar.com/articulo/cultura/exposicion-quijotes-mundo-supera-12000-visitantes/20150808085253159028.html.

Fernández Cordero, Carolina. *Galdós en su siglo XIX: Una novela para el consenso social.* Iberoamericana/Vervuert, 2020.

Fernández Etreros, Carmen, and Guillermo Menéndez Quirós. *Galdós, un escritor en Madrid.* Comunidad de Madrid, 2020.

Fernández Poyatos, María Dolores. "La publicidad de salud en la prensa ilustrada de finales del siglo XIX." *Questiones publicitarias*, vol. 1, no. 16, 2011, pp. 108–24.

Fernández Sanz, Juan José. "Las epidemias de cólera del siglo XIX vistas por Pérez Galdós." *Congresos Internacionales de Estudios Galdosianos*, vol. 2, 1993, pp. 437–51.

Fortunata y Jacinta. Directed by Mario Camus, Radiotelevisión Española, 1980.

Foucault, Michel. *The Birth of the Clinic: An Archeology of Medical Perception.* Translated by A. M. Sheridan Smith, Vintage, 1994.

Fox, Linda C. "Power in the Family and Beyond: Doña Perfecta and Bernarda Alba as Manipulators of Their Destinies." *Hispanófila*, vol. 85, 1985, pp. 57–65.

Franklin, Harper. "1870–1879." *Fashion History Timeline*, Fashion Institute of Technology, State U of New York, 11 Nov. 2019, fashionhistory.fitnyc.edu/1870-1879/.

Franssen, Gaston, and Rick Honings, editors. *Idolizing Authorship: Literary Celebrity and the Construction of Identity, 1800 to the Present.* Amsterdam UP, 2017.

Freedgood, Elaine. *The Ideas in Things: Fugitive Meaning in the Victorian Novel.* U of Chicago P, 2010.

Friedman, Jane. "How to Build an Author's Website: Getting Started Guide." *Jane Friedman*, 1 Sept. 2024, janefriedman.com/author-websites/.

Fuentes Peris, Teresa. *Visions of Filth: Deviancy and Social Control in the Novels of Galdós.* Liverpool UP, 2003.

Furst, Lilian R. *All Is True: The Claims and Strategies of Realist Fiction.* Duke UP, 1995.

———. "Medical History and Literary Texts." Hunsaker Hawkins and McEntyre, pp. 55–64.

"Galdós no es nuestro, es internacional." *Canarias7*, 11 June 2022, www.canarias7.es/cultura/galdos-internacional-20220611190046-nt.html.

Gallagher-Brett, Angela. *Hard Going but Worth It: A Snapshot of Attitudes towards Reading among Language Undergraduates.* Subject Centre for Languages, Linguistics and Area Studies, 2006.

Gallardo, Carmen. *La reina de las lavanderas*. La esfera de los libros, 2012.

Gallud Jardiel, Enrique. *Galdós en los infiernos*. VDB, 2022.

García Lorca, Federico. *La casa de Bernarda Alba*. Edited by H. Ramsden, Manchester UP, 1984.

Garland-Thomson, Rosemarie. "Integrating Disability, Transforming Feminist Theory." *NWSA Journal*, vol. 14, no. 3, Oct. 2002, pp. 1–32.

George, David R., Jr. "'Playing Japanese' in Fin-de-Siécle Zarzuela." *Intersections of Race, Class, and Gender in Fin-de-Siécle Spanish Literature and Culture*, edited by Jennifer Smith and Lisa Nalbone, Taylor and Francis, 2016, pp. 123–45.

George, David R., Jr., and Wan Sonya Tang. Introduction. *Televising Restoration Spain: History and Fiction in Twenty-First-Century Costume Dramas*, Palgrave Macmillan, 2018, pp. 1–19.

Gil, Santiago. *El gran amor de Galdós*. La Palma, 2019.

Gilbert, Sandra M. *The Culinary Imagination: From Myth to Modernity*. W. W. Norton, 2014.

Gilman, Stephen. *Galdos and the Art of the European Novel: 1867–1887*. Princeton UP, 2014.

———. *Galdós y el arte de la novela europea: 1867–1887*. Taurus, 1985.

Gimeno de Flaquer, Concepción. "El problema feminista." 1903. Jagoe et al., pp. 530–35.

Gimferrer, Pere. *Cine y literatura*. Seix Barral, 1999.

Gissing, George. *The Odd Women*. Oxford UP, 2008.

Gogh, Vincent van. *The Potato Eaters*. 1885. Van Gogh Museum, www.vangoghmuseum.nl/en/collection/s0005v1962.

Gonzalez, Jennifer. "Note-taking: A Research Roundup." *Cult of Pedagogy*, 9 Sept. 2018, www.cultofpedagogy.com/note-taking/.

Gordon, Michael. "The Medical Background to Galdós' *La desheredada*." *Anales Galdosianos*, vol. 7, 1972, pp. 67–77.

Graff, Gerald, et al. *"They Say, I Say": The Moves That Matter in Academic Writing*. 2nd ed., W. W. Norton, 2009.

Gramley, Judith D. "Adapting the Novel to Film: The Case of Galdós's *Doña Perfecta*." *Anuario de Cine y Literatura en Español*, vol. 1, 1995, pp. 29–37.

Granjel, Luís S. "Los personajes médicos de Galdós." *Cuadernos Hispanoamericanos*, nos. 250–52, Oct. 1970–Jan. 1971, pp. 656–63.

Grassi, Ángela. "La misión de la mujer." 1857. Jagoe et al., pp. 55–58.

Greg, William R. *Why Are Women Redundant?* N. Trübner, 1869.

Gullón, Germán. "Los cinco finales de Doña Perfecta: Tres novelescos y dos teatrales." *Isidora: Revista de Estudios Galdosianos*, vol. 20, 2012, pp. 9–33.

———. *Galdós: Maestro de las letras modernas*. Valnera, 2020.

———. "La lección del pedagogo Giner de los Ríos al novelista Pérez Galdós." *Bulletin of Spanish Studies*, vol. 95, nos. 9–10, 2018, pp. 63–73.

Hage, Ghassan. "Key Thinkers: Ghassan Hage on Pierre Bourdieu." *YouTube*, uploaded by The Monthly, 3 May 2013, www.youtube.com/watch?v=vn9daX6Jt4g.

Halberstam, Jack. *Female Masculinity.* Duke UP, 1998.

Haydon, Todd, et al. "A Review of the Effectiveness of Guided Notes for Students Who Struggle Learning Academic Content." *Preventing School Failure: Alternative Education for Children and Youth*, vol. 55, no. 4, 2011, pp. 226–31.

Hearn, Jeff. "Men/Masculinities: War/Militarism—Searching (for) the Obvious Connections?" *Making Gender, Making War: Violence, Military and Peacekeeping Practices*, edited by Annica Kronsell and Erika Svedberg, Routledge, 2011, pp. 35–48.

Herlihy-Mera, Jeffrey. "Colonialism in US Spanish Departments." *The Chronicle of Higher Education*, 23 June 2016, www.chronicle.com/blogs/linguafranca/2016/06/23/colonialism-in-u-s-spanish-departments/.

Höglund, Johan. *The American Imperial Gothic: Popular Culture, Empire, Violence.* Ashgate, 2014.

Howes, David. Introduction. *Empire of the Senses: The Sensual Culture Reader*, edited by Howes, Berg Publishers, 2005, pp. 1–17.

"How to Make a Zine—Physically or Digitally." *Santa Clara University Library*, 2025, libguides.scu.edu/c.php?g=1327593&p=9777124.

Hunsaker Hawkins, Anne, and Marilyn Chandler McEntyre, editors. *Teaching Literature and Medicine*, Modern Language Association of America, 2000.

Hutcheon, Linda. *A Theory of Adaptation.* Routledge, 2013.

Ingram, Rebecca. "National Identity and Class Conflict in Pardo Bazán's Cookbooks." Versteeg and Walter, pp. 99–104.

Jaccoud, Sigismond. *Tratado de patología interna.* Translated by Joaquín Gassó and Pablo León y Luque, 2nd ed., Editorial Carlos Bailly-Bailliere, 1875–77. 3 vols.

Jackson, Rosemary. *Fantasy: The Literature of Subversion.* Routledge, 1981.

Jagoe, Catherine. *Ambiguous Angels: Gender in the Novels of Galdós.* U of California P, 1994.

———. "Disinheriting the Feminine: Galdós and the Rise of the Realist Novel in Spain." *Revista de Estudios Hispánicos*, vol. 27, no. 2, 1993, pp. 225–48.

———. "La enseñanza femenina en la España decimonónica." Jagoe et al., pp. 105–45.

———. "La misión de la mujer." Jagoe et al., pp. 21–53.

Jagoe, Catherine, et al., editors. *La mujer en los discursos de género: Textos y contextos en el siglo XIX.* Icaria, 1998.

Jameson, Frederic. *The Antinomies of Realism.* Verso Books, 2013.

Johnson, Randal. Introduction. Bourdieu, *Field*, pp. 1–25.

Johnson, Roberta. *Gender and Nation in the Spanish Modernist Novel.* Vanderbilt UP, 2003.

Johnson, Roberta, and Olga Castro. "First-Wave Spanish Feminism Takes Flight in Castilian-, Catalan-, and Galician-Speaking Spain." Bermúdez and Johnson, pp. 213–20.

"Joven fugada." *El País* [Madrid], 16 Mar. 1900, p. 3.

Kalir, Remi. "Remi Kalir on Social Annotation, Self-Curation, the Connective Tissue of Ideas, Annotation Tools, and Nuance for Synthesis." *Thriving on Overload*, hosted by Ross Dawson, episode 31, 19 Aug. 2022, thrivingonoverload.com/remi-kalir-social-annotation-self-curation-connective-tissue-ideas-annotation-tools-nuance-synthesis-ep31/.

Kalir, Remi, and Antero Garcia. *Annotation.* E-book ed., MIT Press, 2021.

Karlin, Jojo, et al. "Case Study 7: Evolving Manifold Scholarship: From Monographs to OER." *The OER Starter Kit Workbook*, by Abbey K. Elder and Stacy Katz, City U of New York, 2020, cuny.manifoldapp.org/projects/the-oer-starter-kit-workbook.

Kimmel, Michael. *Manhood in America: A Cultural History*. Oxford UP, 2012.

Kirtland Grech, Graziella M. "Subjugation, Rebellion, and Power: The Metonymy of the Slippers in Buñuel's *Tristana*." *Seeing in Spanish: From Don Quixote to Daddy Yankee: Twenty-Two Essays on Hispanic Visual Cultures*, edited by Ryan Prout and Tilmann Altenberg, Cambridge Scholars Publishing, 2011, pp. 32–42.

Kletsel, Greg. "Let's Talk about Zines and Why You Should Make One." *YouTube*, uploaded by Kletsel, 16 Apr. 2021, youtu.be/FPMxDECh6ow?si=gxh-hChgpEj8SOnU.

Labanyi, Jo. "Fetishism and the Problem of Sexual Difference in Buñuel's *Tristana* (1970)." *Spanish Cinema: The Auteurist Tradition*, edited by Peter William Evans, Oxford UP, 1999, pp. 76–91.

———. *Galdós*. Longman Publishers, 1992.

———. "Things in Galdós / Galdós's Things: Use Value and Exchange Value." *Spanish Culture from Romanticism to the Present: Structures of Feeling*, Modern Humanities Research Association, 2019, pp. 52–60.

La Berge, Ann Elizabeth Fowler. *Mission and Method: The Early-Nineteenth-Century French Public Health Movement*. Cambridge UP, 2002.

La de San Quintín. Directed by Juan Antonio Hormigó, Radiotelevisión Española, 1983.

Lang, James. *Small Teaching: Everyday Lessons from the Science of Learning*. Jossey-Bass, 2016.

Larra, Mariano José de. "El castellano viejo." *Artículos varios*, edited by Evaristo Correa Calderón, Castalia, 1986, pp. 311–23.

Laserna, José de. Review of *Electra*, by Benito Pérez Galdós. *El Imparcial*, 31 Jan. 1901, pp. 1–2. *Biblioteca Nacional de España*, hemerotecadigital.bne.es.

La lengua de las mariposas. Directed by José Luis Cuerda, Metrodome, 1999.

Lévi-Strauss, Claude. "The Culinary Triangle." *Partisan Review*, vol. 33, no. 4, 1966, pp. 586–95.

Libro médico azul de fórmulas y notas terapéuticas y reports sobre nuevos adelantos en la química y farmacia. Burroughs, Wellcome, 1883–84. *Wellcome Collection*, wellcomecollection.org/works/mss5cvk2. 2 vols.

Liggans, Emma. *Odd Women? Spinsters, Lesbians and Widows, 1850s–1930s*. Oxford UP, 2016.

Lin, Ying. "Ten Twitter Statistics Every Marketer Should Know in 2023." *Oberlo*, 15 June 2022, www.oberlo.com/blog/twitter-statistics.

Literland [@literlandweb1]. "'Quiero ser algo en el mundo, cultivar un arte, vivir de mí misma. El desaliento me abruma. ¿Será verdad, Dios mío, que pretendo un imposible?' Benito Pérez Galdós, Tristana #Galdos175." *Twitter*, 10 May 2018, twitter.com/literlandweb1/status/994650992443625472.

López, Ignacio Javier. *Caballero de novela: Ensayo sobre el donjuanismo en la novela española moderna, 1880–1930*. Puvill Libros, 1986.

———. Introduction. Pérez Galdós, *Doña Perfecta* [Cátedra], pp. 9–130.

Madrazo y Garreta, Raimundo de. *Manuela de Errazu.* 1870–71. *Museo del Prado,* www.museodelprado.es/coleccion/obra-de-arte/manuela-de-errazu/cfc474ef-69cc-4beb-98d2-5e3695e8aedf.

———. *Ramón de Errazu.* 1879. *Museo del Prado,* www.museodelprado.es/coleccion/obra-de-arte/ramon-de-errazu/88089d52-fdc0-46f8-9f3c-fe763200d49c.

Mañas, José Ángel. *Historias del Kronen,* Destino, 1998.

Manet, Édouard. *Le balcon.* 1868–69, Musée d'Orsay, Paris.

Manne, Kate. *Entitled: How Male Privilege Hurts Women.* Crown, 2020.

Marcus, Sharon. *The Drama of Celebrity.* Princeton UP, 2019.

Marianela. Directed by Angelino Fons, Cámara, 1972.

Márquez, Rosa Luisa. *A-Saltos: El juego como disciplina teatral.* Cuicaloca, 1996.

Marshall, P. David. *Celebrity and Power: Fame in Contemporary Culture.* U of Minnesota P, 2017.

Martínez, Miguel Ángel. *El primer amor de Galdós.* Diputación de Granada, 2020.

Martínez Sierra, María [*published as* Gregorio Martínez Sierra]. *Tú eres la paz.* Espasa-Calpe, 1965.

Massumi, Brian. "The Political Ontology of Threat." *The Affect Theory Reader,* Duke UP, 2010, pp. 52–70.

Matallana-Abril, Juan F. "La herencia del Don Juan Tenorio en el mundo galdosiano de las novelas contemporáneas." *Critica Hispánica,* vol. 18, no. 1, 1996, pp. 141–48.

Mayoral, Carlos. *Un episodio nacional.* Espasa, 2019.

McCloud, Scott. *Entender el cómic: El arte invisible.* Astiberri, 2019.

———. *Understanding Comics: The Invisible Art.* HarperCollins Publishers, 1993.

McKee, Robert. *Story: Substance, Structure, Style, and the Principles of Screenwriting.* Methuen, 1988.

McRuer, Robert. *Crip Theory: Cultural Signs of Queerness and Disability.* New York UP, 2006.

Mellen, Joan, editor. *The World of Luis Buñuel: Essays in Criticism.* Oxford UP, 1978.

Menéndez Onrubia, Carmen. *Introducción al teatro de Benito Pérez Galdós.* Consejo Superior de Investigaciones Científicas, 1983.

Messner, M. A. "When Bodies Are Weapons: Masculinity and Violence in Sport." *International Review for the Sociology of Sport,* vol. 25, no. 3, 1990, pp. 203–20.

Miau. Directed by José Luis Borau, Radiotelevisión Española, 1972.

Miller, Beth. "From Mistress to Murderess: The Metamorphosis of Buñuel's Tristana." *Women in Hispanic Literature: Icons and Fallen Idols,* edited by Miller, U of California P, 1983, pp. 340–60.

Mills, Mara, and Rebecca Sanchez, editors. *Crip Authorship: Disability as Method.* New York UP, 2023.

Miró, Emilio. "*Tristana* o la imposibilidad de ser." *Cuadernos Hispanoamericanos,* nos. 250–52, 1970–71, pp. 505–22.

Mitchell, David T., and Sharon L. Snyder. *Narrative Prosthesis: Disability and Dependencies of Discourse.* U of Michigan P, 2014.

Molina, Mónica. *Los ojos de Galdós.* Edhasa, 2020.

Monlau, Pedro Felipe. *Higiene del matrimonio o El libro de los casados*. Garnier Hermanos, 1898.

Montero, Rosa. "La gloria de los feos." *Amantes y enemigos: Cuentos de parejas*. Alfaguara, 1998, pp. 112–14.

Montesinos, José F. *Galdós*. Castalia, 1980. 3 vols.

Morales, María. "Presencia y significado de la figura de Don Juan Tenorio en la novela de Pérez Galdós." *Horizontes*, vol. 40, no. 79, Oct. 1998, pp. 45–72.

Moreno, Stella. "Amor, deseo y matrimonio en Tristana de Benito Pérez Galdós." *PNCFL Selecta*, vol. 14, 1993, pp. 88–93.

Muñoz-Muriana, Sara. "*Pobre Pierna que Solo Sirve para Andar*: Female (Dis)empowerments, (Dis)ability, and Space in Literary and Filmic 'Tristana.'" *Hispania*, vol. 98, no. 3, 2015, pp. 485–98.

Navarrete, Ramón. *Galdós en el cine español*. T&B Editores, 2003.

Nazarín. Directed by Luis Buñuel, Producciones Barbachano, 1959.

Nicholson, Mervyn. "Food and Power: Homer, Carroll, Atwood and Others." *Mosaic*, vol. 20, no. 3, 1987, pp. 37–55.

Nisbet, Robert A. "The Decline and Fall of Social Class." *The Pacific Sociological Review*, vol. 2, no. 1, 1959, pp. 11–17.

Nogués, Nicko. "De machos a hombres con Nicko Nogués." *Más allá del rosa*, hosted by Jessica Fernández García, 27 June 2022. *YouTube*, www.youtube.com/watch?v=mimxcBLmyN8.

———. *Hackea a tu macho: Diez acciones para hombres que se atreven a desafiar una masculinidad tóxica*. Planeta, 2021.

Offen, Karen. "Defining Feminism: A Comparative Historical Approach." *Signs: Journal of Women in Culture and Society*, vol. 14, no. 1, 1988, pp. 119–57.

"Open Education." *SPARC*. Scholarly Publishing and Academic Resources Coalition, 2025, sparcopen.org/open-education/.

"Open Educational Resources." *CUNY: The City University of New York*, 2025, www.cuny.edu/libraries/open-educational-resources/.

Ortiz-Armengol, Pedro. *Vida de Galdós*. Crítica, 1995.

Otero Luque, Frank. "De pobre huerfanita a despiadada viuda negra: La capacidad de acción (agency) de la mujer en las Tristanas de Pérez Galdós y Buñuel." *Studium: Revista de Humanidades*, vol. 23, 2017, pp. 227–43.

Palacio Atard, Vicente. *La alimentación de Madrid en el siglo XVIII y otros estudios madrileños*. Real Academia de la Historia, 1998.

Paquita la del Barrio. "Rata de dos patas." *YouTube*, uploaded by Discos Musart, 25 Jul 2011.

Pardo Bazán, Emilia. "El antepasado." *Cuentos sacro-profanos, Biblioteca Virtual Miguel de Cervantes*, 2001, www.cervantesvirtual.com/obra-visor/cuentos-sacroprofanos--0/html/fee3469e-82b1-11df-acc7-002185ce6064_3.html#I_30.

———. *La cocina española antigua*. Renacimiento, 1913.

———. Editor's column. *Nuevo Teatro Crítico*, vol. 2, no. 13, Jan. 1892, pp. 77–90.

———. "El estudio de Galdós en Madrid." *Nuevo Teatro Crítico*, vol. 8, Aug. 1891, pp. 65–74.

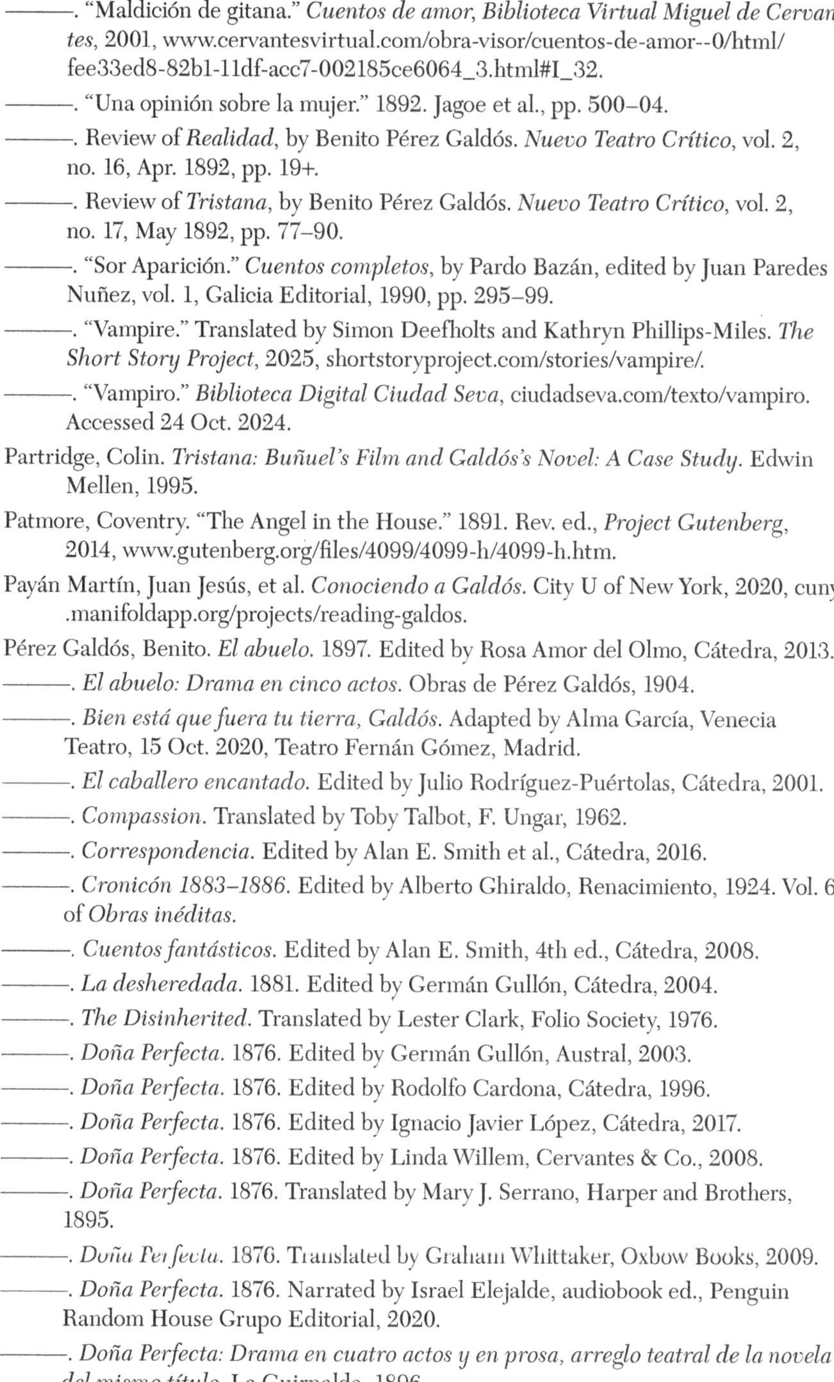

———. "Maldición de gitana." *Cuentos de amor, Biblioteca Virtual Miguel de Cervantes*, 2001, www.cervantesvirtual.com/obra-visor/cuentos-de-amor--0/html/fee33ed8-82b1-11df-acc7-002185ce6064_3.html#I_32.

———. "Una opinión sobre la mujer." 1892. Jagoe et al., pp. 500–04.

———. Review of *Realidad*, by Benito Pérez Galdós. *Nuevo Teatro Crítico*, vol. 2, no. 16, Apr. 1892, pp. 19+.

———. Review of *Tristana*, by Benito Pérez Galdós. *Nuevo Teatro Crítico*, vol. 2, no. 17, May 1892, pp. 77–90.

———. "Sor Aparición." *Cuentos completos*, by Pardo Bazán, edited by Juan Paredes Nuñez, vol. 1, Galicia Editorial, 1990, pp. 295–99.

———. "Vampire." Translated by Simon Deefholts and Kathryn Phillips-Miles. *The Short Story Project*, 2025, shortstoryproject.com/stories/vampire/.

———. "Vampiro." *Biblioteca Digital Ciudad Seva*, ciudadseva.com/texto/vampiro. Accessed 24 Oct. 2024.

Partridge, Colin. *Tristana: Buñuel's Film and Galdós's Novel: A Case Study*. Edwin Mellen, 1995.

Patmore, Coventry. "The Angel in the House." 1891. Rev. ed., *Project Gutenberg*, 2014, www.gutenberg.org/files/4099/4099-h/4099-h.htm.

Payán Martín, Juan Jesús, et al. *Conociendo a Galdós*. City U of New York, 2020, cuny.manifoldapp.org/projects/reading-galdos.

Pérez Galdós, Benito. *El abuelo*. 1897. Edited by Rosa Amor del Olmo, Cátedra, 2013.

———. *El abuelo: Drama en cinco actos*. Obras de Pérez Galdós, 1904.

———. *Bien está que fuera tu tierra, Galdós*. Adapted by Alma García, Venecia Teatro, 15 Oct. 2020, Teatro Fernán Gómez, Madrid.

———. *El caballero encantado*. Edited by Julio Rodríguez-Puértolas, Cátedra, 2001.

———. *Compassion*. Translated by Toby Talbot, F. Ungar, 1962.

———. *Correspondencia*. Edited by Alan E. Smith et al., Cátedra, 2016.

———. *Cronicón 1883–1886*. Edited by Alberto Ghiraldo, Renacimiento, 1924. Vol. 6 of *Obras inéditas*.

———. *Cuentos fantásticos*. Edited by Alan E. Smith, 4th ed., Cátedra, 2008.

———. *La desheredada*. 1881. Edited by Germán Gullón, Cátedra, 2004.

———. *The Disinherited*. Translated by Lester Clark, Folio Society, 1976.

———. *Doña Perfecta*. 1876. Edited by Germán Gullón, Austral, 2003.

———. *Doña Perfecta*. 1876. Edited by Rodolfo Cardona, Cátedra, 1996.

———. *Doña Perfecta*. 1876. Edited by Ignacio Javier López, Cátedra, 2017.

———. *Doña Perfecta*. 1876. Edited by Linda Willem, Cervantes & Co., 2008.

———. *Doña Perfecta*. 1876. Translated by Mary J. Serrano, Harper and Brothers, 1895.

———. *Doña Perfecta*. 1876. Translated by Graham Whittaker, Oxbow Books, 2009.

———. *Doña Perfecta*. 1876. Narrated by Israel Elejalde, audiobook ed., Penguin Random House Grupo Editorial, 2020.

———. *Doña Perfecta: Drama en cuatro actos y en prosa, arreglo teatral de la novela del mismo título*. La Guirnalda, 1896.

———. *The Duchess of San Quintín: A Play in Three Acts*. Translated by Robert M. Fedorchek, Juan de la Cuesta, 2016.

———. *Electra*. Edited by Otis Gridley Bunnell, American Book, 1902. *Project Gutenberg*, 4 Feb. 2009, www.gutenberg.org/ebooks/28002.

———. *Electra*. Biblioteca Nueva, 1998.

———. *Electra*. Dramatic Publishing, 1911.

———. *Electra*. Editorial Hernando, 1981.

———. *Electra*. *Contemporary Spanish Dramatists: Plays by Pérez Galdós, Linares Rivas, Marquina, Zamacois, Dicenta, and the Álvarez Quinteros*, translated by Charles Alfred Turrell, Gorham Press, 1919, pp. 25–126.

———. *Electra*. Translated by Charles Alfred Turrell, Librivox, 25 Apr. 2015. *Internet Archive*, archive.org/details/electra_1504_librivox. Full cast recording.

———. *Episodios nacionales*. Adapted by Carlos Muñiz, Radio Televisión Española, 1973–75.

———. *Episodios nacionales: Quinta serie*. Edited by Francisco Caudet, Cátedra, 2007.

———. *Episodios nacionales: Segunda serie: La España de Fernando VII*. Edited by Dolores Troncoso, Destino, 2006.

———. *The Forbidden*. Translated by Robert S. Rudder and Gloria Chacón Arjona, Cambridge Scholars, 2012.

———. *Fortunata y Jacinta*. 1886–87. Edited by Francisco Caudet, Cátedra, 2011.

———. *Fortunata y Jacinta*. 1886–87. Narrated by Paula Iwasaki, Penguin, 2022.

———. *Fortunata y Jacinta*. 1886–87. Illustrated by Toño Benavides, Reino de Cordelia, 2019.

———. *Fortunata and Jacinta: Two Stories of Married Women*. 1886–87. Translated by Agnes Moncy Gullón, U of Georgia, 1986.

———. "Furor colonial y otros furores." Pérez Galdós, *Cronicón 1883–1886*, pp. 157–62.

———. *Gloria*. Imprenta de J. M. Perez, 1877.

———. *Gloria*. Translated by Nathan Wetherell, Remington, 1879.

———. *The Golden Fountain Café*. Translated by Walter M. Rubin, Latin American Literary Review Press, 1989.

———. *The Grandfather*. Translated by Elizabeth Wallace, R. G. Badger, 1910.

———. *Halma*. Translated by Robert S. Rudder and Ignacio López-Calvo, Cambridge Scholars Publishing, 2014.

———. "Una industria que vive de la muerte." Pérez Galdós, *Cuentos fantásticos*, pp. 39–56.

———. *Inferno*. Translated by Abigail Lee Six, Phoenix House, 1998.

———. *La de San Quintín; Electra*. Edited by Luis F. Díaz Larios, Cátedra, 2002.

———. *León Roch*. Translated by Clara Bell, H. Fertig, 1886.

———. "Los maestros: Don Benito Pérez Galdós." Interview by El Caballero Audaz [José Maria Carretero Novillo], *Por esos mundos*, no. 123, Apr. 1905, pp. 342–50.

———. *Marianela*. 1878. Edited by Francisco Caudet. Cátedra, 2009.

———. *Marianela.* Translated by Gloria Bodtorf Clark, Juan de la Cuesta Hispanic Monographs, 2020.

———. *Marianela.* 1878. Narrated by Elsa Veiga, audiobook ed., Penguin, 2021.

———. *Marianela.* 1878. Santillana, 2009.

———. *Marianela.* 1878. *Textos.info*, 25 Sept. 2016, www.textos.info/benito-perez-galdos/marianela.

———. *Marianela.* Translated by Clara Bell, William S. Gottsberger, 1883.

———. *Marianela: A Story of Spanish Love.* Translated by Helen W. Lester, Translation Publishing, 1923.

———. *Memorias de un desmemoriado.* Verbal, 2021.

———. *Meow.* Translated by Ruth Katz Crispin, Aris and Philips, 2014.

———. *Miau.* 1888. Edited by Francisco Javier Díez de Revenga, Cátedra, 2007.

———. *Miau.* 1888. Translated by J. M. Cohen, Penguin Books, 1966.

———. *Misericordia.* 1897. Edited by Luciano García Lorenzo, Cátedra, 1982.

———. *Misericordia.* Translated by Charles de Salis, Dedalus Press, 2015.

———. *Misericordia.* 1897. Narrated by Israel Elejalde, audiobook ed., Penguin Books, 2019.

———. *Misericordia.* 1897. *Textos.info*, 25 Sept. 2016, www.textos.info/benito-perez-galdos/misericordia.

———. *Nazarín.* 1895. Alianza, 2016.

———. *Nazarín.* Translated by Jo Labanyi, Oxford UP, 1993.

———. "La novela en el tranvía." Pérez Galdós, *Cuentos fantásticos*, pp. 71–104.

———. *Las novelas de Torquemada.* 1889–95. Edited by Ignacio Javier López, Cátedra, 2019.

———. "The Novel on the Tram." *Madrid Tales*, translated by Margaret Jull Costa and Helen Constantine, Oxford UP, 2012.

———. "Nuestros grandes prestigios: Benito Pérez Galdós." Interview by El Bachiller Corchuelo [Enrique González Fiol], *Por esos mundos*, no. 186, July 1910, pp. 27–56.

———. "Observaciones sobre la novela contemporánea." 1870. *Ensayos de crítica literaria*, edited by Laureano Bonet, 2nd ed., Ediciones Península, 1999, pp. 123–39.

———. *Our Friend Manso.* Translated by Robert Russell, Columbia UP, 1987.

———. "La princesa y el granuja." Pérez Galdós, *Cuentos fantásticos*, pp. 157–87.

———. "The Princess and the Street Urchin." *Stories of Enchantment from Nineteenth-Century Spain*, translated by Robert M. Fedorchek, Bucknell UP, 2002, pp. 248–63.

———. Prologue. *La sombra; Celín; Tropiquillos; Theros.* La Guirnalda, 1890, pp. 5–8. *Biblioteca Virtual Miguel de Cervantes*, 2001, www.cervantesvirtual.com/obra/la-sombra-celin-tropiquillos-theros--0/.

———. *La razón de la sinrazón.* Alfar, 2023.

———. *Realidad: Drama en cinco actos.* La Guirnalda, 1892.

———. *Realidad: Novela en cinco jornadas.* La Guirnalda, 1889.

———. *Reality*. Translated by Karen Austin, E. Mellen Press, 1992.

———. *A Royalist Volunteer*. Translated by Lila Wells Guzmán, Edwin Mellen Press, 1993.

———. *The Shadow*. Translated by Karen Austin, Ohio UP, 1980.

———. *La sombra*. Edited by Juan Antonio Molina Foix, Cátedra, 2023.

———. "Some Observations on the Contemporary Novel in Spain." Translated by Nick Caistor. Labanyi, *Galdós*, pp. 29–34.

———. *That Bringas Woman*. Translated by Catherine Jagoe, Everyman, 1996.

———. *Torment*. Translated by J. M. Cohen, Farrar Straus and Young, 1953.

———. *Tormento*. 1884. Alianza Editorial, 2002.

———. *Tormento*. 1884. Edited by David R. George, Jr., Cervantes & Co., 2012.

———. *Tormento*. 1884. Edited by Terez Bajau and Joaquím Parellada, Crítica, 2007.

———. *Torquemada*. Translated by Frances M. López-Morillas, Columbia UP, 1986.

———. *Torquemada at the Stake / Torquemada en la hoguera*. Edited and translated by Stanley Appelbaum, Dover Publications, 2004.

———. *Torquemada en la hoguera*. 1898. Pérez Galdós, *Las novelas de Torquemada*, pp. 77–136.

———. *Tristana*. 1892. Edited by Gordon Minter, Bristol Classical Press, 1996.

———. *Tristana*. 1892. Edited by Isabel Gonzálvez and Gabriel Sevilla, Cátedra, 2023.

———. *Tristana*. 1892. Edited by Susan G. Polansky, Cervantes & Co., 2016.

———. *Tristana*. 1892. Translated by Margaret Jull Costa, New York Review Books, 2014.

———. *Tristana*. 1892. *Textos.info*, 9 Oct. 2016, www.textos.info/benito-perez-galdos/tristana.

———. "Tropiquillos." Pérez Galdós, *Cuentos fantásticos*, pp. 211–30.

Pérez Galdós, Benito, and Juan Pablo García. *El 2 de mayo*. Reino de Cordelia, 2020.

Pope, Randolph D. "Cambio, progreso y transformación: Releyendo *Doña Perfecta* de Galdós." *Anales de la literatura española contemporánea*, vol. 38, nos. 1–2, 2013, pp. 277–92.

Prim: El asesinato de la calle del Turco. Directed by Miguel Bardem, screenplay by Nacho Faerna, Radiotelevisión Española, 2014.

Pulido Rodríguez, Rayco. *Nela*. Astiberri, 2013.

———. "El proceso." *Nunca trabajes solo*, 23 Mar. 2013, nuncatrabajessolo.blogspot.com/2013/03/.

———. "Socartes-Madrid." *Panorama: La novela gráfica española hoy*, edited by Santiago García, Astiberri, 2013, pp. 53–63.

———. "Trabajo. Paisaje. Figura (2)." *Nunca trabajes solo*, 23 Mar. 2013, nuncatrabajessolo.blogspot.com/2013/03/.

Radcliff, Pamela. *Modern Spain, 1808 to the Present*. Wiley-Blackwell, 2017.

Rementería y Fica, Mariano de. *El hombre fino al gusto del día, ó Manual completo de urbanidad, cortesia y buen tono*. Madrid, 1829.

Renoir, Pierre-Auguste. *The Luncheon of the Boating Party*. 1880–81. *The Phillips Collection*, www.phillipscollection.org/collection/luncheon-boating-party.

Respaut, Michèle M. "The Nineteenth Century's Obsession with Medicine: Flaubert's Madame Bovary." Hunsaker Hawkins and McEntyre, pp. 226–32.

"Retratos del autor." *Biblioteca Virtual Miguel de Cervantes*, www.cervantesvirtual.com/portales/benito_perez_galdos/imagenes_retratos/1. Accessed 24 Oct. 2024.

Ríos, Blanca de los. *Las hijas de Don Juan*. Ena Bordonada, pp. 67–125.

Ripoll, Laila. *Fortunata y Benito*. Directed by Ripoll, La Joven Compañía, 7 Feb. 2020, Teatros del Canal, Madrid.

Ripoll, Laila, and Mariano Llorente. *El último viaje de Galdós*. Directed by Mario Vega, Galdós Laboratory, 8 Oct. 2020, Teatro Pérez Galdós, Las Palmas de Gran Canaria.

Rivas, Manuel. *¿Qué me quieres, amor?* Punto de Lectura, 2006.

Roas, David. *Beyond the Frontiers of the Real: A Definition of the Fantastic*. Palgrave Macmillan, 2018.

———. *Tras los límites de lo real: Una definición de lo fantástico*. Páginas de Espuma, 2011.

Robin, Arthur L., et al. "Teaching Note-Taking Skills to Underachieving College Students." *The Journal of Educational Research*, vol. 71, no. 2, 1977, pp. 81–85.

Robles, Federico Carlos Sáinz de. "Ensayo de un censo de los personajes galdosianos comprendidos en novelas, cuentos y teatro." *Obras completas*, by Pérez Galdós, vol. 4, Aguilar, 1958, pp. 1700–2078.

Rodriguez, Erika. "Care and Cultural Exclusion in Restoration Spain." *Revista Canadiense de Estudios Hispánicos*, vol. 44, no. 3, 2020, pp. 691–714.

Rodríguez-Galindo, Vanesa. *Madrid on the Move: Feeling Modern and Visually Aware in the Nineteenth Century*. Manchester UP, 2021.

Rueda, Ana. "La *Electra* de Galdós y sus redes de conducción eléctrica." *Anales Galdosianos*, vol. 54, 2019, pp. 59–72.

Rugg, Marilyn D. "The Women of Orbajosa: Patriarchy as the Definitive Ideology in Galdós's *Doña Perfecta*." *Mediterranean Studies*, vol. 16, 2007, pp. 191–223.

Ruiz, Mario E. "El idealismo Platónico en 'Marianela' de Galdós." *Hispania*, vol. 53, no. 4, 1970, pp. 870–80. *JSTOR*, https://doi.org/10.2307/337853.

Sáez de Melgar, Faustina. "El Ateneo de Señoras." 1869. Jagoe et al., pp. 160–63.

Said, Edward. *Orientalism*. Vintage Books, 1979.

Salaün, Serge. "El cuerpo tiene la palabra: Influencias simbolistas en el teatro español hacia 1900." *Albores españoles de una modernidad europea*, edited by Jochen Mecke, Vervuert, 2012, pp. 287–303.

Sánchez Noriega, José Luis. *De la literatura al cine: Teoría y análisis de la adaptación*. Paidós, 2000.

Sandner, David, editor. *Fantastic Literature: A Critical Reader*. Bloomsbury Publishing, 2004.

Sangre de mayo. Directed by José Luis Garci, Nickel Odeon / Telemadrid, 2008.

"Sanguijuela." *Farmacopea oficial Española*. 6th ed., Tipografía de Gregorio Estrada, 1884, pp. 91–92.

Schweik, Susan M. *The Ugly Laws: Disability in Public*. New York UP, 2009.

Shubert, Adrian. *A Social History of Modern Spain*. 1990. E-book ed., Taylor and Francis, 2003.

Sinnigen, John H. "Benito Pérez Galdós en el cine mexicano: El caso de *Doña Perfecta*." *Galdós y el siglo XX: Actas del VIII Congreso Internacional Galdosiano*, edited by Yolanda Arencibia et al., Museo Pérez Galdós, 2009, pp. 799–813.

———. *Benito Pérez Galdós en el cine mexicano: Literatura y cine*. Universidad Nacional Autónoma de México, 2008.

———. "*Doña Perfecta*: Política, sexo y literatura en dos restauraciones." *Confluencia*, vol. 20, no. 3, 2015, pp. 136–48.

Sinnigen, John H., and Claudia Medina Ramírez. "Galdós para una pandemia: Festival virtual de cine mexicano y argentino." *Cuadernos Associazione Ispanisti Italiani*, vol. 17, 2021, pp. 191–208.

Sinués de Marco, María del Pilar. *El ángel del hogar*. Madrid, 1857.

———. "Un libro para las damas." 1875. Jagoe et al., pp. 89–95.

Smith, Jennifer. "Doña Perfecta como entrada al análisis de la polarización político-social estadounidense." XII Congreso Internacional Galdosiano: Coda a un centenario: Galdós, miradas y perspectivas, 20 June 2022, Casa de Colón, Las Palmas de Gran Canaria. Conference presentation.

"Social Brand University 2023 Research: Impact of University Social Media on U.S. College Bound Students' Decision-Making Process." *Businesswire*, 11 Apr. 2023, www.businesswire.com/news/home/20230411005005/en/Social-Brand-University-2023-Research-Impact-of-University-Social-Media-on-U.S.-College-Bound-Students'-Decision-Making-Process.

Sorolla y Bastida, Joaquín. *Comida en la barca*. 1898. *Academia Colecciones*, www.academiacolecciones.com/pinturas/inventario.php?id=0804.

Stam, Robert. "The Theory and Practice of Adaptation." Introduction. *Literature and Film: A Guide to the Theory and Practice of Film Adaptation*, edited by Stam and Alessandra Raengo, Blackwell, 2005, pp. 1–52.

Stannard, Michael W. *Galdós and Medicine*. Peter Lang, 2015.

Stassi, Claudio. *Nada*. Planeta Cómic, 2021.

Surwillo, Lisa. *Monsters by Trade: Slave Traffickers in Modern Spanish Literature and Culture*. Stanford UP, 2014.

Sutherland, Erika M. "Una industria desheredada: Las sanguijuelas en la España decimonónica." *Literatura y medicina: Teoría y práxis, 1800–1930*, edited by Jorge Avilés-Diz and José Goñi Pérez, vol. 2, Ediciones de la Torre, 2021, pp. 221–55.

———. "Naturalism, Medicine, and *Un viaje de novios*." Versteeg and Walter, pp. 78–85.

———. "Las sanguijuelas y la medicina de Galdós: Literatura y la medicina popular." Muhlenberg College, 1 July 2023, docs.google.com/presentation/d/10y3_7Ig9fzcN9oqoii_pYxOEzDGDrUFI/edit?usp=sharing&ouid=101071606047672699003&rtpof=true&sd=true.

Tang, Wan Sonya. *Specters, Monsters, and the Damned: Fantastic Threats to the Social Order in Nineteenth-Century Spanish Fiction*. Vanderbilt UP, 2024.

Teicher, Jordan. "The Lost Art of the Mid-Range Blog Post." *Contently*, Jan. 14, 2019, contently.com/2019/01/14/mid-range-blog-post/.

"Ten Unbelievable Benefits of Social Media for Students." *Cambridge International Education*, May 9, 2024, cambridgeinternationalschoolguwahati.com/benefits-of-social-media-for-students/.

Tesh, Sylvia. "Political Ideology and Public Health in the Nineteenth Century." *International Journal of Health Services*, vol. 12, no. 2, 1982, pp. 321–42.

Tijoux, Ana. "Ana Tijoux—Antipatriarca (Official Music Video)." *YouTube*, uploaded by Nacional Records, 29 May 2015, www.youtube.com/watch?v=RoKoj8bFg2E.

Todorov, Tzvetan. *The Fantastic: A Structural Approach to a Literary Genre*. Translated by Richard Howard, Cornell UP, 1975.

Tolliver, Joyce. *Cigar Smoke and Violet Water: Gendered Discourse in the Stories of Emilia Pardo Bazán*. Bucknell UP, 1998.

———. "'Sor Aparición' and the Gaze: Pardo Bazán's Gendered Reply to the Romantic Don Juan." *Hispania*, vol. 77, no. 3, Sep. 1994, pp. 394–405.

Tormento. Directed by Pedro Olea, José Frade Producciones Cinematográficas, 1973.

Torres, David. "Galdós y la pierna de Tristana." *Publico*, 19 Feb. 2020, publico.es/opinion/columnas/galdos-pierna-tristana.html.

Tristana. Directed by Luis Buñuel, Mercurio Films, 1970.

Tsuchiya, Akiko. *Marginal Subjects: Gender and Deviance in Fin-de-siècle Spain*. U of Toronto P, 2011.

———. "The Struggle for Autonomy in Galdós's *Tristana*." *Modern Language Notes*, vol. 104, no. 2, 1989, pp. 330–50.

Turner, Harriet S. "Benito Pérez Galdós." *The Cambridge History of Spanish Literature*, edited by David T. Gies, Cambridge UP, 2004, pp. 392–409.

Twenge, Jean, et al. "Trends in U.S. Adolescents' Media Use, 1976–2016: The Rise of Digital Media, the Decline of TV, and the (Near) Demise of Print." *Psychology of Popular Media Culture*, 20 Aug. 2018, *APA PsycNet*, https://doi.org/10.1037/ppm0000203.

Unamuno, Miguel de. "Nada menos que todo un hombre." *Novelas completas*, by Unamuno, edited by Juan Antonio Garrido Ardila, Cátedra, 2017, pp. 839–68.

Urrechea, Federico. Review of *Realidad*, by Benito Pérez Galdós. *El Imparcial*, 16 Mar. 1892, p. 1. *Biblioteca Nacional de España*, hemerotecadigital.bne.es.

Valis, Noel. *The Culture of Cursilería: Bad Taste, Kitsch, and Class in Modern Spain*. Duke UP, 2003.

———. *Sacred Realism: Religion and the Imagination in Modern Spanish Narrative*. Yale UP, 2010.

Varey, John E. *Pérez Galdós:* Doña Perfecta. Grant and Cutler, 1971.

Vega Alfaro, Eduardo de la. "Origins, Development and Crisis of the Sound Cinema (1929–64)." *Mexican Cinema*, edited by Paulo Antonio Paranaguá, British Film Institute, 1995, pp. 79–93.

Velázquez, Diego. *La rendición de Breda*. 1635, Museo del Prado, Madrid.

Versteeg, Margot, and Susan Walter, editors. *Approaches to Teaching the Writings of Emilia Pardo Bazán*. Modern Language Association of America, 2017.

Viridiana. Directed by Luis Buñuel, Films 59, 1960.

Wellbery, Caroline. "The Value of Medical Uncertainty?" *The Lancet*, vol. 375, 15 May 2010, pp. 1686–87.

Willem, Linda M. *Adapting Spanish Classics for the New Millennium: The Nineteenth-Century Novel Remediated*. Palgrave, 2022.

———. "Writing and Adapting Disability: Galdós' *Marianela* and Pablo Messiez's *Los ojos*." *Bulletin of Spanish Studies*, vol. 95, nos. 9–10, 2018, pp. 109–20.

Wolters, Nicholas. "Secondhand: The Used Clothing Trade and Narrative Ragpicking in Galdós's El Doctor Centeno." *Anales Galdosianos*, vol. 53, 2018, pp. 55–75.

Woodbridge, Hensley C. "Benito Pérez Galdós: A Selected Annotated Bibliography." *Hispania*, vol. 53, no. 4, 1970, pp. 899–971.

Yudkin, Joshua. "A Renewed Call to Safeguard Public Health Epistemology." *International Journal of Public Health*, vol. 6, May 2021, pp. 40–41.

Yxart, José. *El arte escénico en España*. Vol. 1, Alta Fulla, 1987.

Zaviezo, Gabriela. "Las masculinidades en transición de don Lope Garrido en Tristana." *Decimonónica*, vol. 11, no. 1, 2014, pp. 77–88.

Zedd, Eliot. "Social Media Has Turned College Students into Mass Consumers." *The Breeze*, 9 Feb. 2023, www.breezejmu.org/opinion/opinion-social-media-has-turned-college-students-into-mass-consumers/article_65ac8052-a7d9-11ed-9930-272f82cad2b1.html.

"Zines at the Library of Congress." *Library of Congress*, 31 May 2019, guides.loc.gov/zines/introduction.

Zorrilla, José. *Don Juan Tenorio*. Edited by David T. Gies, Clásicos Castalia, 1994.

———. Prologue to "La pasionaria." *Cuentos fantásticos del siglo XIX*, edited by David Roas, Mare Nostrum, 2003, p. 187.

Zurro, Alfonso. *Galdós enamorado*. Directed by Zurro, 25 Mar. 2020, Teatro Pérez Galdós, Las Palmas de Gran Canaria.